Betty Crocker's
Best-Loved Recipes

Macmillan • USA

IDG BOOKS WORLDWIDE, INC.

An International Data Group Company
919 E. Hillsdale Boulevard
Suite 400
Foster City, CA 94404

 The IDG Books Worldwide logo is a registered trademark under exclusive license to IDG Books Worldwide, Inc., from International Data Group, Inc.

BETTY CROCKER, Bisquick, Fiber One, Wondra, Gold Medal, Potato Buds, and Hamburger Helper are registered trademarks of General Mills, Inc.

Photo appearing on page 58 courtesy of *Lafayette Journal and Courier*.

For general information on IDG Books Worldwide's books in the U.S., please call our Consumer Customer Service department at 800-762-2974. For reseller information, including discounts and premium sales, please call our Reseller Customer Service department at 800-434-3422.

Library of Congress Cataloging-in-Publication Data

Crocker, Betty.
   [Best-Loved Recipes]
   Betty Crocker's Best-Loved Recipes.
      p. cm.
   Includes index.
   ISBN 0-7645-6071-9
   1. Cookery, American. 2. Cookery—Competitions—United States.
3. Cooks—United States—Biography   I. Title.
TX715.C921379   1988
641.5973—dc21   98-38261
                                                                 CIP

GENERAL MILLS, INC.

Betty Crocker Kitchens

Director: Marcia Copeland

Managing Editor: Lois Tlusty

Recipe Development: Betty Crocker Kitchens Home Economists

Food Stylists: Betty Crocker Kitchens Food Stylists

Photography: Photographic Services Department

Cover: Paul Costello

Design: Nancy Freeborn/Freeborn Design

For consistent baking results, the Betty Crocker Kitchens recommend Gold Medal Flour.

Manufactured in the United States of America
10 9 8 7 6 5 4 3 2

First Edition

Contents

Betty Crocker
Your Best Friend
in the Kitchen

For over seventy-five years, Betty Crocker has touched so many of our lives—whether being by our side when we tried our first recipe in the kitchen or helping us out with our questions about homemaking and cooking—that our kitchens seem warmer just by the mention of her name.

In the following pages, you'll read the history of this great woman and discover all the people—from homemakers to home economists—that make Betty Crocker who she is today.

The Beginning of a Legend

Betty Crocker
1998

In 1921, General Mills, then a small milling company in Minnesota, held a puzzle contest and to their surprise, they received more than just contest entrees. They found themselves faced with the challenge of how best to respond to thousands of questions and requests for recipes as well as baking and cooking advice. They created Betty Crocker to do the job, and what a great job she did! Thanks to her helpful advice, she became known as a friend for trusted information about keeping a home and creating delicious food.

Although Betty was never a real person, she became real to homemakers through the years. Even today, she still receives marriage proposals! The spirit of Betty Crocker—its warmth and hospitality—lives on not only with the advice and fellowship she shares with people every day, but also through the seventy-five inspirational essays and specially chosen recipes in this book. You, too, will feel the friendship, trust, and confidence that Betty gives to all of us.

The Spirit of Betty Crocker Contest

For Betty's most recent portrait and seventy-fifth anniversary, The Spirit of Betty Crocker Contest, a nationwide essay contest was launched by General Mills to identify seventy-five exceptional women of diverse backgrounds and ages. Each contestant had to embody Betty Crocker's joy of cooking and baking, commitment to family and friends, resourcefulness and creativity in daily life, and community involvement. General Mills asked Americans to nominate special women who personify these characteristics. Choosing from among the thousands of entries received was difficult, but finally the seventy-five winners were identified.

Photographs of these lucky winners were loaded into a computer and blended together to create a composite. Artist John Stuart Ingle used the composite to paint today's Betty Crocker. This new portrait is truly a reflection of all of us! If you look closely, you'll see part of yourself there—maybe it is the friendly eyes or welcoming smile—since we all share the spirit of Betty in our hearts.

Throughout this book, you'll meet with the seventy-five extraordinary women that won The Spirit of Betty Crocker Contest. You'll get to know them by reading the loving essays written by their family and friends and the women themselves. By sharing their time, energy, love, and recipes, these remarkable women demonstrate the spirit of Betty Crocker that makes them found in the heart of the kitchen and the lives they touch! These women represent today's Betty Crocker: feeding the homeless, baking cookies for the dormitory, taking in foster children, inspiring kids to stay in school, creating a strong support system for the family—sometimes as a single parent—and all the while sharing love through the food they make. These uncommon heroines come from all walks of life, and each and every one embodies the exceptional characteristics that we know in a mother or sister, friend or teacher who has made a positive difference in our lives.

Reflections of Betty Crocker

Women certainly have changed over the years, and so has Betty Crocker! Her first official portrait appeared in 1936 to celebrate the fifteenth "birthday" of her creation. Artist Neysa McMein blended the features of several of the home economists working in the Betty Crocker Kitchens at that time in an effort to create an appearance that would instill confidence in young homemakers. Since then, Betty has had seven other portraits, all striving to make her reflect the look of contemporary women and show her spirit to the women who seek her timely help.

1936

1955

1965

1968

1972

1980

Betty has changed through the years to reflect the hairstyles and fashions of women of the time, but you've probably noticed she always wears red with a touch of white at her neck. She appears friendly, and trustworthy, much like your best friend. She is an approachable person who makes you feel that you can do it and who will be happy for your success. She is all women—whether young or more mature, a businesswoman or a homemaker, dressed for success or for the carpool—Betty Crocker symbolizes the warmth and love people express when they gather and share wonderful homemade meals.

Betty Crocker Doesn't Do It Alone

Over the years, the hundreds of professional women and men who have worked in the Betty Crocker Kitchens created the trust we have in Betty's advice and help. They represent a wide cross-section of the population—from young working moms and dads to empty nesters and singles—and all are dedicated to developing reliable recipes and providing the best food information possible to help you keep pace with your busy lifestyle. The Betty Crocker Kitchen staff writes the recipes so they are easy to use and understand. These recipes are created in kitchens that are like yours, using the same pans and appliances that you have, so Betty Crocker can guarantee the recipes will work as well for you as they do for the Betty Crocker Kitchens.

One of the biggest challenges in the kitchen is anticipating what you'll want to serve your family and guests in the future. We don't have crystal balls to see into everyone's homes, but we do have the Betty Crocker Kitchens collected experience and intuition. We watch for emerging new flavors and health trends and keep current with the latest cookware and equipment. We monitor menus and dishes from restaurants that are setting the latest eating trends. We sample new ingredients and exotic fruits and vegetables, and we keep current with the latest food-safety information. This way, we can offer you the most up-to-date information, acquaint you with the interesting, new foods and ingredients that are appearing in your local supermarket, and offer new flavor twists to meals.

Betty and You

Betty Crocker has spent her entire existence helping people like you who enjoy cooking. Think about how your food choices and cooking methods and interests have formed over the years. Betty has noticed these new developments, too, and has tried to respond accordingly. The Betty Crocker Kitchens are aware of how your

1986

changing lifestyle affects your cooking and eating habits. And we enjoy sharing recipes and information so you can continue to create delicious, healthful meals for you, your family, and friends.

As you read through the pages of this book, you will discover Betty's best-loved recipes, those most-requested dishes that evoke the wonderful memories of home and loved ones. You may even recognize some signature dishes of your own. These tried-and-true recipes have earned Betty Crocker the reputation of being your best friend in the kitchen, providing you with great recipes that turn out just right and taste great, too! So savor these recipes and enjoy the visits you will have with the seventy-five women who are part of today's Betty Crocker. You'll discover what you always may have guessed—and what we have always known—that there is a little bit of Betty Crocker in all of us.

Great Women, Great Food

In 1996, General Mills launched a nationwide search, The Spirit of Betty Crocker Contest, for her seventy-fifth anniversary. The purpose of the contest was to find seventy-five women who personify the characteristics of Betty Crocker—women who enjoy cooking and baking and who are committed to family and friends, resourceful and creative in handling everyday tasks, and involved in the community. Thousands of entrees were received and seventy-five women from across the nation were chosen. Now it's your chance to meet these extraordinary women as they share their stories and some of their best-loved Betty Crocker recipes with you. We think you'll discover there is a little bit of Betty Crocker in all of us.

Winner's Name*	Residence	Recipe
Baer, Mary	Hallandale, FL	Cashew Brownie Bars
Baldwin, Fran	Dublin, OH	Beef Brisket Barbecue
Birks, Elaine	Minneapolis, MN	Blueberry Streusel Muffin
Brammer, Mary Jane (Dottie)	Fairmont, MN	Popovers
Brannen, Lisa	Glenville, GA	Cream of Broccoli Soup
Busch, Nancy	Pittsburgh, PA	Brown Sugar Drops
Chow, Sally	Clarksdale, MS	Banana Bread
Cockrell, Carmelina	Beaverton, OR	Honey–Whole Wheat Bread
Collins-Burnham, Sandra	Eagle River, AK	Chocolate Chip Cookies
Comerford, Betty	Larchmount, NY	Sour Cream Coffee Cake

*In alphabetical order

Great Women, Great Food

Winner's Name	Residence	Recipe
Crocker, Betty	Salt Lake City, UT	Snickerdoodles
Dawdy, Marilyn	Sulphur, LA	Best Buttermilk Pancakes
DeCerce, Samantha	Colts Neck, NJ	Cornmeal Chicken with Casera Sauce
Deutsch, Becky	Evansville, IN	Willamsburg Orange Cake
Devlin, Heidi	Lebanon, PA	Best Chocolate Cake
Douglas, Penny	West Lafayette, IN	Caramel-Pecan Sticky Rolls
Drake, Emily	West Jordan, UT	Seven-Layer Salad
Edwards, Dorothy Jane (D.J.)	Santa Rosa, CA	French Breakfast Puffs
Gilbert, Marie	London, Ontario, CN	Cranberry-Raspberry Salad
Gordon, Diann	Brownsville, TX	Zesty Pork Tenderloin
Guay, Marielle	St. Philippe, Argenteuil	Savory Chicken and Rice
Hatch, Teri	Merillville, IN	Sunflower Seven-Grain Bread
Haugen, Tiffany	Walterville, OR	Strawberry Rhubarb Pie
Hui, Susanna	Woodbury, MN	Glazed Lamb Chops
Ivory, Loretta	Denver, CO	Golden Corn Pudding
Jones, Barbara (B.J.)	Albuquerque, NM	Deluxe Sugar Cookies
Kennedy, Waiyee	Utica, NY	Chicken Pot Stickers
Kettel, Camille	Algonac, MI	Spinach Phyllo Pie
Kurtz, Kathie	Carterville, IL	Shrimp Fajitas
Kyburz, Sheilah	Bloomington, MN	Wild Rice- and Almond-Stuffed Pork
Lawson, Evelyn	Victorville, CA	Almond Honey–Whole Wheat Bread

Great Women, Great Food

Winner's Name	Residence	Recipe
Leviner, Julie	Wilmington, NC	Classic Beef Stroganoff
Lewis, Susana	Carrabelle, FL	Black and White Turkey Chili
Licón, Connie	Kankakee, IL	Fresh Peach Cobbler
Loftus, Katherine	Lostine, OR	Beef Enchiladas
Logan, Ann	Rutherfordton, NC	Pepperoni Pizza-Hamburger Pie
Manning, Delores (Sis)	Sloatsburg, NY	Spaghetti with White Clam Sauce
McBrien, Rose	Staten Island, NY	Macaroni and Cheese
McKell, Marie	Ukiah, CA	Savory Spaghetti
Megel, Jeanne	Colorado Springs, CO	Hummus
Molzan, Susan	Houston, TX	Garlic Smashed Potatoes
Moses, Carrie	Portland, OR	Peach-Custard Kuchen
Murphy, Eddie	Buena Park, CA	Oatmeal Spice Cake with Browned Butter
Muthig, Joyce	Parksville, NY	Country Ribs
Nemitz, Dawn	Minooka, IL	Spanish Rice
O'Neill, Christine Fotré	Chicago, IL	Meatball Porcupines
Pardue, Kristi	Boise, ID	Turkey Divan
Peterson, Laurie	New Richmond, WI	Creamy Scalloped Potatoes
Pope, Debbie Hedrick	Williamsburg, WV	Stuffed Chicken Breasts
Putnam, Cora	Port St. Lucie, FL	Almond Puffs
Rasmussen, Peggy	Hamel, MN	Bonnie Butter Cake
Rechsteiner, Marion Kallfelz	Wilmington, DE	Blueberry Buckle Coffee Cake

Great Women, Great Food

Winner's Name	Residence	Recipe
Rowell, Mary	Kansas City, MO	Chicken Cacciatore
Schwarz, Sofia	Seattle, WA	Mahogany Chiffon Cake
Segura, Margot M.	El Sobrante, CA	Creamy Fettuccine Alfredo
Senes, Susan	Trumbull, CT	Apple Pie
Shannon, Jill	Prairie Village, KS	Chicken and Dumplings
Simerly, Kathy	Johnson City, TN	Chunky Tomato Soup
Smith, Linda	Shorewood, IL	Heartland Three-Bean Salad
Solum, Gloria	Hector, MN	Three-Bean Casserole
Stauffer, Sue	Rockford, IL	Cheesecake with Cherry Glaze
Vacarro, Delores	Pueblo, CO	Oatmeal-Raisin Cookies
Vincent, Jo Ann	Metairie, LA	Old-Fashioned Meat Loaf
Washington, Lillian	Steubenville, OH	New England Clam Chowder
Weiner, Mary Lou	Meridian, ID	Cranberry–Wild Rice Bake
Weitzman, Carol	Cleveland, OH	Fajitas
White, Sharon	Durham, NC	Chicken in Cream
Wilson, Correna	Wilson, OK	Chocolate Brownies
Winter-Hartley, Cindy	Cary, NC	Mexican Beef and Bean Casserole
Work, Sandi	St. Louis, MO	Bountiful Twice-Baked Potatoes
Wright, Cottie	Gainesville, FL	Spinach Gourmet

Great Women, Great Food

Winner's Name	Residence	Recipe
Young, Roxyanne	San Diego, CA	Impossible Broccoli 'n Cheddar Pie
Zach, Margaret (Marge)	Portland, OR	Overnight Cinnamon Rolls
Zietlow, Marcille Faye	Oshkosh, WI	Cranberry-Orange Pound Cake
Zimmerman, Thea Palmer	Rockville, MD	Egg Salad Stacks

CHAPTER ONE

Breakfast Corner

Whether lingering over coffee or hosting a brunch, nothing beats a nourishing, wholesome breakfast. It's a wonderful way to start the day with your family or friends. Any day of the week, breakfast time is something to look forward to. And if it's the weekend, all the better! Lounge and enjoy the fat Sunday paper. It's one of the week's high points, an occasion that calls for a treat. Pancakes, waffles, and French toast fit the bill. Dressed up or down, eggs are glorious in every guise. Here they are, all your favorite recipes—along with a host of ideas for sweet breads, coffee cakes and muffins to accompany any mid-morning break, especially alongside a steaming cup of coffee or cocoa.

Strawberry Muffins (page 45)

Egg Dishes

Baked Vegetable Omelet
(page 17)

Baked Vegetable Omelet

This omelet is chock-full of fresh vegetables. What a great way to eat a serving of vegetables. Make it for breakfast or even for dinner—you'll love the results.

1 cup shredded Monterey Jack cheese (4 ounces)

1 1/2 cups chopped broccoli or 1 package (10 ounces) frozen chopped broccoli, thawed and drained

2 medium tomatoes, coarsely chopped

2 cups shredded Cheddar cheese (8 ounces)

1 cup milk

1/4 cup all-purpose flour

1/2 teaspoon salt

3 eggs

1. Heat oven to 350°.

2. Layer Monterey Jack cheese, broccoli, tomatoes and Cheddar cheese in ungreased square baking dish, 8 x 8 x 2 inches. Beat milk, flour, salt and eggs until smooth; pour over cheese.

3. Bake uncovered until egg mixture is set, 40 to 45 minutes. Let stand 10 minutes before cutting.

1 SERVING: Calories 315 (Calories from Fat 200); Fat 22g (Saturated 13g); Cholesterol 165mg; Sodium 610mg; Carbohydrates 10g (Dietary Fiber 1g); Protein 20g.

Ham and Egg Brunch Bake

This dish is certain to be a real crowd-pleaser when served for breakfast or brunch. For a cheesier flavor, you might want to try a sharp cheddar. To enhance the smoky flavor of the ham, use smoked Gouda.

6 cups frozen (unthawed) hash brown potatoes

2 cups diced fully cooked ham

2 cups shredded Swiss cheese (8 ounces)

1 jar (7 ounces) roasted red bell peppers, drained and chopped

1 jar (4 1/2 ounces) sliced mushrooms, drained

6 eggs

1/3 cup milk

1 cup small curd creamed cottage cheese

1/4 teaspoon pepper

1. Heat oven to 350°. Grease rectangular baking dish, 13 x 9 x 2 inches.

2. Sprinkle 3 cups of the potatoes evenly in baking dish. Layer with ham, Swiss cheese, bell peppers and mushrooms. Sprinkle remaining potatoes over mushrooms.

3. Beat eggs, milk, cottage cheese and pepper with fork or wire whisk until blended; pour over potatoes. Bake uncovered 45 to 50 minutes or until light golden brown and set in center.

1 SERVING: Calories 310 (Calories from Fat 145); Fat 16g (Saturated 8g); Cholesterol 210mg; Sodium 800mg; Carbohydrates 19g (Dietary Fiber 2g); Protein 25g.

Ham and Cheddar Strata

Choose this recipe if you want to make a dish the night before, then pop it in the oven while the guests arrive. Feel free to use any kind of bread here—a whole-grain bread will add a nice texture to the dish.

12 slices bread

2 cups cut-up fully cooked smoked ham

2 cups shredded Cheddar cheese (8 ounces)

4 medium green onions, sliced

2 cups milk

1 teaspoon dry mustard

1/4 teaspoon red pepper sauce

6 eggs

Paprika

1. Trim crusts from bread. Arrange 6 bread slices in greased rectangular baking dish, 13 x 9 x 2 inches. Layer ham, cheese and onions on bread in dish. Cut remaining bread slices diagonally into halves; arrange on onions.

2. Beat milk, mustard, pepper sauce and eggs until smooth; pour evenly over bread. Sprinkle with paprika. Bake immediately, or cover and refrigerate up to 24 hours.

3. Heat oven to 300° degrees. Bake uncovered until center is set and bread is golden brown, 60 to 70 minutes. Let stand 10 minutes before cutting.

1 SERVING: Calories 475 (Calories from Fat 225); Fat 25g (Saturated 12g); Cholesterol 285mg; Sodium 1280mg; Carbohydrates 31g (Dietary Fiber 2g); Protein 33g.

Potatoes and Eggs Sunny-Side Up

Show your sunny side by serving this filling favorite on a weekend morning when you have a little extra time to relax with your family. What's best—you bake it, making it easy to fix and serve.

12 ounces bulk pork sausage

1 small onion, chopped

3 cups frozen shredded hash brown potatoes

1 teaspoon herb-seasoned salt

1 1/2 cups shredded Swiss cheese (6 ounces)

6 eggs

1. Heat oven to 350°.

2. Cook and stir sausage and onion in 10-inch skillet over medium heat until sausage is brown; drain. Stir in frozen potatoes and herb-seasoned salt. Cook, stirring constantly, just until potatoes are thawed, about 2 minutes. Remove from heat; stir in cheese. Spread in ungreased rectangular baking dish, 11 x 7 x 1 1/2 inches.

3. Make 6 indentations in potato mixture with back of spoon; break 1 egg into each indentation. Sprinkle with pepper if desired. Bake uncovered until eggs are desired doneness, 20 to 25 minutes.

1 SERVING: Calories 355 (Calories from Fat 190); Fat 21g (Saturated 9g); Cholesterol 260mg; Sodium 730mg; Carbohydrate 23g (Dietary Fiber 2g); Protein 21g.

Brunch Oven Omelet with Canadian Bacon

12 SERVINGS

Linger over your morning cup of coffee with your guests while the maple-flavored bacon and golden omelet tend themselves in the oven.

Oven Canadian Bacon (right)

1/4 cup margarine or butter

18 eggs

1 cup sour cream

1 cup milk

2 teaspoons salt

4 medium green onions, chopped (1/4 cup)

Chopped fresh parsley

1. Heat oven to 325°.

2. Prepare Oven Canadian Bacon; set aside. Melt margarine in rectangular baking dish, 13 x 9 x 2 inches, in oven; tilt dish to coat bottom.

3. Beat eggs, sour cream, milk and salt with fork or wire whisk until blended. Stir in onions. Pour into baking dish.

4. Bake omelet mixture and bacon about 35 minutes or until eggs are set but moist and bacon is hot. Arrange omelet and bacon on large platter. Sprinkle with parsley.

OVEN CANADIAN BACON

1 pound Canadian-style bacon, cut into twenty-four 1/8-inch slices

1/4 cup maple-flavored syrup

Reassemble slices of bacon on aluminum foil. Pour syrup over bacon. Wrap in foil; place in shallow pan.

1 SERVING: Calories 265 (Calories from Fat 160); Fat 18g (Saturated 7g); Cholesterol 350mg; Sodium 1030mg; Carbohydrates 6g (Dietary Fiber 0g); Protein 18g.

It's in the Bag

Today, we often take for granted the recipes that appear on nearly every Betty Crocker package. How did that get started? In 1928, the Washburn Crosby Company, under the leadership of James Ford Bell, joined with a number of other flour mills to become a larger, expanded company, now known as General Mills, Inc. To mark the occasion, Gold Medal® flour began a long-standing tradition of packing recipes in the bags. Consumers ever since have had the luxury of new recipes whenever they buy a bag of flour, although today's recipes are printed on the bag.

Cheese and Egg Pie with Bacon

6 SERVINGS

Yes! We've used an easy-to-make cornflake crust for this savory pie. The wonderful corn flavor complements the cheese and smoky bacon in this egg dish.

1 cup coarsely crushed cornflakes

2 tablespoons margarine or butter, melted

1/4 cup margarine or butter

8 eggs

1/2 cup milk

1 tablespoon snipped chives

1/2 teaspoon seasoned salt

1/8 teaspoon pepper

6 slices bacon, crisply cooked and crumbled

3 slices process American cheese, cut diagonally into halves

Cheese and Egg Pie with Bacon

1. Mix cornflakes and 2 tablespoons melted margarine; reserve 1/4 cup. Spread remaining cornflake mixture in ungreased pie plate, 9 x 1 1/4 inches, or quiche dish, 9 x 1 1/2 inches. Heat 1/4 cup margarine in 10-inch skillet over medium heat until melted.

2. Beat eggs, milk, chives, seasoned salt and pepper with hand beater. Pour egg mixture into skillet; add bacon. Cook over low heat, stirring gently, until eggs are almost set. Quickly spoon into pie plate. Arrange cheese, overlapping slightly, around edge of plate. Sprinkle with reserved cornflake mixture.

3. Bake uncovered in 375° oven until cheese is melted and eggs are firm, 10 to 15 minutes.

1 SERVING: Calories 225 (Calories from Fat 145); Fat 16g (Saturated 6g); Cholesterol 300mg; Sodium 450mg; Carbohydrates 6g (Dietary Fiber 0g); Protein 14g.

The First Cookbook

The very first cookbook issued by General Mills's predecessor, the Washburn Crosby Company, was *Miss Parloa's New Cook Book, A Guide to Marketing and Cooking*, published in 1880. Maria Parloa was a noted cooking instructor at the Boston Cooking School, and she had quite an extensive list of necessary kitchen equipment. Among those nearly 100 necessary items were a fish kettle, a larding needle, a trussing needle, a variety of flour barrels and covers, a pail for cleaning, a blacking brush, and a bean pot. How many of those do you have in your kitchen?

Spring Vegetable Frittata

6 SERVINGS

The frittata comes to us from Italy. The ingredients are mixed all together and slowly cooked over a low heat until golden brown rather than folded inside, like a French omelet. The golden brown crust helps keep the inside of the frittata moist.

1/2 cup chopped onion

1 clove garlic, finely chopped

2 tablespoons margarine or butter

1 green or red bell pepper, chopped

1/4 teaspoon salt

1/4 teaspoon pepper

1 small tomato, chopped

2 small zucchini, chopped

6 eggs, beaten

1/4 cup grated Parmesan cheese

1. Heat oven to 375°.

2. Cook and stir onion and garlic over medium-high heat in margarine in 10-inch ovenproof skillet 3 minutes. Add bell pepper; cook over medium heat about 2 minutes until crisp-tender. Add remaining ingredients except eggs and cheese; cook 4 minutes, stirring occasionally. Add eggs.

3. Bake 10 to 12 minutes or until set in center. Sprinkle top with cheese.

1 SERVING: Calories 140 (Calories from Fat 90); Fat 10g (Saturated 3g); Cholesterol 215mg; Sodium 280mg; Carbohydrates 5g (Dietary Fiber 1g); Protein 9g.

Spring Vegetable Frittata

Tomato-Basil Omelet

2 SERVINGS

Two of the best flavors from the garden—vine-ripened tomatoes and sweet, fragrant basil—combine to make a savory omelet bursting with summertime flavor.

1 teaspoon olive or vegetable oil

4 medium green onions, chopped (1/4 cup)

1 medium tomato, chopped (3/4 cup)

1 tablespoon chopped fresh or 1 teaspoon dried basil leaves

4 eggs or 1 cup fat-free cholesterol-free egg product

Freshly ground pepper

1. Heat oil in 8-inch nonstick skillet over medium heat. Cook onions in oil 2 minutes, stirring occasionally. Stir in tomato and basil. Cook about 1 minute, stirring occasionally, until tomato is heated through. Beat eggs thoroughly with fork or wire whisk; pour over tomato mixture.

2. As mixture begins to set at bottom and side, gently lift cooked portions with spatula so that thin, uncooked portion can flow to bottom. Avoid constant stirring. Cook 3 to 4 minutes or until eggs are thickened throughout but still moist. Sprinkle with pepper.

1 SERVING: Calories 190 (Calories from Fat 115); Fat 13g (Saturated 4g); Cholesterol 425mg; Sodium 140mg; Carbohydrates 6g (Dietary Fiber 1g); Protein 13g.

Country Egg Scramble

4 TO 6 SERVINGS

Scramble up this morning-time favorite and top it with salsa, hot sauce, or a dollop of sour cream for an added touch of color.

1 pound new red potatoes, cubed (6 or 7)

6 eggs

1/3 cup milk

1/4 teaspoon salt

1/8 teaspoon pepper

2 tablespoons margarine or butter

4 medium green onions, slices (1/2 cup)

6 slices bacon, crisply cooked and crumbled

1. Heat 1 inch water to boiling in 2-quart saucepan. Add potatoes. Cover and heat to boiling; reduce heat to medium-low. Cover and cook 6 to 8 minutes or until potatoes are tender; drain.

2. Beat eggs, milk, salt and pepper with fork or wire whisk until a uniform yellow color; set aside.

3. Melt margarine in 10-inch skillet over medium-high heat. Cook potatoes in margarine 3 to 5 minutes, turning potatoes occasionally, until light brown. Stir in onions. Cook 1 minute, stirring constantly.

4. Pour egg mixture into skillet. As mixture begins to set at bottom and side, gently lift cooked portions with spatula so that thin, uncooked portion can flow to bottom. Avoid constant stirring. Cook 3 to 4 minutes or until eggs are cooked throughout but still moist. Sprinkle with bacon.

1 SERVING: Calories 320 (Calories from Fat 160); Fat 18g (Saturated 6g); Cholesterol 330mg; Sodium 480mg; Carbohydrates 26g (Dietary Fiber 2g); Protein 15g.

Country Egg Scramble, Buttermilk Biscuits (page 301)

Pancakes, Waffles, &French Toast

Ultimate Pancakes

ABOUT 16 PANCAKES

Who doesn't love pancakes? These light, fluffy pancakes are great hot off the griddle. For something special, try these favorite mix-ins: raspberries, blueberries, sliced peaches, chocolate chips, sliced bananas, toasted nuts. Gently mix them into the batter or sprinkle them on top of the pancake after pouring the batter and before flipping them over.

2 cups Bisquick® Original or Reduced Fat baking mix

1 cup milk

2 eggs

2 tablespoons lemon juice

4 teaspoons sugar

2 teaspoons baking powder

1. Heat griddle or skillet over medium heat or to 375°. Grease heated griddle, if necessary. To test griddle, sprinkle with a few drops of water. If bubbles skitter around, heat is just right. Stir all ingredients until blended.

2. Pour batter by scant 1/4 cupfuls onto hot griddle.

3. Cook until edges are dry. Turn; cook until golden.

1 PANCAKE: Calories 80 (Calories from Fat 25); Fat 3g (Saturated 1g); Cholesterol 30mg; Sodium 290mg; Carbohydrates 11g (Dietary Fiber 0g); Protein 2g.

Buckwheat Pancakes

TEN 4-INCH PANCAKES

Pile these wholesome and hearty pancakes high on your plate and serve with Citrus-Banana Compote (page 49) alongside. You'll find buckwheat flour in the flour section of many supermarkets or natural foods stores.

1 egg

1/2 cup buckwheat flour

1/2 cup whole wheat flour

1 cup milk

1 tablespoon sugar

3 teaspoons baking powder

2 tablespoons shortening, melted, or vegetable oil

1/2 teaspoon salt

Whole bran or wheat germ, if desired

1. Beat egg with hand beater until fluffy; beat in remaining ingredients just until smooth.

2. Heat griddle or skillet over medium heat or to 375°. Grease heated griddle, if necessary. To test griddle, sprinkle with a few drops water. If bubbles skitter around, heat is just right.

3. For each pancake, pour about 3 tablespoons batter from tip of large spoon or from pitcher onto hot griddle. Cook pancakes until puffed and dry around edges. Sprinkle each pancake with 1 teaspoon whole bran. Turn and cook other sides until golden brown.

1 PANCAKE: Calories 90 (Calories from Fat 35); Fat 4g (Saturated 1g); Cholesterol 25mg; Sodium 280mg; Carbohydrates 11g (Dietary Fiber 1g); Protein 3g.

Marilyn Dawdy
Sulphur, Louisiana

Marilyn has always teased us about her having won the "Betty Crocker" award in high school. (She has the statue to prove it!) Marilyn decided to get a pharmacy degree. Her other love, cooking, won over. Marilyn gave up a lucrative salary as a pharmacist to start a small catering service and has owned and operated

Marilyn's Flowers and Catering for seventeen years. Having fourteen full-time employees along with five part-time employees can sometimes be a lot. She will sit there and laugh with you when times are at their highest, and she will sit there with her loving arms wrapped around you while you are crying and at your lowest. No wonder most of the employees at Marilyn's have stayed so long.

Marilyn and her husband Ed, an elementary school principal, have been married for twenty-seven years. They have three children. No matter how busy she is, there is always time for her friends, especially when they need her. Not only is Marilyn devoted and committed to her friends, but they feel the same about her. Her eighty-year-old father also lives with her, but she manages to always have time for dear Papaw.

Marilyn was the first woman Rotarian of the Sulphur Rotary Club, becoming president in 1994. She is on the board of the West Calcasieu Chamber of Commerce and the Brimstone Historical Museum. She is an active member of Our Lady Prompt Succor Catholic Church. Several times, Marilyn was awarded the Small Business Award and was nominated for the State of Louisiana Small Business Person of the Year.

Marilyn is always there for anyone that needs her anytime. She is very understanding and very forgiving. She has been not only a great rock to lean on and a very good friend, but most of all, a teacher like no other could be. I have learned many things from her—mostly about life, a lot about work, and most of all, how to make it in this world.

Best Buttermilk Pancakes

NINE 4-INCH PANCAKES

Drizzle these tender, golden pancakes with rich chocolate sauce, pile on the fresh juicy red raspberries and top them off with a dusting of powdered sugar. Your family will be in seventh heaven.

1 egg

1 cup all-purpose or whole wheat
  flour

1 cup buttermilk

1 tablespoon granulated or packed
  brown sugar

2 tablespoons vegetable oil

1 teaspoon baking powder

1/2 teaspoon baking soda

1/4 teaspoon salt

1. Beat egg in medium bowl with hand beater until fluffy. Beat in remaining ingredients just until smooth. (For thinner pancakes, stir in 1 to 2 tablespoons milk.)

2. Heat griddle or skillet over medium heat or to 375°. Grease heated griddle, if necessary. To test griddle, sprinkle with a few drops of water. If bubbles jump around, heat is just right.

3. For each pancake, pour slightly less than 1/4 cup batter from cup or pitcher onto hot griddle. Cook pancakes until puffed and dry around edges. Turn and cook other sides until golden brown.

1 PANCAKE: Calories 105 (Calories from Fat 35); Fat 4g (Saturated 1g); Cholesterol 25mg; Sodium 220mg; Carbohydrates 14g (Dietary Fiber 0g); Protein 3g.

How Did Betty Get Her Name?

When the Washburn Crosby Company (now General Mills) ran a contest in an ad in the *Saturday Evening Post* in 1921, the company got more than it bargained for. Along with the nearly thirty thousand correct responses, it received requests for recipes and advice about baking problems. Who best to respond to these letters? Company officials decided to create a fictitious woman to sign the responses. They chose the name "Betty" because it sounded friendly and "Crocker" to honor a popular company director, William C. Crocker.

Oatmeal Pancakes with Strawberry Sauce

6 SERVINGS

Start your day off right with the wholesome goodness of fiber-packed oat pancakes. Topped with strawberries, they're a sweet beginning to any morning.

1 cup quick-cooking oats

3 1/2 cups milk

2 cups all-purpose flour

1/4 cup margarine or butter, melted

3 tablespoons sugar

1 tablespoon baking powder

2 eggs

Strawberry Sauce (right)

1. Mix oats and milk in large bowl; let stand 5 minutes. Add remaining ingredients except Strawberry Sauce. Beat mixture on medium speed until well blended.

2. Heat griddle or skillet over medium heat or to 375°. Grease heated griddle, if necessary. To test griddle, sprinkle with a few drops of water. If bubbles jump around, heat is just right. For each pancake, pour 3 tablespoons batter onto hot griddle. Cook pancakes until puffed and dry around edges. Turn and cook other side until golden brown. Serve with warm Strawberry Sauce.

STRAWBERRY SAUCE

1 package (10 ounces) frozen sliced strawberries, thawed

2 teaspoons cornstarch

Drain strawberries; reserve liquid. Combine liquid and cornstarch in small saucepan. Cook over medium heat about 1 minute or until mixture boils. Stir in strawberries; cook 1 minute.

1 SERVING: Calories 320 (Calories from Fat 90); Fat 10g (Saturated 3g); Cholesterol 60mg; Sodium 330mg; Carbohydrates 51g (Dietary Fiber 3g); Protein 10g.

"First Lady of Food"

During the Great Depression and the war years of the 1940s, Betty rose to the challenge of helping America's families. Using her radio program, newspaper columns, and booklets (7 million copies of her booklet *Your Share* were distributed), she advised families on maintaining an adequate diet despite diminished wages and war-rationed foods. She was so respected that the United States Office of War Information asked her to do a special radio show on the NBC network called *Our Nation's Rations.* Her popularity soared (in 1945 she was the second best-known woman in America after Eleanor Roosevelt!), and she was pronounced the "First Lady of Food."

Cocoa Pancakes with Strawberries

EIGHT 4-INCH PANCAKES

Who can resist chocolate and strawberries together? What is great is that these pancakes are good for you, too.
They are low in fat and cholesterol!

2 egg whites or 1/4 cup fat-free cholesterol-free egg
    product

3/4 cup milk

1 tablespoon margarine or butter, melted

3/4 cup all-purpose flour

1/4 cup sugar

2 tablespoons baking cocoa

1 teaspoon baking powder

1/8 teaspoon salt

1/8 teaspoon ground nutmeg

1 cup vanilla fat-free yogurt, if desired

1 cup sliced strawberries

Cocoa Pancakes with Strawberries

1. Beat egg whites in medium bowl with hand
   beater until foamy. Beat in milk and margarine
   until smooth. Stir in remaining ingredients
   except yogurt and strawberries.

2. Spray griddle or skillet with nonstick cooking
   spray. Heat over medium heat or to 375°. To
   test griddle, sprinkle with a few drops of water.
   If bubbles jump around, heat is just right.

3. For each pancake, pour slightly less than 1/4 cup
   batter from cup or pitcher onto hot griddle.
   Cook pancakes until puffed and dry around
   edges. Turn and cook other sides until golden
   brown. Serve with yogurt and strawberries.

1 PANCAKE: Calories 95 (Calories from Fat 20); Fat 2g (Saturated 1g); Cholesterol 2mg; Sodium 140mg; Carbohydrates 17g
(Dietary Fiber 1g); Protein 3g.

Banana Pecan Pancakes

TWENTY-SEVEN 4-INCH PANCAKES

No time for pancakes in the mornings? Try the breakfast-for-dinner approach and make sure these wonderful pancakes are on your menu.

2 eggs

2 cups all-purpose flour

2 cups buttermilk

2 cups mashed ripe bananas (4 medium)

1/4 cup granulated or packed brown sugar

1/4 cup vegetable oil

2 teaspoons baking powder

1 teaspoon baking soda

1/2 teaspoon salt

1 cup chopped pecans, toasted, if desired

3 medium bananas, sliced

3 cups strawberry halves

Maple-flavored syrup

Sweetened whipped cream, if desired

Ground nutmeg, if desired

1. Beat eggs in medium bowl with hand beater until fluffy. Beat in flour, buttermilk, mashed bananas, sugar, oil, baking powder, baking soda and salt just until smooth. Stir in pecans. (For thinner pancakes, stir in addition 1 to 2 tablespoons milk.)

2. Heat griddle or skillet over medium heat or to 375°. Grease heated griddle, if necessary. To test griddle, sprinkle with a few drops of water. If bubbles jump around, heat is just right.

3. For each pancake, pour slightly less than 1/4 cup batter from cup or pitcher onto hot griddle. Cook pancakes until puffed and dry around edges. Turn and cook other sides until golden brown.

4. Serve pancakes with sliced bananas and strawberry halves. Drizzle with syrup. Top with whipped cream; sprinkle with nutmeg.

1 PANCAKE: Calories 105 (Calories from Fat 25); Fat 3g (Saturated 1g); Cholesterol 15mg; Sodium 150mg; Carbohydrates 18g (Dietary Fiber 1g); Protein 2g.

Dear Betty . . .

One of the many ways that Betty Crocker stayed in touch with American homemakers was through her weekly newspaper column. In 1939, she was dispensing advice and answering questions in about 400 newspapers across the country. The column hasn't run continuously, but in the late 1990s, it was carried by about 970 newspapers. Today's consumers are still seeking advice from their favorite food authority!

Banana Pecan Pancakes

Cinnamon French Toast

French toast doesn't get much better than this! Use cinnamon-raisin bread for a real treat, or sprinkle the golden slices of cinnamon bread with raisins.

3 eggs

3/4 cup milk

1 tablespoon sugar

1/4 teaspoon vanilla

1/8 teaspoon salt

8 slices cinnamon or plain sandwich bread

1. Beat eggs, milk, sugar, vanilla and salt with hand beater until smooth.

2. Heat griddle or skillet over medium-low heat or to 375°. Grease heated griddle, if necessary. To test griddle, sprinkle with a few drops of water. If bubbles jump around, heat is just right.

3. Dip bread into egg mixture, coating both sides. Place on griddle. Cook about 4 minutes on each side or until golden brown.

1 SLICE: Calories 105 (Calories from Fat 25); Fat 3g (Saturated 1g); Cholesterol 80mg; Sodium 210mg; Carbohydrates 16g (Dietary Fiber 1g); Protein 5g.

Surprise French Toast

Add an extra "surprise" to your French toast. Spread some tangy orange marmalade and some chunky peanut butter, along with the cream cheese in the recipe. Or any of your favorite jams or jellys would work.

1 package (3 ounces) cream cheese

16 slices (1/2 inch thick) French bread

1 cup milk

4 eggs

2 tablespoons margarine or butter

Powdered sugar

Syrup

1. Spread 1 tablespoon cream cheese on each of 8 bread slices; top with second bread slice. Whisk together milk and eggs in large bowl.

2. Heat griddle or large skillet over medium heat or to 350°. Melt margarine.

3. Dip sandwiches in egg mixture; carefully place on griddle. Cook about 8 minutes on a side until golden brown. Sprinkle with powdered sugar; serve with syrup.

1 SLICE: Calories 485 (Calories from Fat 205); Fat 23g (Saturated 9g); Cholesterol 240mg; Sodium 820mg; Carbohydrates 54g (Dietary Fiber 3g); Protein 19g.

Mom's Best Waffles

TWELVE 4-INCH WAFFLE SQUARES

Mom, you'll get rave reviews when you serve these waffles. They're perfect for weekend breakfasts. If you have any leftover, just put them in the freezer or refrigerator, so they are ready to pop in the toaster for another delicious breakfast anytime during the week.

2 eggs

2 cups all-purpose or whole wheat flour

1 3/4 cups milk

1/2 cup vegetable oil

1 tablespoon granulated or packed brown sugar

4 teaspoons baking powder

1/4 teaspoon salt

1. Spray nonstick waffle iron with nonstick cooking spray, if necessary. Heat waffle iron.

2. Beat eggs in large bowl with hand beater until fluffy. Beat in remaining ingredients just until smooth.

3. Pour about 1/2 cup batter from cup or pitcher onto center of hot waffle iron. (Waffle irons vary in size; check manufacturer's directions for recommended amount of batter.) Close lid of waffle iron.

4. Bake about 5 minutes or until steaming stops. Carefully remove waffle.

1 WAFFLE SQUARE: Calories 190 (Calories from Fat 100); Fat 11g (Saturated 2g); Cholesterol 40mg; Sodium 240mg; Carbohydrates 19g (Dietary Fiber 0g); Protein 4g.

Nut Waffles

TWELVE 4-INCH WAFFLE SQUARES
(THREE 9-INCH WAFFLES)

Your family will be nutty for these waffles. The kind of nuts you can use is endless—walnuts, pecans, almonds or even pistachios. They're great!

2 eggs

2 cups all-purpose or whole wheat flour

1/2 cup vegetable oil or margarine or butter, melted

1 3/4 cups milk

1 tablespoon granulated or brown sugar

4 teaspoons baking powder

1/4 teaspoon salt

2 tablespoons coarsely chopped or broken nuts

1. Spray nonstick waffle iron with nonstick cooking spray, if necessary. Heat waffle iron.

2. Beat eggs with hand beater in medium bowl until fluffy. Beat in remaining ingredients just until smooth.

3. Pour batter from cup or pitcher onto center of hot waffle iron. Immediately sprinkle with nuts. (Waffle irons vary in size; check manufacturer's directions for recommended amount of batter.) Close lid of waffle iron.

4. Bake about 5 minutes or until steaming stops. Carefully remove waffle.

1 WAFFLE SQUARE: Calories 195 (Calories from Fat 110); Fat 12g (Saturated 3g); Cholesterol 40mg; Sodium 240mg; Carbohydrates 19g (Dietary Fiber 1g); Protein 4g.

Rise and Shine Waffles

You won't believe these flavor-packed waffles are also a low-fat, low-cholesterol breakfast. Top off with a spoonful of creamy maple-flavored yogurt—we're sure you'll love them.

3/4 cup old-fashioned oats

1/4 cup packed brown sugar

1 cup milk

2 egg whites, slightly beaten, or 1/4 cup fat-free cholesterol-free egg product

3 tablespoons margarine or butter, melted

2/3 cup all-purpose flour

2 tablespoons wheat germ

2 teaspoons baking powder

1/4 teaspoon baking soda

1 teaspoon grated orange peel

Maple Yogurt Topping (right)

Grated orange peel, if desired

Chopped cranberries, if desired

1. Mix oats, brown sugar and milk in large bowl; let stand 10 minutes. Stir in egg whites and margarine. Stir in flour, wheat germ, baking powder, baking soda and 1 teaspoon orange peel.

2. Spray nonstick waffle iron with nonstick cooking spray; heat waffle iron. Pour about 1 cup batter from cup or pitcher onto center of hot waffle iron. (Waffle irons vary in size; check manufacturer's directions for recommended amount of batter.) Close lid of waffle iron.

3. Bake 4 to 5 minutes or until steaming stops. Carefully remove waffle. Top with Maple Yogurt Topping. Garnish with orange peel and cranberries.

MAPLE YOGURT TOPPING

1 cup plain fat-free yogurt

1/4 cup maple-flavored syrup

Mix ingredients until well blended.

1 WAFFLE SQUARE: Calories 200 (Calories from Fat 55); Fat 6g (Saturated 2g); Cholesterol 5mg; Sodium 270mg; Carbohydrates 31g (Dietary Fiber 1g); Protein 6g.

"Kitchen Tested"

Did you ever wonder what was meant by "Kitchen Tested" on the packages of Gold Medal flour? In 1925, company officials decided to have home economists in the company kitchens test the performance of Gold Medal flour in typical household baked goods. Once proven that the flour was of high quality, it could be shipped and sold to homemakers who could depend on it to produce high-quality foods for their families.

Rise and Shine Waffles

Banana and Chocolate Chip Waffles

TWELVE 4-INCH WAFFLE SQUARES

Mmmmm! Bananas and chocolate together make a winning breakfast combination.
Freeze any over-ripe bananas you might have sitting on your counter and you will always have them on hand
when the urge hits to make these luscious pancakes.

2 eggs

2 cups all-purpose flour

1/2 cup mashed ripe banana (1 medium)

1 1/2 cups milk

1/3 cup vegetable oil or 1/3 cup margarine or butter, melted

1 tablespoon sugar

4 teaspoons baking powder

1/4 teaspoon salt

1/2 cup miniature semisweet chocolate chips

2 medium bananas, sliced

2 tablespoons miniature semisweet chocolate chips

Strawberry-flavored syrup

1. Spray nonstick waffle iron with nonstick cooking spray; heat waffle iron.

2. Beat eggs in medium bowl with electric mixer on medium speed 1 minute. Beat in flour, mashed banana, milk, oil, sugar, baking powder and salt just until smooth. Stir in 1/2 cup chocolate chips.

3. Pour about 1/2 cup batter from cup or pitcher onto center of hot waffle iron. (Waffle irons vary in size; check manufacturer's directions for recommended amount of batter.) Close lid of waffle iron.

4. Bake about 5 minutes or until steaming stops. Carefully remove waffle.

5. Serve waffles with sliced bananas and 2 tablespoons chocolate chips. Drizzle with syrup.

1 WAFFLE SQUARE: Calories 210 (Calories from Fat 90); Fat 10g (Saturated 4g); Cholesterol 40mg; Sodium 240mg; Carbohydrates 31g (Dietary Fiber 1g); Protein 5g.

Betty Crocker Kitchens Resource Center

One of the more interesting areas in the Betty Crocker Kitchens is the Resource Center, affectionately known as the "cookbook library." It is actually a collection of many different types of resources—2,000 cookbooks; over 100 food reference books, encyclopedias and dictionaries; nearly 500 files of articles and recipes clippings; electronic and CD-ROM cookbooks; and more than sixty food and women's magazines—available to the staff who work in the kitchens. It began about fifty years ago as a small collection of cookbooks, but grew and is now staffed by a professional Information Specialist. All this helps the Betty Crocker Kitchens staff better understand the wants and needs of our consumers.

Banana and Chocolate Chip Waffles

Maple-Pecan Waffles

6 SERVINGS

Waffles are such a treat in the morning. The combination of maple and pecans is hard to beat, especially with date-butter and sweet syrup cascading down your stack of steaming, hot waffles!

4 eggs

4 cups all-purpose flour

2 cups milk

1 1/2 cups maple-flavored syrup

1 cup margarine or butter, melted

1/4 cup chopped pecans

2 tablespoons baking powder

Date Butter (right)

1. Spray nonstick waffle iron with nonstick cooking spray; heat waffle iron.

2. Beat eggs until fluffy in large bowl; beat in remaining ingredients except Date Butter just until smooth.

3. Pour batter from cup or pitcher onto center of hot waffle iron. (Waffle irons vary in size; check manufacturer's directions for recommended amount of batter.) Close lid of waffle iron.

4. Bake until steaming stops, about 5 minutes. Remove waffle carefully. Serve with Date Butter.

DATE BUTTER

1/2 cup margarine or butter

1/4 cup chopped dates

Mix margarine and dates in small bowl until well blended.

1 WAFFLE SQUARE: Calories 265 (Calories from Fat 125); Fat 14g (Saturated 3g); Cholesterol 40mg; Sodium 300mg; Carbohydrates 32g (Dietary Fiber 1g); Protein 4g.

Radio Betty

Did you ever listen to Betty Crocker on the radio? Many folks did. In 1924, the *Betty Crocker Cooking School of the Air* began on a local radio station in Minneapolis. The station was a way for Betty to help and inspire women in their quest to make a happy home for their families. The show became so popular that it began broadcasting nationally in 1927, and it even occasionally featured celebrity interviews with the likes of Cary Grant, Joan Crawford, and Clark Gable. Betty had connections! She continued to dispense advice over the air for over twenty-four years, providing millions of listeners with recipes and tips. In 1998, the program was revived in a different format, in keeping with the busy lives of today's listeners. It airs Monday through Friday in ninety-second spots and focuses on innovative, topical food themes.

Muffins & Sweet Cakes

Orange-Currant Scones
(page 49)

Brown Sugar Muffins

12 MUFFINS

Make these easy and delicious muffins on a morning when you want to wake up the family with enticing smells wafting from the kitchen.

1 cup quick-cooking oats

1/2 cup milk

3/4 cup packed brown sugar

1/4 cup margarine or butter, melted

1 egg

1 cup all-purpose flour

1/2 cup chopped walnuts

2 teaspoons baking powder

1. Heat oven to 400°. Grease 12 medium muffin cups, 2 1/2 x 1 1/4 inches, or line with paper baking cups.

2. Mix oats, milk and brown sugar in large bowl; let stand 5 minutes. Add margarine and egg; blend well. Stir in remaining ingredients just until moistened.

3. Fill muffin cups two-thirds full. Bake 15 or 20 minutes or until toothpick inserted in center comes out clean.

1 MUFFIN: Calories 195 (Calories from Fat 70); Fat 8g (Saturated 1g); Cholesterol 20mg; Sodium 150mg; Carbohydrates 28g (Dietary Fiber 1g); Protein 4g.

Apple-Buckwheat Muffins

18 MUFFINS

Not only are these robust muffins—with bits of juicy apples and crunchy nuts—great for breakfast, you can also serve them piping hot for lunch, with a bowl of hearty soup.

1 1/2 cups all-purpose flour

1/2 cup buckwheat or whole wheat flour

1/2 cup sugar

1 tablespoon baking powder

1/4 teaspoon salt

3/4 cup apple juice

1/4 cup margarine or butter, melted

1 egg

1 cup chopped walnuts

1 large tart apple, peeled, cored and chopped

1. Heat oven to 400°. Grease bottoms only of 18 medium muffin cups, 2 1/2 x 1 1/4 inches, or line with paper baking cups.

2. Mix all-purpose flour, buckwheat flour, sugar, baking powder and salt in large bowl. Stir in apple juice, margarine and egg just until blended (batter will be lumpy). Stir in walnuts and chopped apple.

3. Divide batter evenly among muffin cups, filling two-thirds full. Bake 20 to 25 minutes or until toothpick inserted in center comes out clean. Cool 5 minutes; remove from pan.

1 MUFFIN: Calories 145 (Calories from Fat 65); Fat 7g (Saturated 1g); Cholesterol 10mg; Sodium 150mg; Carbohydrates 19g (Dietary Fiber 1g); Protein 3g.

Praline Peach Muffins

12 MUFFINS

When the sweet aroma of fresh, ripe peaches welcomes you at the supermarket, you'll be glad you have this recipe. If you are planning on using fresh peaches, be sure to choose freestone peaches instead of clingstone. Freestone peaches will release the pit without much effort.

Topping (right)

1/2 cup packed brown sugar

1/2 cup milk

1/3 cup vegetable oil

1 teaspoon vanilla

1 egg

1 2/3 cups all-purpose flour

2 teaspoons baking powder

1/4 teaspoon salt

1 cup chopped fresh or frozen (thawed and drained) or canned (well drained) peaches

1/2 cup coarsely chopped pecans

1. Heat oven to 400°. Grease bottoms only of 12 medium muffin cups, 2 1/2 x 1 1/4 inches, or line with paper baking cups.

2. Prepare Topping; set aside. Beat brown sugar, milk, oil, vanilla and egg in large bowl. Stir in flour, baking powder and salt just until flour is moistened. Fold in peaches and pecans.

3. Divide batter evenly among muffin cups (cups will be almost full). Sprinkle with Topping.

4. Bake 18 to 20 minutes or until golden brown. Immediately remove from pan to wire rack. Serve warm if desired.

TOPPING

1 tablespoon firm margarine or butter

1/4 cup packed brown sugar

1/4 cup chopped pecans

Cut margarine into remaining ingredients, using pastry blender or crisscrossing 2 knives, until crumbly.

1 MUFFIN: Calories 245 (Calories from Fat 115); Fat 13g (Saturated 2g); Cholesterol 20mg; Sodium 160mg; Carbohydrates 30g (Dietary Fiber 1g); Protein 3g.

Elaine Birks
Minneapolis, Minnesota

The name Betty Crocker has been in our household since I can remember. My memories are of a red-and-white three-ring book with Betty Crocker written on the front. Some of the pages still have small spatters of cake batter and cookie dough on them. The Lemon Meringue Pie recipe holds three generations of very

special memories, particularly for my mother. My great grandmother made this recipe for very special occasions, and my mother was allowed to do the measuring and make the meringue. It was a great lesson.

Cooking has been a part of my life since I can remember. As I matured I began to wonder if my friends and family enjoyed my dishes so much, others could also. So with that in mind, Grandma's Skillet Catering Services came to fruition. Family tradition is baked into each delectable dish I prepare. This is my way of continuing to share family traditions and values with the community. My most recent project is collecting family recipes and incorporating them into a fun-filled cookbook.

Grandma's Skillet is a community-based business, and each year we will be donating two events to assist in supporting preferably a youth program. In addition, Grandma's Skillet has formed a positive and productive relationship with the Hubert H. Humphrey Job Corp Culinary program. This program allows me to give young people the opportunity to get work experience in a minority-owned catering business. It gives them the opportunity to learn how to make typically ethnic dishes.

Blueberry Streusel Muffins

12 MUFFINS

No streusel for you? That's fine. You can make these muffins without the streusel topping if you like—the baking time will be the same.

Streusel Topping (below)

1 cup milk

1/4 cup vegetable oil

1/2 teaspoon vanilla

1 egg

2 cups all-purpose or whole
   wheat flour

1/3 cup sugar

3 teaspoons baking powder

1/2 teaspoon salt

1 cup fresh or canned (drained)
   blueberries*

STREUSEL TOPPING

2 tablespoons firm stick
   margarine or butter

1/4 cup all-purpose flour

2 tablespoons packed brown
   sugar

1/4 teaspoon ground cinnamon

1. Heat oven to 400°. Grease bottoms only of 12 medium muffin cups, 2 1/2 x 1 1/4 inches, with shortening, or line with paper baking cups.

2. Prepare Streusel Topping; set aside.

3. Beat milk, oil, vanilla and egg in large bowl. Stir in flour, sugar, baking powder and salt all at once just until flour is moistened (batter will be lumpy). Fold in blueberries. Divide batter evenly among muffin cups. Sprinkle each with about 2 teaspoons topping.

4. Bake 20 to 25 minutes or until golden brown. Immediately remove from pan to wire rack. Serve warm if desired.

STREUSEL TOPPING

Cut margarine into flour, brown sugar and cinnamon in medium bowl, using pastry blender or crisscrossing 2 knives, until crumbly.

1 MUFFIN: Calories 195 (Calories from Fat 70); Fat 8g (Saturated 1g); Cholesterol 20mg; Sodium 250mg; Carbohydrates 29g (Dietary Fiber 1g); Protein 3g.

*3/4 cup frozen (thawed and well drained) blueberries can be substituted for the fresh or canned blueberries.

Mountain Bran Muffins

12 MUFFINS

Freshly baked muffins from a homemade mix can be a real boon to busy families. This handy mix—based on a cherished bran bread recipe from the Colorado mountains—can be stored in a cool, dry place. The next time you're longing for a rich, moist bran muffin packed with walnuts and raisins, you'll be all ready to go! The Mountain Bran Mix makes about 7 1/2 cups of the mix—which is enough for 3 dozen muffins!

1 cup buttermilk

1 egg

2 1/2 cups Mountain Bran Mix (right)

1/2 cup chopped walnuts

1/2 cup raisins

1. Heat oven to 400°. Grease bottoms only of 12 medium muffin cups, 2 1/2 x 1 1/4 inches, or line with paper baking cups.

2. Beat buttermilk and egg in large bowl. Stir in Mountain Bran Mix just until moistened; fold in walnuts and raisins.

3. Divide batter evenly among muffin cups (about seven-eighths full). Bake until golden brown or toothpick inserted in center comes out clean, 18 to 20 minutes. Let stand 3 minutes; remove muffins from pan.

MOUNTAIN BRAN MIX

3 cups all-purpose flour

3 cups Fiber One® cereal, finely crushed

2 cups packed brown sugar

1 1/2 teaspoons baking soda

1 1/2 teaspoons baking powder

1 1/2 teaspoons salt

1/2 cup shortening

Mix flour, cereal, brown sugar, baking soda, baking powder and salt in 4-quart bowl. Cut in shortening until mixture resembles coarse crumbs. Cover and store in cool, dry place no longer than 1 month.

1 MUFFIN: Calories 190 (Calories from Fat 65); Fat 7g (Saturated 1g); Cholesterol 20mg; Sodium 220mg; Carbohydrates 31g (Dietary Fiber 3g); Protein 4g.

Strawberry Muffins

12 MUFFINS

Stir a little honey into some softened butter and serve it with these muffins, fresh from the oven. It's delicious!

3/4 cup milk

1/2 cup vegetable oil

1 tablespoon grated orange peel

1 egg

2 cups all-purpose flour

1 cup chopped strawberries

1/3 cup sugar

1 tablespoon baking powder

1/4 teaspoon salt

Pecan Streusel Topping (right)

1. Heat oven to 400°. Grease 12 medium muffin cups, 2 1/2 x 1 1/4 inches, or line with paper baking cups.

2. Mix milk, oil, orange peel and egg in large bowl until well blended. Stir in remaining ingredients except Pecan Streusel Topping, just until moistened.

3. Prepare Pecan Streusel Topping. Fill muffin cups two-thirds full with batter. Sprinkle batter with Pecan Streusel Topping. Bake 15 to 20 minutes or until toothpick inserted in center comes out clean.

PECAN STREUSEL TOPPING

1/2 cup chopped pecans

1/2 cup packed brown sugar

1/4 cup all-purpose flour

2 tablespoons melted margarine or butter

Mix all ingredients until well blended.

1 MUFFIN: Calories 285 (Calories from Fat 135); Fat 15g (Saturated 2g); Cholesterol 20mg; Sodium 210mg; Carbohydrates 35g (Dietary Fiber 1g); Protein 4g.

Strawberry Muffins

Marion Kallfelz Rechsteiner

Wilmington, Delaware

There is no one more youthful and full of zest for life and spirit than the seventy-three-year-young Marion Kallfelz Rechsteiner, attorney-at-law and president of Delaware Press Women.

While earning a B.A. degree at Syracuse University, Marion lived in a cooperative house, where she often had to cook for twenty women. Two weeks after graduation, Marion replaced a man as editor of a weekly newspaper, where she claims she got her real journalism education, doing every imaginable job but sweeping the floor. In her career as a journalist, Marion proved—in an era when it was uncommon—that a woman could do a man's job as editor of a weekly paper.

A bridal shower gift of the famous *Betty Crocker's Picture Cook Book* proved invaluable with its basic instructions, especially when she and Leo moved to Wilmington, Delaware, and had three daughters. At Christmas they made good use of *Betty Crocker's Cookie Carnival* book. Both show signs of great wear and use.

Marion enrolled, at age sixty, in the Antioch School of Law, Washington, D.C., and subsequently in the Widener University School of Law. Marion serves as an attorney for Legal Aid of Chester County, Pennsylvania, helping clients with personal problems such as housing, divorce, custody, and debt collection.

Because of a strong commitment to her community, she is a volunteer for the Hagley Museum and Library; she serves on the board of the Delaware Interfaith Coalition on Aging; she is a member of the advisory committee for a neighborhood group home for people from the state mental hospital; and she continues to serve as a lector at her church. Marion has received numerous honors and awards for cooking and baking and for her commitment to her community and her profession. When asked the secret to leading such a fast-paced and productive life, Marion said, "It's better to wear out than rust out."

Blueberry Buckle Coffee Cake

This "buckle" is made by tossing summer fruit into a sweet cake batter and sprinkling with a buttery crumb topping. The juicy blueberries will bubble and ooze up through the cake batter and add a bit of summery sweetness in each bite of this delicious cake.

2 cups all-purpose flour

3/4 cup sugar

2 1/2 teaspoons baking powder

3/4 teaspoon salt

1/4 cup shortening

3/4 cup milk

1 egg

2 cups fresh or frozen (thawed and drained) blueberries

Crumb Topping (below)

Glaze (below)

1. Heat oven to 375°. Grease square pan, 9 x 9 x 2 inches, or round pan, 9 x 1 1/2 inches.

2. Blend flour, sugar, baking powder, salt, shortening, milk and egg; beat 30 seconds. Carefully stir in blueberries. Spread butter in pan; sprinkle with Crumb Topping.

3. Bake 45 to 50 minutes or until toothpick inserted in center comes out clean. Drizzle with Glaze. Serve warm.

CRUMB TOPPING

1/2 cup sugar

1/3 cup all-purpose flour

1/2 teaspoon ground cinnamon

1/4 cup margarine or butter, softened

CRUMB TOPPING

Mix all ingredients until crumbly.

GLAZE

1/2 cup powdered sugar

1/4 teaspoon vanilla

1 1/2 to 2 teaspoons hot water

GLAZE

Mix all ingredients until drizzling consistency.

1 SERVING: Calories 380 (Calories from Fat 110); Fat 12g (Saturated 5g); Cholesterol 40mg; Sodium 390mg; Carbohydrates 65g (Dietary Fiber 2g); Protein 5g.

Sweet Corn Bread Muffins

12 MUFFINS

Cornmeal is available in textures ranging from fine to coarse. You'll find grocery stores commonly carry a finely ground cornmeal which will make a light, soft bread. The coarser cornmeals, often called stone ground, give breads a stronger flavor and coarser texture. Stone-ground cornmeal is delicious in this recipe.

1 cup milk

1/4 cup margarine or butter, melted

1 egg

1 1/4 cups cornmeal

1 cup all-purpose flour

1/2 cup sugar

1 tablespoon baking powder

1/2 teaspoon salt

1. Heat oven to 400°. Grease bottoms only of 12 medium muffin cups, 2 1/2 x 1 1/4 inches, or line with paper baking cups.

2. Beat milk, margarine and egg in 3-quart bowl. Stir in remaining ingredients all at once just until flour is moistened (batter will be lumpy).

3. Fill muffin cups about three-fourths full. Bake until golden brown and toothpick inserted in center comes out clean, 20 to 25 minutes.

1 MUFFIN: Calories 175 (Calories from Fat 45); Fat 5g (Saturated 1g); Cholesterol 20mg; Sodium 290mg; Carbohydrates 29g (Dietary Fiber 1g); Protein 4g.

Lemon and Poppy Seed Scones

8 SCONES

Did you know it takes over 900,000 poppy seeds to make one pound? You'll find their crunchy texture and nutty flavor pleasing in these scones.

2 cups all-purpose flour

3 teaspoons baking powder

1/4 teaspoon salt

1/4 cup sugar

1 tablespoon poppy seed

1/3 cup firm margarine or butter

1/3 cup currants

2 tablespoons lemon juice

3/4 cup milk

1. Heat oven to 425°. Spray cookie sheet with non-stick cooking spray.

2. Mix flour, baking powder, salt, sugar and poppy seed in large bowl. Cut in margarine, using pastry blender or crisscrossing 2 knives, until mixture resembles fine crumbs. Stir in currants. Mix lemon juice and milk; stir into flour mixture.

3. Turn dough onto lightly floured surface. Knead lightly 10 times. Pat or roll into 9-inch circle on ungreased cookie sheet. Brush with milk and sprinkle with sugar if desired. Cut into 8 wedges, but do not separate.

4. Bake 12 to 15 minutes or until golden brown. Immediately remove from cookie sheet; carefully separate wedges. Serve warm.

1 SCONE: Calories 240 (Calories from Fat 80); Fat 9g (Saturated 2g); Cholesterol 2mg; Sodium 360mg; Carbohydrates 37g (Dietary Fiber 1g); Protein 4g.

Orange-Currant Scones

ABOUT 20 SCONES

Currants look like tiny, dark raisins. If they are unavailable, you can always substitute dark or golden raisins for the currants. If you want to add a sweet-tart twist, mix in dried cranberries or blueberries for the currants.

1/2 cup currants

1/3 cup margarine or butter

1 3/4 cups all-purpose flour

3 tablespoons sugar

2 1/2 teaspoons baking powder

1/4 teaspoon salt

1 tablespoon grated orange peel

1 egg, beaten

4 to 6 tablespoons half-and-half

1 egg white, beaten

1. Heat oven to 400°.

2. Soak currants in warm water for 10 minutes to soften; drain. Cut margarine into flour, sugar, baking powder and salt with pastry blender until mixture resembles fine crumbs. Stir in orange peel, egg, currants and just enough half-and-half until dough leaves side of bowl.

3. Turn dough onto lightly floured surface. Knead lightly 10 times. Divide dough into 2 parts. Roll or pat into two 6-inch circles about 1/2 inch thick. Place on ungreased cookie sheet; brush with beaten egg white.

4. Bake 10 to 12 minutes or until golden brown. Immediately remove from cookie sheet. Cut into wedges to serve.

1 SCONE: Calories 95 (Calories from Fat 35); Fat 4g (Saturated 1g); Cholesterol 10mg; Sodium 140mg; Carbohydrates 13g (Dietary Fiber 0g); Protein 2g.

Citrus-Banana Compote

6 SERVINGS

This sweet compote is wonderful over pancakes or even as a dessert topping spooned over ice cream, pound cake or angel food cake. Even better—the lime juice and oranges keep the sliced banana fresh-looking.

1/2 cup sugar

1/2 cup water

2 tablespoons grated orange peel

2 tablespoons grated lime peel

4 bananas, peeled and sliced

2 oranges, peeled and cut into sections

2 tablespoons lime juice

1. Heat sugar and water to boiling in small saucepan over medium heat. Stir in orange peel and lime peel; boil 2 minutes, stirring occasionally. Let mixture stand 5 minutes.

2. Mix bananas and oranges with lime juice in medium bowl. Pour warm syrup over fruit. Serve fruit warm.

1 SERVING: Calories 155 (Calories from Fat 0); Fat 0g (Saturated 0g); Cholesterol 0mg; Sodium 0mg; Carbohydrates 41g (Dietary Fiber 3g); Protein 1g.

Dorothy Jane (D.J.) Edwards

Santa Rosa, California

My mom is seventy-five years old, the same age as Betty Crocker. She married in 1941, baked her first yeast bread from a Betty Crocker recipe, and never bought a loaf of store-bought bread the first year she was married. She has been cooking with Betty Crocker ever since and says Betty Crocker taught her HOW to cook and bake.

She still uses a tiny, dog-eared copy of the *Betty Crocker Cook Book of All-Purpose Baking*, (1942), and the *Betty Crocker Picture Cook Book* (1950) was what she used to teach me and my sister our way around the kitchen. I still remember that one of the family traditions she started when we were little was baking the Christ Child's Birthday Cake—a small, star-shaped Betty Crocker cake that was served on Christmas Eve, lighted with candles. She says she learned early on that it is important to find a source of recipes you can trust, so you know the product will "turn out" okay.

My two brothers also came in for their share of instruction from Mother. After they left home, Malcolm surprised her by serving brownies he had baked from a Betty Crocker mix in his college apartment kitchen. Martin says he was brought up with the idea that the name Betty Crocker is synonymous with good food! . . . And now her grandchildren are getting acquainted with Betty Crocker, baking Betty Crocker brownies, biscuits, and having fun with various cake mixes.

D.J. has a background of work with Girl Scouts, Boy Scouts, PTA, and especially her church. She is currently on its Finance and Management Board and helps write the church newsletter. She is also well known as a creative solo liturgical dancer, and choreographs original dances, which she performs in worship services in churches across the country. She writes and publishes The Grand Kids Newsletter for her ten grandchildren and their parents, trying to encourage communication between far-flung cousins.

French Breakfast Puffs

15 PUFFS

The recipe for these sweet buns was first published in the 1920s on Washburn-Crosby flour recipe cards. The recipe came from Miss Esoline Beauregard in Florida, who sent it to Washburn-Crosby urging them to try her mother's wonderful recipe.

1/3 cup shortening

1/2 cup sugar

1 egg

1 1/2 cups all-purpose flour

1 1/2 teaspoons baking powder

1/2 teaspoon salt

1/4 teaspoon ground nutmeg

1/2 cup milk

1/2 cup sugar

1 teaspoon ground cinnamon

1/2 cup margarine or butter,
    melted

1. Heat oven to 350°. Grease 15 muffin cups, 2 1/2 x 1 1/4 inches.

2. Mix shortening, 1/2 cup sugar and egg thoroughly. Mix flour, baking powder, salt and nutmeg; stir into egg mixture alternately with milk.

3. Fill muffin cups two-thirds full. Bake 20 to 25 minutes or until golden brown. Mix 1/2 cup sugar and cinnamon. Roll hot muffins immediately in melted butter, then in sugar-cinnamon mixture. Serve hot.

1 PUFF: Calories 205 (Calories from Fat 100); Fat 11g (Saturated 5g); Cholesterol 30mg; Sodium 180mg; Carbohydrates 24g (Dietary Fiber 0g); Protein 2g.

Cinnamon Biscuit Fans

8 BISCUITS

Looking for a shortcut? A fast and easy way to cut margarine into flour mixture is to slice the margarine into smaller pieces and place all the ingredients into the bowl of a food processor. With a few quick pulses, the flour mixture and margarine will cut in perfectly.

1/3 cup firm margarine or butter

2 cups all-purpose flour

2 tablespoons sugar

3 teaspoons baking powder

1/2 teaspoon salt

About 3/4 cup milk

3 tablespoons margarine or butter, softened

3 tablespoons sugar

1 teaspoon ground cinnamon

Glaze (right)

1. Heat oven to 425°. Grease 8 medium muffin cups, 2 1/2 x 1 1/4 inches.

2. Cut 1/3 cup margarine into flour, 2 tablespoons sugar, the baking powder and salt in large bowl, using pastry blender or crisscrossing 2 knives, until mixture resembles fine crumbs. Stir in just enough milk so dough leaves side of bowl and forms a ball.

3. Turn dough onto lightly floured surface. Knead lightly 10 times. Roll into rectangle, 12 x 10 inches. Spread 3 tablespoons margarine over rectangle. Mix 3 tablespoons sugar and the cinnamon; sprinkle over rectangle. Cut rectangle crosswise into 6 strips, 10 x 2 inches. Stack strips; cut crosswise into 8 pieces. Place cut sides up in muffin cups.

4. Bake 16 to 18 minutes or until golden brown. Immediately remove from pan. Drizzle Glaze over warm biscuits. Serve warm.

GLAZE

1/2 cup powdered sugar

2 to 2 1/2 teaspoons milk

Mix ingredients until smooth and thin enough to drizzle.

1 BISCUIT: Calories 295 (Calories from Fat 115); Fat 13g (Saturated 3g); Cholesterol 2mg; Sodium 480mg; Carbohydrates 41g (Dietary Fiber 0g); Protein 4g.

Cinnamon Biscuit Fans

Cora Putnam

Port St. Lucie, Florida

Cora Putnam is a package of energy, love, fortitude, concern, and confidence. She has a glow, a warmth about her, that has touched one and all.

Days and nights were bursting with child care as each child had severe health problems. Her seven children developed into responsible, hardworking adults through her sole guidance, her constant endurance, and vigorous love. When the children eventually grew up and left to answer destiny's call, she found herself raising two granddaughters.

Her jobs found her as a nurses aide, a waitress, and a restaurant manager. She baked cakes at home and local restaurants sold them as their own "homemade" desserts. Her *Betty Crocker Cookbook* was a constant companion. She worked three jobs to pay the bills and keep a roof over their heads. But dinnertime was always an adventure in food—her beautifully done roasts, at the very least three vegetables, and always two home-baked desserts.

The hard work never stopped. Her spirit never wavered. She attacked each day with vigor and might. Her neighbors and friends benefited from her constant generosity. Senior citizens were the recipients of glorious meals and scrumptious desserts year after year. Church raffles increased due to her cakes being auctioned off. Especially enjoyed was her Betty Crocker pound cake made with loving hands.

Now she has moved to Florida. Moving to a new state has meant meeting new friends and receiving visits from old ones. So there is Cora still making scrumptious meals and her wonderful special cakes.

Almond Puffs

MAKES 16 TO 20 PUFFS

With bits of almonds peppered through the sweet dough, plus the extra crunch on top, no one can resist the almondy goodness of this breakfast treat. What's great, you bake them in muffin tins, so they are easy to transport and share.

1 package active dry yeast

3/4 cup warm water (105° to
    115°)

1/4 cup sugar

1/4 cup shortening, margarine
    or butter, softened

1 teaspoon salt

1 egg

2 1/4 cups all-purpose flour

2/3 cup chopped blanched
    almonds

3 tablespoons sugar

1. Grease 16 to 20 medium muffin cups, 2 1/2 x 1 1/4 inches.

2. Dissolve yeast in warm water in large bowl. Add 1/4 cup sugar, the shortening, salt, egg, and 1 cup flour. Blend with electric mixer on low speed 1/2 minute, scraping bowl constantly. Beat on medium speed 2 minutes scraping bowl occasionally. Stir in remaining flour and 1/3 cup almonds.

3. Spoon batter into muffin cups filling each 1/2 full. Mix remaining 1/3 cup almonds and 3 tablespoons sugar; sprinkle on batter.

4. Cover and let rise in warm place about 1 hour or until double. Dough is ready if indention remains when touched.

5. Heat oven to 350°.

6. Bake 15 to 20 minutes or until golden brown.

1 PUFF: Calories 355 (Calories from Fat 110); Fat 12g (Saturated 5g); Cholesterol 40mg; Sodium 250mg; Carbohydrates 60g (Dietary Fiber 1g); Protein 3g.

Danish Puff

The next time you want to treat your co-workers to a little something special, bring in this puff and watch it disappear!

1/2 cup margarine or butter, softened

1 cup all-purpose flour

2 tablespoons water

1/2 cup margarine or butter

1 cup water

1 teaspoon almond extract

1 cup all-purpose flour

3 eggs

Powdered Sugar Glaze (right)

Sliced almonds or chopped nuts

1. Heat oven to 350°.

2. Cut 1/2 cup margarine into 1 cup flour until particles are size of small peas. Sprinkle 2 tablespoons water over mixture; mix with fork. Gather pastry in ball; divide in half. Pat each half into rectangle, 12 x 3 inches, about 3 inches apart on ungreased cookie sheet.

3. Heat 1/2 cup margarine and 1 cup water to rolling boil in 2-quart saucepan; remove from heat. Stir in almond extract and 1 cup flour quickly. Stir vigorously over low heat about 1 minute or until mixture forms a ball; remove from heat. Add eggs; beat until smooth.

4. Spread half of the topping over each rectangle. Bake about 1 hour or until topping is crisp and brown; cool.

5. Spread with Powdered Sugar Glaze; sprinkle with nuts.

POWDERED SUGAR GLAZE

1 1/2 cups powdered sugar

2 tablespoons margarine or butter, softened

1 1/2 teaspoons vanilla

1 to 2 tablespoons warm water

Mix all ingredients until smooth and spreadable.

1 PUFF: Calories 385 (Calories from Fat 215); Fat 24g (Saturated 14g); Cholesterol 120mg; Sodium 160mg; Carbohydrates 38g (Dietary Fiber 1g); Protein 5g.

Danish Puff

Sweet Breakfast Rolls

Let the wake-up call be the smell of freshly baked cinnamon rolls wafting through the house. It will be our little secret that you did not have to get up at the crack of dawn to prepare them.

3 1/2 to 4 cups all-purpose flour

1/3 cup granulated sugar

1 teaspoon salt

2 packages active dry yeast

1 cup very warm milk (120° to 130°)

1/3 cup margarine or butter, softened

1 egg

2 tablespoons margarine or butter, softened

2 tablespoons granulated sugar

2 tablespoons packed brown sugar

1 teaspoon ground cinnamon

Glaze (page 47)

1. Mix 2 cups of the flour, 1/3 cup granulated sugar, the salt and yeast in large bowl. Add milk, 1/3 cup butter and the egg.

2. Beat on low speed 1 minute, scraping bowl frequently. Stir in enough remaining flour, 1 cup at a time, to make dough easy to handle.

3. Turn dough onto lightly floured surface; knead about 5 minutes or until smooth and elastic. Place in greased bowl; turn greased side up. Cover and let rise in warm place about 1 1/2 hours or until double. (Dough is ready if indentation remains when touched.)

4. Grease rectangular pan, 13 x 9 x 2 inches.

5. Punch down dough. Flatten with hands or rolling pin into rectangle, 15 x 10 inches; spread with 2 tablespoons butter. Mix the brown sugar and cinnamon. Sprinkle evenly over rectangle. Roll up tightly, beginning at 15-inch side. Pinch edge of dough into roll to seal. Stretch and shape to make even.

6. Cut roll into fifteen 1-inch slices. Place slightly apart in pan. Wrap pan tightly with heavy-duty aluminum foil. Refrigerate at least 12 hours but no longer than 48 hours. (To bake immediately, do not wrap. Let rise in warm place about 30 minutes or until double. Bake as directed in step 7.)

7. Heat oven to 350°. Bake uncovered 30 to 35 minutes or until golden brown. Drizzle rolls with Glaze.

1 ROLL: Calories 380 (Calories from Fat 145); Fat 16g (Saturated 3g); Cholesterol 15mg; Sodium 320mg; Carbohydrates 55g (Dietary Fiber 1g); Protein 5g.

Penny Douglas
West Lafayette, Indiana

Mrs. Douglas's love for cooking was discovered when she was a very young girl, as she grew up on a ranch in the Sandhills of Nebraska. Harvesting, haying, and doing chores often found the rest of her family outdoors. Her mother trusted her to make the meals for the hungry brood, and everyone soon realized the talent that was there. She picked up a degree in home economics from the University of Nebraska and followed her new husband into the military. She promptly began teaching bread and pastry classes out of her home and entertained people with her baked delights. She has participated in baking contests (winning several prizes)and began a bread-baking business that has hungry customers waiting each week for "bread day."

Those who know Penny know of her commitment to family and friends. Probably Penny's greatest commitment was shown just a few years ago to a dear neighbor dying of cancer. Penny baked her goods on a weekly basis not only to provide an opportunity to visit and cheer her but also to meet her needs for fighting the disease itself.

She has trained her family to be a great team that supports many areas of home management. In a day of waning commitment on the part of schools to the field of home economics, she has vowed that each of her offspring will have a good background and love for the "kitchen."

Mrs. Douglas is an active member of her local church and a ten-year leader in a local 4-H club. She is also an active member of the American Sewing Guild; the latest project was making clothes for children born prematurely at the local hospital. In her church she is the group leader for a number of wives who meet bimonthly to enjoy each other's company and to improve their marriages. By her actions Mrs. Douglas has blessed her family, and we have enjoyed sharing her with others.

Caramel-Pecan Sticky Rolls

MAKES 15 ROLLS

Save time tomorrow by preparing these rolls today! Prepare dough as directed, but do not let the dough rise after placing rolls in pan. Just cover the pan tightly with heavy-duty aluminum foil and pop it in the refrigerator for at least 12 hours but no longer than 24 hours. In the morning, bake them as directed in the recipe.

3 1/2 to 4 cups all-purpose or bread flour

1/3 cup granulated sugar

1 teaspoon salt

2 packages active dry yeast

1 cup very warm milk (120° to 130°)

1/3 cup stick margarine or butter, softened

1 egg

1 cup packed brown sugar

1/2 cup stick margarine or butter, softened

1/4 cup dark corn syrup

1 cup pecan halves (4 ounces)

2 tablespoons stick margarine or butter, softened

1/2 cup chopped pecans or raisins, if desired

1/4 cup granulated or packed brown sugar

1 teaspoon ground cinnamon

1. Mix 2 cups of the flour, 1/3 cup granulated sugar, the salt and yeast in large bowl. Add warm milk, 1/3 cup margarine and the egg. Beat with electric mixer on low speed 1 minute, scraping bowl frequently. Beat on medium speed 1 minute, scraping bowl frequently. Stir in enough remaining flour to make dough easy to handle.

2. Turn dough onto lightly floured surface. Knead about 5 minutes or until smooth and elastic. Place in greased bowl and turn greased side up. Cover and let rise in warm place about 1 hour 30 minutes or until double. Dough is ready if indentation remains when touched.

3. Heat 1 cup brown sugar and 1/2 cup margarine to boiling in 2-quart saucepan, stirring constantly; remove from heat. Stir in corn syrup. Pour into ungreased rectangular pan, 13 x 9 x 2 inches. Sprinkle with pecan halves.

4. Punch down dough. Flatten with hands or rolling pin into rectangle, 15 x 10 inches, on lightly floured surface. Spread with 2 tablespoons margarine. Mix chopped pecans, 1/4 cup granulated sugar and the cinnamon; sprinkle evenly over margarine. Roll rectangle up tightly, beginning at 15-inch side. Pinch edge of dough into roll to seal. Stretch and shape until even. Cut roll into fifteen 1-inch slices. Place slightly apart in pan. Cover and let rise in warm place about 30 minutes or until double.

5. Heat oven to 350°.

6. Bake 30 to 35 minutes or until golden brown. Immediately turn upside down onto heatproof tray or serving plate. Let stand 1 minute so caramel will drizzle over rolls; remove pan. Serve warm.

1 ROLL: Calories 370 (Calories from Fat 155); Fat 17g (Saturated 3g); Cholesterol 15mg; Sodium 300mg; Carbohydrates 51g (Dietary Fiber 2g); Protein 5g.

Chocolate Caramel Rolls

Gooey chocolate chips melted in between sweet dough! It doesn't get much better than this. These rolls make a nice treat for coffee break or anytime you want a little snack.

3 1/2 cups all-purpose flour

1/2 cup baking cocoa

1/3 cup granulated sugar

1/2 teaspoon salt

2 packages active dry yeast

1 cup very warm milk (120° to 130°)

1/3 cup margarine or butter, softened

1 egg

1 cup packed brown sugar

1/2 cup margarine or butter

1/4 cup dark corn syrup

3/4 cup pecan halves

2 tablespoons margarine or butter, softened

1/2 cup miniature semisweet chocolate chips

2 tablespoons packed brown sugar

1 teaspoon ground cinnamon

1. Mix 2 cups of the flour, the cocoa, granulated sugar, salt, and yeast in large bowl. Add milk, 1/3 cup margarine, and the egg. Beat with electric mixer on low speed 1 minute, scraping bowl frequently. Beat on medium speed 1 minute, scraping bowl frequently. Stir in the remaining flour (dough will be stiff).

2. Turn dough onto lightly floured surface. Knead about 5 minutes or until smooth and elastic. Place in greased bowl and turn greased side up. Cover and let rise in warm place about 1 1/2 hours or until double. (Dough is ready if indentation remains when touched.)

3. Heat 1 cup brown sugar and 1/2 cup margarine to boiling in 2-quart saucepan, stirring constantly; remove from heat. Stir in corn syrup. Pour into ungreased rectangular pan, 13 x 9 x 2 inches. Sprinkle with pecan halves.

4. Punch down dough. Flatten with hands or rolling pin into rectangle, 15 x 10 inches, on lightly floured surface. Spread with 2 tablespoons margarine. Mix chocolate chips, 2 tablespoons brown sugar and the cinnamon; sprinkle evenly over margarine. Roll up tightly, beginning at 15-inch side. Pinch edge of dough into roll to seal. Stretch and shape until even. Cut roll into fifteen 1-inch slices. Place slightly apart in pan. Cover and let rise in warm place about 30 minutes or until double.

5. Heat oven to 350°.

6. Bake 30 to 35 minutes or until dark brown. Immediately turn pan upside down into heatproof tray or serving plate. Let stand 1 minute so caramel will drizzle over rolls; remove pan.

1 ROLL: Calories 390 (Calories from Fat 160); Fat 18g (Saturated 4g); Cholesterol 15mg; Sodium 260mg; Carbohydrates 54g (Dietary Fiber 3g); Protein 6g.

Margaret (Marge) Zach
Portland, Oregon

I always thought my mother was Betty Crocker. Mom was raised on a farm, walking every day to a one-room school. Her young life was filled with many trials and tribulations until she met, fell in love with, and married my father. With a hungry husband and five children to follow, she learned to make satisfying meals.

In 1967, we all moved west to Portland, Oregon, where Mom began her career in the restaurant business. Over the years, she owned two small diners where regular customers raved over every dish she prepared. There were people who couldn't start their day without one of her caramel rolls. I think work crews fight over who gets to do work on Mom's street, just because they know of the hot rolls and coffee they will be served.

I am proud to say that as large as our family has grown, we still get everyone together for every occasion. Mom fixes a fantastic feast of hors d'oeurves, dinner, and dessert. Of course, she cooks enough for an army, so there are care packages for each of us to take home and enjoy.

Mom has a magical way of taking what is available in her kitchen and fixing a wonderful meal. The greatest part of it is how she enjoys it. We all have our own special way of showing our love to people—Mom's is with cooking. She enjoys cooking and baking for others and does it in such a loving way that it makes everyone in her life feel special.

I could go on and on. She is one in a million.

Overnight Cinnamon Rolls

MAKES 24 ROLLS

Don't want to wait all night for these cinnamon rolls? You don't have to. Just skip the part about wrapping them in Step 5. Instead, let the rolls rise in warm place about 30 minutes or until they double in size. Then, just bake them as directed in Step 6 and enjoy.

2 packages active dry yeast

1/2 cup warm water
  (105° to 115°)

2 cups very warm milk
  (120° to 130°)

1/3 cup sugar

1/3 cup vegetable oil or
  shortening

3 teaspoons baking powder

2 teaspoons salt

1 egg

6 1/2 to 7 1/2 cups all-purpose
  flour

4 tablespoons margarine or
  butter, softened

1/2 cup sugar

1 tablespoon plus 1 teaspoon
  ground cinnamon

Powdered Sugar Frosting (below)

POWDERED SUGAR
FROSTING

2 cups powdered sugar

2 tablespoons milk

1 teaspoon vanilla

1. Dissolve yeast in warm water in large bowl. Stir in milk, 1/3 cup sugar, the oil, baking powder, salt, egg and 3 cups of the flour. Beat until smooth. Stir in enough remaining flour, 1 cup at a time, to make dough easy to handle.

2. Turn dough onto well-floured surface. Knead about 10 minutes or until smooth and elastic. Place in greased bowl and turn greased side up. Cover and let rise in warm place about 1 1/2 hours or until double. Dough is ready if indentation remains when touched.

3. Grease bottom and sides of 2 rectangular pans, 13 x 9 x 2 inches.

4. Punch down dough and divide in half. Flatten one half with hands or rolling pin into rectangle, 12 x 10 inches, on lightly floured surface. Spread with 2 tablespoons of the margarine. Mix 1/2 cup sugar and the cinnamon; sprinkle half of the sugar-cinnamon mixture over rectangle. Roll up, beginning at 12-inch side. Pinch edge of dough into roll to seal. Stretch and shape until even.

5. Cut roll into 12 slices. Place slightly apart in pan. Wrap pan tightly with heavy-duty aluminum foil. Repeat with other half of dough. Refrigerate at least 12 hours but no longer than 24 hours. (To bake immediately, do not wrap. Let rise in warm place about 30 minutes or until double. Bake as directed in step 6.)

6. Heat oven to 350°. Remove foil from pans. Bake 30 to 35 minutes or until golden. Frost with Powdered Sugar Frosting while warm.

POWDERED SUGAR FROSTING

Mix all ingredients until smooth and spreadable.

1 ROLL: Calories 250 (Calories from Fat 55); Fat 6g (Saturated 2g); Cholesterol 15mg; Sodium 280mg; Carbohydrates 45g (Dietary Fiber 1g); Protein 5g

Betty Comerford
Larchmont, New York

Betty Comerford, a friend and co-worker, truly personifies the Betty Crocker of today. Betty manages to balance her time between family, work, and community while always keeping time for cooking and baking.

I can't think of anyone who loves to be in the kitchen cooking and baking more than Betty, some-

thing she's loved since she was a child and has now passed on to her three children. Betty was brought up by a mother who loved to be in the kitchen. When Betty was fourteen years old, her mother passed away, and she immediately took over full responsibility for cooking and baking all the meals for her father and four older brothers.

But her passion for cooking didn't stop there. She was awarded the grand champion of the fair with her Cinnamon Rolls three years straight, taking many of her entries on to the state fair. Her love of cooking and baking continued into college, where she majored in home economics education. While student teaching, she developed new classes such as bachelor living—convincing young men to take interest in the practical side of home economics and learn how to cook,

clean, and decorate.

And even today, with her three children, she makes time to cook and bake. She has made it an annual event to spend all day Christmas Eve making her homemade cinnamon rolls and delivering them to her friends' houses that evening, all prepared but unbaked so they can be baked on Christmas morning filling all the houses with the wonderful aroma of homemade baked goods. She has even made it a priority to take off from work to go to her child's school to bake with the class.

She's an active member of the Junior League, whose mission is developing programs and projects that benefit children. Also she's been involved in renovating and setting up several after school centers and shelters that benefit underprivileged children. In sum, I can't think of anyone who better demonstrates the qualities of Betty Crocker today.

Sour Cream Coffee Cake

Layered with a delicious nut filling and drizzled with a pretty powdered sugar glaze, this coffee cake is an easy and popular cake to serve at morning get-togethers.

Cinnamon Filling or Almond
   Filling (below)

1 1/2 cups sugar

3/4 cup (1 1/2 sticks) margarine
   or butter, softened

1 1/2 teaspoons vanilla

3 eggs

3 cups all-purpose or whole
   wheat flour

1 1/2 teaspoons baking powder

1 1/2 teaspoons baking soda

3/4 teaspoon salt

1 1/2 cups sour cream

1/2 cup powdered sugar

1/4 teaspoon vanilla

1 to 2 teaspoons milk

1. Heat oven to 325°. Grease tube pan, 10 x 4 inches, or 12-cup bundt cake pan.

2. Prepare Cinnamon Filling; set aside.

3. Beat sugar, margarine, vanilla and eggs in 2 1/2-quart bowl on medium speed, scraping bowl occasionally, 2 minutes. Beat in flour, baking powder, baking soda and salt alternately with sour cream on low speed.

4. Spread one-third of the batter (about 2 cups) in pan; sprinkle with one-third of the filling (about 1/3 cup). Repeat 2 times.

5. Bake until toothpick inserted near center comes out clean, about 1 hour. Cool 20 minutes; remove from pan. Mix remaining ingredients until smooth and of desired consistency; drizzle over coffee cake.

CINNAMON FILLING

1/2 cup packed brown sugar

1/2 cup finely chopped nuts

1 1/2 teaspoons ground cinnamon

ALMOND FILLING

1/2 package (7- to 8.8-ounce
   size) almond paste, cut into
   small pieces

1/2 cup powdered sugar

1/4 cup (1/2 stick) margarine or
   butter

1/2 cup sliced almonds

CINNAMON FILLING

Mix all ingredients.

ALMOND FILLING

Cook almond paste, powdered sugar and margarine over medium heat, stirring constantly, until smooth; stir in almonds.

1 SERVING: Calories 340 (Calories from Fat 145); Fat 16g (Saturated 5g); Cholesterol 55mg; Sodium 410mg; Carbohydrates 47g (Dietary Fiber 3g); Protein 5g.

CHAPTER TWO

Lunch Favorites

Scrumptious sandwiches, snappy fresh salads, and soul-satisfying soups are right here. These are your favorite lunchtime meals. Stack them high or wrap them up, you'll find easy-to-make sandwiches that give an irresistible spin to American classics. Robust or delicately flavored, the soups are one-pot meals for every season or mood. A meal in itself, there's nothing like a salad to satisfy our craving for variety, texture, and complex flavors. If you "brown bag" it at the office or are looking for great picnic ideas, all your lunch favorites are here, waiting for you to enjoy.

Sandwiches

Broiled Burgers with Mushrooms and Onions

4 SERVINGS

Punch up the flavor of the mushrooms on your burger! Why not try using 1/4 cup sliced fresh mushrooms— try button, portobello, or shiitake—for the canned.

1 pound ground beef

3 tablespoons finely chopped onion

3 tablespoons water

3/4 teaspoon salt

1/8 teaspoon pepper

Mushrooms and Onions (below)

1. Mix ground beef, onion, water, salt and pepper. Shape mixture into 4 patties, each about 3/4 inch thick.

2. Set oven control to broil. Place patties on rack in broiler pan. Broil with tops about 3 inches from heat until desired doneness, 5 to 7 minutes on each side for medium. Prepare Mushrooms and Onions; spoon over hamburgers.

MUSHROOMS AND ONIONS

1 medium onion, thinly sliced

1 tablespoon margarine or butter

1 can (4 ounces) mushroom stems and pieces, drained

1/2 teaspoon Worcestershire sauce

Cook onion in margarine over medium heat, stirring occasionally, until tender. Stir in mushrooms and Worcestershire sauce; heat until mushrooms are hot.

1 SERVING: Calories 275 (Calories from Fat 170); Fat 19g (Saturated 7g); Cholesterol 65mg; Sodium 660mg; Carbohydrates 5g (Dietary Fiber 1g); Protein 22g.

Grilled Coney Island Burgers

6 SERVINGS

If you can't decide if you want a chili dog or a burger, here's a recipe for you! It's a hot dog and burger wrapped up in one.

1 pound ground beef

1 can (7 1/2 ounces) chili with beans

1 tablespoon chopped green chilies

6 frankfurter buns, split and warmed

1. Shape ground beef into 6 rolls, each about 5 inches long and 3/4 inch thick. Mix chili and green chilies in small grill pan; heat on grill until hot.

2. Grill ground beef rolls about 4 inches from medium coals, turning once, until desired doneness, 3 to 5 minutes on each side for medium. Serve in frankfurter buns; spoon about 2 tablespoons chili mixture into each bun.

1 SERVING: Calories 310 (Calories from Fat 135); Fat 15g (Saturated 6g); Cholesterol 50mg; Sodium 450mg; Carbohydrates 26g (Dietary Fiber 2g); Protein 20g.

Grilled Teriyaki Burgers

We love how versatile these burgers are since we can also use ground chicken or turkey for the ground beef. The poultry flavor blends nicely with the soy and ginger, making these delightful sandwichs.

1 pound ground beef

2 tablespoons soy sauce

1 teaspoon salt

1/4 teaspoon crushed gingerroot or 1/8 teaspoon ground ginger

1 clove garlic, crushed

1. Shape ground beef into 4 patties, each about 3/4 inch thick. Mix remaining ingredients; spoon onto patties. Turn patties; let stand 10 minutes.

2. Grill patties about 4 inches from medium coals, turning once, until desired doneness, 5 to 7 minutes on each side for medium. Serve on toasted sesame seed buns if desired.

1 SERVING: Calories 230 (Calories from Fat 145); Fat 16g (Saturated 6g); Cholesterol 65mg; Sodium 1100mg; Carbohydrates 1g (Dietary Fiber 0g); Protein 21g

Grilled Teriyaki Burgers

Hamburgers Parmigiana

Parmigiana describes a food made with Parmesan cheese. And who can say no to cheese and tomato sauce? Jazz up your mealtime with these tasty patties.

1 pound ground beef

1 small onion, chopped

2 tablespoons grated Parmesan cheese

1/2 teaspoon garlic salt

1 jar (15 1/2 ounces) chunky-style spaghetti sauce

1/2 cup shredded mozzarella cheese

4 slices French bread, toasted, or 2 hamburger buns, split and toasted

1. Mix ground beef, onion, Parmesan cheese and garlic salt. Shape into 4 patties, each about 1/2 inch thick.

2. Cook in 10-inch skillet over medium heat, turning frequently, until desired doneness; drain.

3. Pour spaghetti sauce over patties, heat until hot. Top each patty with 2 tablespoons mozzarella cheese; let stand until cheese begins to melt. Serve on French bread.

1 SERVING: Calories 465 (Calories from Fat 215); Fat 24g (Saturated 9g); Cholesterol 75mg; Sodium 980mg; Carbohydrates 35g (Dietary Fiber 2g); Protein 30g.

Beef and Veggie Pitas

4 SERVINGS

Make one or both of our super-easy cheesy or creamy sauces to dip or dunk your sandwich in. Of course, this sandwich also is delicious with turkey instead of roast beef.

Cheese Sauce (below) or Creamy Italian Sauce (right)

Lettuce leaves

3/4 pound thinly sliced roast beef

1 medium cucumber, thinly sliced

1 medium tomato, thinly sliced

1 medium bell pepper, cut into rings

1 medium zucchini, thinly sliced

4 thin slices red onion

4 pita breads (6 inches in diameter), cut crosswise in half

Prepare desired sauce. Layer lettuce, beef, cucumber, tomato, bell pepper, zucchini and onion in pita bread halves. Serve with sauce.

CHEESE SAUCE

1 jar (8 ounces) process cheese spread

2 tablespoons milk

1/4 cup chopped tomato

1/4 cup sliced green onions (3 medium)

Heat cheese spread and milk in 1-quart saucepan over medium heat, stirring constantly, until smooth. Stir in tomato and onions. Serve warm.

CREAMY ITALIAN SAUCE

1/2 cup creamy Italian dressing

1/4 cup sour cream

1/4 cup mayonnaise or salad dressing

1/4 cup milk

Mix all ingredients.

1 SERVING: Calories 515 (Calories from Fat 160); Fat 18g (Saturated 10g); Cholesterol 105mg; Sodium 1300mg; Carbohydrates 46g (Dietary Fiber 3g); Protein 45g.

Beef and Veggie Pitas

Rachel Sandwiches

Rachel sandwiches could be the sister sandwich to the Reuben, which is topped with sauerkraut instead of coleslaw. For lunch away from home, pack the meat, cheese and coleslaw in separate containers in an insulated lunchbag or cooler and assemble each sandwich when you're ready to eat!

12 slices dark rye bread

4 ounces sliced Swiss cheese

1/4 pound sliced corned beef

3 cups deli coleslaw

Butter 1 side of each bread slice if desired. Layer cheese, beef and coleslaw on buttered side of each of 6 bread slices. Top with remaining bread slices. Cut sandwiches in half.

1 SANDWICH: Calories 435 (Calories from Fat 260); Fat 29g (Saturated 8g); Cholesterol 50mg; Sodium 730mg; Carbohydrates 33g (Dietary Fiber 5g); Protein 16g.

No-Bake Pesto Chicken Pizza

4 SERVINGS

For a change of pace, pita breads make a delicious alternative to the Italian bread shells. Or fill 4 pita bread halves with the chicken mixture for a meal on the go.

1 tablespoon olive or vegetable oil

1 medium stalk celery, chopped (1/2 cup)

1 cup cut-up cooked chicken

1/3 cup pesto

1 package (8 ounces) Italian bread shells (6 inches in diameter)

2 tablespoons freshly shredded Parmesan cheese

1/2 cup shredded lettuce

1. Heat oil in 10-inch skillet over medium-high heat. Cook celery in oil 4 to 5 minutes, stirring occasionally, until crisp-tender; reduce heat. Stir in chicken and pesto. Cook, stirring occasionally, until hot.

2. Spoon chicken mixture onto bread shells. Mix cheese and lettuce; sprinkle over chicken mixture. Cut each bread shell in half.

1 SERVING: Calories 535 (Calories from Fat 225); Fat 25g (Saturated 6g); Cholesterol 45mg; Sodium 760mg; Carbohydrates 52g (Dietary Fiber 1g); Protein 27g.

No-Bake Pesto Chicken Pizza

Deli Turkey Stack

Here's the secret for those perfect hard-cooked eggs with a tender white surrounding a golden yellow yolk: Heat the water and eggs to boiling, then remove from heat, cover and let stand 18 minutes. Immediately cool eggs in cold water to prevent further cooking.

8 slices pumpernickel bread, cut in half

Lettuce leaves

12 ounces thinly sliced cooked turkey

2 medium tomatoes, cut into wedges

2 hard-cooked eggs, sliced

1/2 cup reduced-fat Thousand Island dressing

Whole ripe olives

Top 4 bread halves with one-fourth of the lettuce, turkey, tomatoes, eggs and dressing. Garnish with olives. Repeat with remaining ingredients.

1 SANDWICH: Calories 355 (Calories from Fat 100); Fat 11g (Saturated 3g); Cholesterol 175mg; Sodium 790mg; Carbohydrates 34g (Dietary Fiber 4g); Protein 34g.

Mexican Layered Sandwiches

You can find prepared guacamole in the deli or frozen-food section of your supermarket. Of course, you can always use your favorite guacamole recipe.

1/2 cup guacamole

4 pita breads (6 inches in diameter)

6 ounces thinly sliced cooked turkey

2 cups shredded lettuce

1 medium tomato, chopped (3/4 cup)

3/4 cup shredded Monterey Jack cheese (3 ounces)

Creamy Salsa (below)

Spread guacamole over pita breads. Top with turkey, lettuce, tomato and cheese. Top with Creamy Salsa. Sprinkle with sliced ripe olives or chopped green onions, if desired.

CREAMY SALSA

3 tablespoons sour cream

1 tablespoon salsa

1 tablespoon chopped green onions

Mix all ingredients.

1 SANDWICH: Calories 385 (Calories from Fat 135); Fat 15g (Saturated 7g); Cholesterol 60mg; Sodium 660mg; Carbohydrates 40g (Dietary Fiber 3g); Protein 25g.

Mexican Layered Sandwiches

Thea Palmer Zimmerman

Rockville, Maryland

I first got to know Thea several years ago around the time of my daughter's birthday. I was wishing that I could decorate her birthday cake myself. Thea kindly offered to teach me. I learned enough to produce a beautiful cake full of roses, and I made a new friend in the process.

Since that time, I've learned so much from Thea that I often tell her she should have her own local radio spot called "Thank you, Thea," in which she offers her practical know-how to a larger audience. Thanks to Thea, my freezer is filled with potential. I've got eight containers of frozen fresh blueberries that are already mixed with the other filling ingredients. When I need a pie, I can simply prepare a fresh crust, toss in the frozen filling and bake. I have six containers of frozen fresh-picked raspberries, which I plan to use in coffee cakes this winter.

Thea has solutions to seemingly every problem or situation concerning the home. She sews clothing for her children and herself, and with every leftover piece of fabric that's big enough, she serges a table napkin. Her children enjoy fresh colorful napkins at every meal. When it was time this summer to make 110 pennants for members of the swim team, Thea volunteered to help and serged her way through the donated sheets to create an "awesome" spectacle of team spirit.

Thea is a modern woman who gave America Online to her mother so that they can now correspond by E-mail. She regularly corresponds with her mother, her brother, and her sister over the Internet.

Thea is a Girl Scout troop leader. She is active in her church. She is the B-team rep. for her children's summer swim team. She volunteers many hours at her children's elementary school. She has taken ice-skating lessons for two years and swims year-round.

You have to meet her to believe her. She is a wonder. Thea Zimmerman is Betty Crocker.

Egg Salad Stacks

2 SERVINGS

Yum! These "stacks" make a nice change from typical egg salad. Mixing yogurt and mayonnaise together reduces the calories and fat but still gives you the great flavor of a creamy egg salad.

4 hard-cooked eggs, chopped

2 medium green onions, sliced

1/4 cup shredded carrot

2 tablespoons mayonnaise or salad dressing

2 tablespoons plain low-fat yogurt

1/4 teaspoon curry powder

1/8 teaspoon salt

Dash of pepper

4 leaves romaine

2 English muffins, split and toasted, or 2 slices bread

4 rings yellow or green bell pepper

2 tablespoons alfalfa sprouts

Mix eggs, onions, carrot, mayonnaise, yogurt, curry powder, salt and pepper. Place 1 romaine leaf on each muffin half. Top with egg mixture, bell pepper rings and alfalfa sprouts.

1 SERVING: Calories 400 (Calories from Fat 200); Fat 22g (Saturated 5g); Cholesterol 435mg; Sodium 630mg; Carbohydrates 35g (Dietary Fiber 3g); Protein 19g.

Betty's TV Show

Betty Crocker on TV? In the early 1950s, Betty appeared on a weekly program that dramatized cooking problems drawn from letters she received. After a problem was spelled out, Betty would demonstrate a solution. The actress who portrayed Betty was Adelaide Hawley, who also had been Betty's voice on the radio. Due to Betty's popularity, celebrities were happy to appear on the show. In one episode, viewers watched as Betty taught Gracie Allen and George Burns how to bake a cake! Do you think they ever used the skills she taught them?

Summertime Shrimp Rounds

8 OPEN-FACE SANDWICHES

If you can't find garlic-and-herb spreadable cheese, mix 4 ounces cream cheese, softened, 1 tablespoon mayonnaise, 1 teaspoon each dried basil and oregano leaves and 1/4 teaspoon garlic powder.

1 container (5 ounces) garlic-and-herb or herb soft spreadable cheese

4 onion or plain bagels, cut horizontally in half

32 medium shrimp, cleaned and cooked

1 small cucumber, cut lengthwise in half and sliced 1/4 inch thick

1/4 cup chopped green onions or red onion

8 cherry tomatoes

Spread 1 tablespoon cream cheese on each bagel half. Arrange 4 shrimp and 4 cucumber slices on each. Sprinkle with onions. Insert toothpicks into cherry tomatoes. Place in sandwiches.

1 OPEN-FACE SANDWICH: Calories 180 (Calories from Fat 55); Fat 6g (Saturated 3g); Cholesterol 125mg; Sodium 320mg; Carbohydrates 17g (Dietary Fiber 1g); Protein 16g.

Summertime Shrimp Rounds

Mozzarella and Tomato Melts

4 OPEN-FACE SANDWICHES

You'll be craving these melts in the summer when the tomatoes are so juicy and ripe you'll hardly be able to wait the few minutes it takes to make these sandwiches!

4 slices Italian bread, each 1 inch thick

8 ounces part-skim mozzarella cheese, sliced

2 medium tomatoes, thinly sliced

Salt and freshly ground pepper to taste

1/2 cup pesto

1. Set oven control to broil. Place bread on rack in broiler pan. Broil with tops about 4 inches from heat until golden brown; turn. Divide cheese among bread slices. Broil just until cheese begins to melt.

2. Arrange tomatoes on cheese. Sprinkle with salt and pepper. Top with pesto. Garnish with fresh basil leaves if desired.

1 OPEN-FACE SANDWICH: Calories 435 (Calories from Fat 270); Fat 30g (Saturated 10g); Cholesterol 35mg; Sodium 860mg; Carbohydrates 22g (Dietary Fiber 2g); Protein 21g.

Roasted Vegetable Wraps with Garlic Mayonnaise

Wrap up lots of flavor in these neat-to-eat sandwiches. Check out the refrigerated section in your grocery store to find different flavored flour tortillas, such as sun-dried tomato or pesto. They're delicious!

1 medium bell pepper

1 medium red onion, cut into 1/2-inch wedges

1 medium zucchini, cut lengthwise in half, then cut crosswise into 1/4-inch slices

1/4 pound mushrooms, cut into fourths

3 tablespoons olive or vegetable oil

1/2 teaspoon dried basil leaves

1/4 teaspoon salt

1/4 teaspoon coarsely ground pepper

Garlic Mayonnaise (right)

6 flour tortillas (8 or 10 inches in diameter)

1 1/2 cups shredded lettuce

1. Heat oven to 450°. Spread bell pepper, onion, zucchini and mushrooms in ungreased jelly roll pan, 15 1/2 x 10 1/2 x 1 inch.

2. Mix oil, basil, salt and pepper; brush over vegetables. Bake uncovered 12 to 15 minutes or until crisp-tender; cool slightly.

3. Spread about 2 teaspoons Garlic Mayonnaise down center of each tortilla to within 2 inches of bottom. Top with vegetables, spreading to within 2 inches of bottom of tortilla. Top with 1/4 cup lettuce.

4. Fold one end of tortilla up about 1 inch over filling; fold right and left sides over folded end, overlapping. Fold remaining end down.

GARLIC MAYONNAISE

1/4 cup mayonnaise or salad dressing

1 tablespoon finely chopped fresh parsley

1 teaspoon chopped garlic or 1/4 teaspoon garlic powder

Mix all ingredients.

1 SANDWICH: Calories 280 (Calories from Fat 155); Fat 17g (Saturated 3g); Cholesterol 5mg; Sodium 360mg; Carbohydrates 29g (Dietary Fiber 2g); Protein 5g.

Home Recipe Test Panel

Were you ever a Betty Crocker home recipe tester? As early as 1925, the Betty Crocker Kitchens started asking homemakers to help ensure the quality of recipes by testing them in their own homes. Later, visitors to the Betty Crocker Kitchens were asked to sign up, and some tested recipes for many years. Other home testers were recruited by marketing research firms to join the panel, which at one time was composed of about 2,000 testers. The home economists in the kitchens found the feedback from the testers to be very informative, and the program was active for almost sixty-five years.

Grilled Three-Cheese Sandwiches

2 SANDWICHES

Grilled cheese sandwiches are always a hit, so why stop at one cheese? If you have a little pesto in the refrigerator, try spreading some between the cheese layers instead of the spicy mustard. Mmmm. Yum!

2 tablespoons spicy mustard

4 slices whole wheat or rye bread

1 tablespoon sunflower nuts

1 slice (1 1/2 ounces) mozzarella cheese, cut in half

1 slice (1 1/2 ounces) Swiss cheese, cut in half

1 slice (1 1/2 ounces) Cheddar cheese, cut in half or
   2 slices (3/4 ounce each) process American cheese

2 tablespoons margarine, butter or spread, softened

1. Spread mustard over 1 side of each bread slice. Sprinkle nuts over mustard on 2 bread slices. For each sandwich, place one half piece each of mozzarella cheese, Swiss cheese and Cheddar cheese on nuts. Top with remaining bread, mustard side down. Spread half of the margarine over tops of bread.

2. Place sandwiches, margarine sides down, in 10-inch skillet. Spread remaining margarine over tops of bread. Cook uncovered over medium heat about 5 minutes or until bottoms are golden brown, turn. Cook 2 to 3 minutes until bottoms are golden brown and cheese is melted.

1 SANDWICH: Calories 500 (Calories from Fat 295); Fat 33g (Saturated 14g); Cholesterol 55mg; Sodium 920mg; Carbohydrates 30g (Dietary Fiber 3g); Protein 24g.

Betty on the World Wide Web

During the summer of 1997, Betty went high-tech with the launching of her award-winning home page on the World Wide Web. In case you've missed it, the address is <http://www.bettycrocker.com>, and if you have Internet access, you'd better check it out. You can search for recipes by category; you can enter the food items you have languishing in your pantry and find a recipe that'll use them for you; you can use Betty's menu plans for the week or customize the plan to fit your family's needs. You can even just have fun testing your Betty knowledge by playing the portrait game. If you have a question, you can E-mail Betty, and she'll get right back to you with an answer. In fact, we get about a thousand E-mail messages a month. Even in cyberspace, Betty is seen as a reliable resource.

Pita Sandwiches

8 SANDWICHES

The great thing about pita sandwiches is that you can stuff whatever you like inside. For a Mediterranean twist, spoon some Hummus (page 273) into a split pita and top with ripe tomatoes, a little red onion, some crumbled feta cheese and top it off with lettuce. It's so yummy!

8 pita breads (6 inches in diameter)

1/2 pound cooked sliced turkey

1/2 pound cooked sliced roast beef

8 tomato slices

1/2 cup alfalfa sprouts

Peppery Mustard Sauce (below)

Horseradish Sauce (right)

Split each pita bread halfway around edge with knife; separate to form pocket. Place 2 slices turkey or roast beef in each pocket; top with tomato slice and sprouts. Serve sandwiches with Peppery Mustard Sauce and Horseradish Sauce.

PEPPERY MUSTARD SAUCE

3/4 cup olive oil

3 tablespoons lemon juice

2 tablespoons grainy mustard

1 teaspoon cracked black pepper

Combine all ingredients in blender or food processor; cover and blend or process until smooth. Store tightly covered in refrigerator.

HORSERADISH SAUCE

1/2 cup sour cream

2 tablespoons prepared horseradish

2 tablespoons apple cider

Mix all ingredients in small bowl. Refrigerate covered until chilled.

1 SERVING: Calories 470 (Calories from Fat 235); Fat 26g (Saturated 5g); Cholesterol 55mg; Sodium 420mg; Carbohydrates 37g (Dietary Fiber 2g); Protein 24g.

Salads

Italian Chicken Salad
(page 83)

Tarragon-Chicken Salad

4 SERVINGS

Have some leftover chicken from dinner? Try this fla-vorful salad for lunch the next day. You can even make it the day before—just cover and refrigerate. Stir in honeydew balls just before serving.

1/2 cup mayonnaise

1/2 cup plain yogurt

2 tablespoons tarragon vinegar

1 tablespoon chopped fresh or 1 teaspoon dried
   tarragon leaves

4 cups cut-up cooked chicken

1 cup toasted, chopped pecans

2 cups honeydew balls

Lettuce

Melon slices

Mix mayonnaise, yogurt, vinegar and tarragon in large bowl; toss with chicken, pecans and honeydew balls. Serve salad on lettuce-lined plates with slices of melon.

1 SERVING: Calories 710 (Calories from Fat 475); Fat 53g (Saturated 8g); Cholesterol 140mg; Sodium 300mg; Carbohydrates 17g (Dietary Fiber 3g); Protein 44g.

Italian Chicken Salad

4 SERVINGS

The pre-mixed salad greens gives this refreshing pasta salad its "Italian" flair. If you have some fresh basil growing in your garden, pick a few leaves and thinly slice them to garnish each serving.

3/4 cup uncooked fusilli or rotini pasta

1/2 cup zesty Italian dressing

1 medium yellow or green bell pepper, chopped
   (1 cup)

1 medium carrot, shredded (2/3 cup)

4 boneless, skinless chicken breast halves
   (about 1 pound)

6 cups Italian blend salad mix or 6 cups bite-size
   pieces mixed salad greens

1. Cook and drain pasta as directed on package. Toss pasta and 1/3 cup of the dressing. Stir in bell pepper and carrot.

2. Cover and grill chicken 4 to 6 inches from medium coals 15 to 20 minutes, brushing with remaining dressing and turning occasionally, until juice of chicken is no longer pink when centers of thickest pieces are cut. Cut chicken diagonally into 1-inch strips.

3. Divide salad greens among 4 serving plates. Top with pasta mixture and chicken. Sprinkle with pepper if desired.

1 SERVING: Calories 380 (Calories from Fat 160); Fat 18g (Saturated 3g); Cholesterol 60mg; Sodium 300mg; Carbohydrates 27g (Dietary Fiber 2g); Protein 29g.

Turkey Taco Salad

What a great salad to serve at your next fiesta! For beef lovers, use lean ground beef instead of the turkey. Have colorful bowls of additional toppings, such as sliced black olives, sour cream, and sliced jalapeño peppers for those who like it "hot."

1 pound ground turkey

3/4 cup water

2 teaspoons chili powder

1/2 teaspoon salt

1/2 teaspoon ground cumin

1 small onion, finely chopped (1/4 cup)

1 clove garlic, finely chopped

1 can (11 ounces) whole kernel corn, drained

6 cups corn tortilla chips (about 3 ounces)

4 cups shredded iceberg lettuce

1 medium tomato, chopped (1/4 cup)

1 cup salsa

1. Cook turkey, water, chili powder, salt, cumin, onion and garlic in 10-inch skillet over medium-high heat 10 to 12 minutes, stirring frequently, until turkey is no longer pink and liquid is absorbed. Stir in corn. Cover and keep warm over low heat.

2. Arrange tortilla chips on large serving plate. Top with lettuce, tomato, turkey mixture and salsa.

1 SERVING: Calories 395 (Calories from Fat 160); Fat 18g (Saturated 4g); Cholesterol 75mg; Sodium 1160mg; Carbohydrates 35g (Dietary Fiber 5g); Protein 28g.

Curried Turkey Salad

Did you know curry isn't just one spice, but is a mixture of up to 20 different spices, including cardamom, nutmeg, cinnamon, cloves, coriander, black pepper. In India, people grind their fresh curry powder daily. The flavor of those curries can vary dramatically from region to region.

1 1/2 cups uncooked elbow macaroni (6 ounces)

1 package (10 ounces) frozen green peas

3/4 cup mayonnaise or salad dressing

2 teaspoons curry powder

2 cups cut-up cooked turkey breast

1/2 cup shredded Cheddar cheese (2 ounces)

4 medium green onions, sliced (1/4 cup)

1 medium stalk celery, sliced (1/2 cup)

Lettuce leaves, if desired

1. Cook and drain macaroni as directed on package. Rinse with cold water; drain. Rinse frozen peas with cold water to separate; drain.

2. Mix mayonnaise and curry powder in large bowl. Stir in macaroni, peas and remaining ingredients except lettuce. Cover and refrigerate 2 to 4 hours to blend flavors. Serve on lettuce.

1 SERVING: Calories 465 (Calories from Fat 250); Fat 28g (Saturated 6g); Cholesterol 60mg; Sodium 290mg; Carbohydrates 34g (Dietary Fiber 4g); Protein 23g.

Curried Turkey Salad

Pasta Salad with Salmon and Dill

4 SERVINGS

You'll be surprised how easy it is to cut carrots and zucchini into thin slices with a vegetable peeler. For more control when cutting, be sure the vegetables are lying on a flat surface, such as a cutting board or counter top.

8 ounces uncooked fettuccine

2 medium carrots

2 medium zucchini

1 can (7 1/2 ounces) boneless, skinless red sockeye salmon, drained and flaked

1 container (8 ounces) refrigerated dill dip

3/4 teaspoon lemon pepper

1. Cook and drain fettuccine as directed on package. Rinse with cold water; drain.

2. Cut carrots and zucchini lengthwise into thin slices, using vegetable peeler.

3. Toss all ingredients. Serve immediately or refrigerate 1 to 2 hours or until chilled.

1 SERVING: Calories 390 (Calories from Fat 135); Fat 15g (Saturated 7g); Cholesterol 95mg; Sodium 760mg; Carbohydrates 46g (Dietary Fiber 3g); Protein 20g.

Pasta Salad with Salmon and Dill

Seafood-Rice Salad

10 SERVINGS

Looking for a shortcut? If your supermarket offers a salad bar, you'll find freshly steamed broccoli flowerets waiting for you there. Just purchase the amount you need and toss this fresh, lemony salad together in no time.

Lemon Vinaigrette (below)

2 pounds scallops, cooked

1 pound medium shrimp, cooked and cleaned

4 cups cooked rice

3 cups broccoli flowerets, cooked

2 packages (6 ounces each) frozen crabmeat, thawed and drained

1. Prepare Lemon Vinaigrette.

2. Mix all ingredients in large bowl except Lemon Vinaigrette. Toss salad with Lemon Vinaigrette.

LEMON VINAIGRETTE

1/2 cup vegetable oil

1/2 cup lemon juice

2 tablespoons chopped fresh chives

1 tablespoon grated lemon peel

1 teaspoon Dijon mustard

1 teaspoon sugar

Mix all ingredients.

1 SERVING: Calories 295 (Calories from Fat 115); Fat 13g (Saturated 2g); Cholesterol 90mg; Sodium 270mg; Carbohydrates 22g (Dietary Fiber 1g); Protein 24g.

Stuffed Tuna Shells

6 SERVINGS (3 SHELLS EACH)

Looking for a change from tuna sandwiches for lunch? You can even vary the stuffing by using canned chicken or salmon in place of the tuna.

18 uncooked jumbo pasta shells (about half of 12-ounce package)

1 cup frozen green peas

1/4 cup plain yogurt

1/4 cup mayonnaise or salad dressing

2 cans (6 ounces each) tuna packed in water, drained

2 tablespoons finely chopped onion

1 teaspoon lemon juice

1/2 teaspoon dried basil leaves

1/2 teaspoon dried oregano leaves

1/4 teaspoon lemon pepper

Salt and pepper to taste

Dash of paprika

1. Cook and drain pasta shells as directed on package; pat dry.

2. Rinse frozen peas with cold water to separate; drain and pat dry. Mix yogurt and mayonnaise in medium bowl. Stir in remaining ingredients except paprika. Gently fold in peas.

3. Spoon 1 heaping tablespoonful tuna mixture into each shell. Sprinkle with paprika before serving. Serve chilled or at room temperature.

1 SERVING: Calories 255 (Calories from Fat 80); Fat 9g (Saturated 2g); Cholesterol 25mg; Sodium 280mg; Carbohydrates 26g (Dietary Fiber 2g); Protein 19g.

Stuffed Tuna Shells

Shrimp-Pasta Salad Toss

2 SERVINGS

If your favorite deli pasta salad is too thick for this recipe, thin it by stirring in a tablespoon of milk until you get the consistency you like. This recipe is perfect to double, or even triple, if you want to serve more people.

6 ounces frozen cooked shrimp, thawed

2 cups bite-size pieces spinach

1/2 pint deli pasta salad (1 cup)

1/2 cup cherry tomatoes, cut in half

2 tablespoons sliced ripe olives

Toss all ingredients.

1 SERVING: Calories 300 (Calories from Fat 115); Fat 13g (Saturated 2g); Cholesterol 175mg; Sodium 630mg; Carbohydrates 26g (Dietary Fiber 3g); Protein 23g.

Shrimp-Pasta Salad Toss

Snappy Seafood Salad

4 SERVINGS

It's a snap to put this summer seafood salad together. Dress it up and add a nice texture and flavor with tender, young salad greens that you can purchase pre-mixed in place of the lettuce.

2 cups uncooked medium pasta shells (5 ounces)

2/3 cup mayonnaise or salad dressing

1 tablespoon chili sauce or cocktail sauce

1/3 cup small pitted ripe olives

3 cups bite-size pieces lettuce

1 package (8 ounces) frozen seafood chunks (imitation crabmeat), thawed

1 small tomato, cut into 8 wedges

1. Cook and drain pasta as directed on package. Rinse with cold water; drain.

2. Mix mayonnaise and chili sauce in large bowl. Add pasta and olives; toss. Add lettuce and seafood; toss. Serve with tomato wedges.

1 SERVING: Calories 480 (Calories from Fat 290); Fat 32g (Saturated 5g); Cholesterol 40mg; Sodium 870mg; Carbohydrates 36g (Dietary Fiber 2g); Protein 14g.

Snappy Seafood Salad

Pesto Macaroni Salad

6 SERVINGS

Here's a fresh and tasty twist on traditional macaroni salad. Even better, oil and vinegar is used in place of mayonnaise, making it perfect to pack for picnic lunches.

3 cups uncooked medium shell macaroni

1 tablespoon olive or vegetable oil

1 container (8 ounces) pesto

4 Italian plum tomatoes, each cut into 4 wedges

1/2 cup small pitted ripe olives

1/4 cup white wine vinegar

4 cups coarsely shredded spinach

Grated Parmesan cheese

1. Cook macaroni as directed on package; drain. Rinse in cold water; drain and toss with oil.

2. Mix pesto, tomatoes, olives and vinegar in large bowl. Arrange 2 cups of the macaroni and 2 cups of the spinach on pesto mixture; repeat with remaining macaroni and spinach.

3. Cover and refrigerate at least 2 hours but no longer than 24 hours. Toss; sprinkle with cheese.

1 SERVING: Calories 470 (Calories from Fat 215); Fat 24g (Saturated 15g); Cholesterol 150mg; Sodium 220mg; Carbohydrates 56g (Dietary Fiber 5g); Protein 13g.

Vegetable-Pasta Salad

10 SERVINGS

Keep your vegetables fresh and bright by blanching them. It's not hard. Just place vegetables in a wire basket or a blancher, and drop basket into boiling water. Cover and cook vegetables for about a minute, until just slightly tender. Then remove the basket from the boiling water and immediately plunge the vegetables into iced water to stop cooking.

1 package (16 ounces) pasta shells, cooked and drained

1 1/2 pounds fresh asparagus, blanched, cut into 4-inch pieces

1 pound fresh sugar snap peas, blanched

6 green onions, sliced

1 yellow bell pepper, cut into julienne strips

Lemon Mayonnaise (below)

Mix all ingredients except Lemon Mayonnaise in large bowl; toss. Stir in Lemon Mayonnaise until well mixed. Cover and refrigerate until ready to serve.

LEMON MAYONNAISE

1 cup mayonnaise

1/2 cup plain yogurt

1/4 cup lemon juice

2 tablespoons chopped fresh or 2 teaspoons dried tarragon leaves

1/2 teaspoon salt

Mix all ingredients until well blended.

1 SERVING: Calories 365 (Calories from Fat 170); Fat 19g (Saturated 3g); Cholesterol 15mg; Sodium 260mg; Carbohydrates 43g (Dietary Fiber 4g); Protein 10g.

Soups

Creamy Tomato-Beef
Noodle Soup (page 94)

Kathy Simerly
Johnson City, Tennessee

I have yet to meet a person who doesn't think Kathy is one of the best, most decent people they know. When friends have problems, it is often Kathy whom they call first, because they know she will always have time for them, encourage them, and offer good advice.

We have a blended family of four children—two each by a former marriage. The kids respect her as a parent, mentor, and friend. Kathy is also devoted to her mom, who lives nearby and is never too busy to talk with her or run over for a visit.

She has a master's degree in psychology and uses that talent to counsel cancer patients. She serves on the board of directors of our local American Cancer Society (ACS) and helped organize and served as a committee chairman for our community's first "Relay for Life," which raised over thirteen thousand dollars for the ACS. Kathy also volunteers for anything the school asks her to do. She supports her church and depends upon her faith for her strength.

Her creativity is most evident in the ways she shows her love for us all. Often I open my briefcase or suitcase to find a love note or short message of encouragement. The same is true of the kids. If there is some special event, she always makes a big fuss. When they win some event or accomplish a goal they come home to a bedroom bedecked with ribbons or balloons.

Kathy makes every effort to continue the traditional family dinner each evening. No matter how hectic her day, she sees that a healthful meal is on the table, and we sit down together. She garnishes most dishes and sets a formal table in the dining room on a regular basis. All this extra work is done because of two things: she loves her family and she enjoys cooking. If there was a real-life Betty Crocker, she might well be living inside Kathy.

Chunky Tomato Soup

A quick whirl in a blender or food processor will smooth out this soup without sacrificing any flavor. Kids will love it if you stir in some cooked alphabet noodles for some lunchtime fun.

2 tablespoons olive or vegetable oil

2 cloves garlic, chopped

2 medium stalks celery, coarsely chopped (1 cup)

2 medium carrots, coarsely chopped (1 cup)

2 cans (28 ounces each) whole Italian-style tomatoes, undrained

2 cups water

1 teaspoon dried basil leaves

1/2 teaspoon pepper

2 cans (14 1/2 ounces each) chicken broth

8 slices hard-crusted Italian or French bread, each 1 inch thick, toasted

Grated Parmesan cheese, if desired

1. Heat oil in Dutch oven over medium-high heat. Cook garlic, celery and carrots in oil 5 to 7 minutes, stirring frequently, until carrots are crisp-tender.

2. Stir in tomatoes, breaking up tomatoes coarsely. Stir in remaining ingredients except toast and cheese. Heat to boiling; reduce heat. Cover and simmer 1 hour, stirring occasionally.

3. Place 1 slice toast in each of 8 bowls. Ladle soup over toast. Sprinkle with cheese. Serve immediately.

1 SERVING: Calories 175 (Calories from Fat 55); Fat 6g (Saturated 1g); Cholesterol 0mg; Sodium 840mg; Carbohydrates 26g (Dietary Fiber 3g); Protein 7g.

Betty's Kitchen Is Just Like Yours!

Part of the responsibility of the Betty Crocker Kitchens is to make sure that our products and recipes will work just as well in *your* kitchen as they work for us in Betty's kitchens. In order to do that, the home economists and technicians use the same appliances, utensils, and cookware that you may use. We test on both gas and electric stoves and ovens, and one kitchen has a variety of microwave ovens. It looks a little odd to see so many microwaves in one kitchen, but it is important to try our products in as many different types of microwaves as possible because performance varies so much. Another kitchen is responsible for testing bread machines. What fun to see as many as eight of these machines lined up in various stages of processing, testing our latest bread machine recipes. And the delicious aromas . . . mmm!

Creamy Tomato-Beef Noodle Soup

This is a creamy tomato soup that makes a great lunch or light supper. Kids will love slurping up the noodles and dunking in bits of breadsticks.

1 pound ground beef

1 small onion, chopped (1/4 cup)

1/2 cup frozen green peas

2 cups tomato juice

1 1/4 cups water

3/4 teaspoon chopped fresh or 1/4 teaspoon dried
   marjoram leaves

1/8 teaspoon pepper

1 bay leaf

1 can (10 3/4 ounces) condensed cream of celery
   soup

1 cup uncooked egg noodles (2 ounces)

1. Cook beef and onion in Dutch oven over medium heat about 10 minutes, stirring occasionally, until beef is brown; drain.

2. Stir in remaining ingredients except noodles. Heat to boiling. Stir in noodles; reduce heat. Simmer uncovered about 10 minutes, stirring occasionally, until noodles are tender. Remove bay leaf.

1 SERVING: Calories 370 (Calories from Fat 180); Fat 20g (Saturated 8g); Cholesterol 85mg; Sodium 1080mg; Carbohydrates 24g (Dietary Fiber 2g); Protein 25g.

Vegetable-Beef Soup

Want to make this soup in a snap? Use 4 cups canned beef broth and 3 cups cut-up cooked beef for the Beef and Broth. You can also keep it speedy by using 1 cup each frozen corn kernels, peas and green beans for the fresh.

Beef and Broth (below)

1 ear corn

2 medium potatoes, cubed (2 cups)

2 medium tomatoes, chopped (1 1/2 cups)

1 medium carrot, thinly sliced (1/2 cup)

1 medium stalk celery, sliced (1/2 cup)

1 cup 1-inch pieces green beans

1 cup shelled green peas

1/4 teaspoon pepper

1. Prepare Beef and Broth. Add enough water to broth to measure 5 cups. Return strained beef and broth to Dutch oven.

2. Cut kernels from corn. Stir corn and remaining ingredients into broth. Heat to boiling; reduce heat to low. Cover and simmer about 30 minutes or until vegetables are tender.

BEEF AND BROTH

2 pounds beef shank cross-cuts or soup bones

6 cups cold water

1 teaspoon salt

1/4 teaspoon dried thyme leaves

1 medium carrot, cut up

1 medium stalk celery with leaves, cut up

1 small onion, cut up

5 peppercorns

3 whole cloves

3 sprigs parsley

1 bay leaf

1. Remove marrow from center of bones. Heat marrow in Dutch oven over low heat until melted, or heat 2 tablespoons vegetable oil until hot. Cook beef shanks over medium heat until brown on both sides.

2. Add water; heat to boiling. Skim foam from broth. Stir in remaining ingredients; heat to boiling. Skim foam from broth; reduce heat to low. Cover and simmer 3 hours.

3. Remove beef from broth. Cool beef about 10 minutes or just until cool enough to handle. Strain broth through cheesecloth-lined sieve; discard vegetables and seasonings.

4. Remove beef from bones. Cut beef into 1/2-inch pieces. Skim fat from broth. Use immediately, or cover and refrigerate broth and beef in separate containers up to 24 hours or freeze for future use.

1 SERVING: Calories 235 (Calories from Fat 80); Fat 9g (Saturated 4g); Cholesterol 50mg; Sodium 440mg; Carbohydrates 19g (Dietary Fiber 3g); Protein 22g.

Chicken Noodle Soup

4 SERVINGS

What's better when you're feeling a little under the weather than a warm, soothing bowl of golden chicken noodle soup? Even better, this soup can be made in under 30 minutes!

2 tablespoons olive or vegetable oil

2 cloves garlic, finely chopped

2 medium green onions, chopped (2 tablespoons)

1 medium carrot, sliced (1/2 cup)

2 cups cubed cooked chicken

1 cup 2-inch pieces uncooked spaghetti or 4 ounces uncooked egg noodles

1 tablespoon chopped fresh parsley or 1 teaspoon dried parsley flakes

1/2 teaspoon ground nutmeg

1/4 teaspoon pepper

1 bay leaf

3 cans (14 1/2 ounces each) chicken broth

1. Heat oil in 3-quart saucepan over medium heat. Cook garlic, onions and carrot in oil about 4 minutes, stirring occasionally, until carrot is crisp-tender.

2. Stir in remaining ingredients. Heat to boiling; reduce heat. Cover and simmer about 15 minutes, stirring occasionally, until spaghetti is tender.

3. Remove bay leaf.

1 SERVING: Calories: 360 (Calories from Fat 125); Fat 14g (Saturated 3g); Cholesterol 55mg; Sodium 1120mg; Carbohydrate 30g (Dietary Fiber 2g), Protein 31g

Chicken Noodle Soup (front), Chunky Tomato Soup (page 93)

Chicken Tortellini Soup

Cheese-stuffed tender pastas floating in steamy chicken broth will provide comfort and warmth to rejuvenate your soul. Some hot, homemade buttery biscuits (pages 300–304) might help, too.

1/4 cup margarine or butter

1/2 cup finely chopped onion

1/2 cup finely chopped celery

4 boneless, skinless chicken breast halves, cut into
1-inch pieces (about 1 1/2 pounds)

1/4 cup all-purpose flour

1/2 teaspoon pepper

4 1/2 cups chicken broth

1 package (16 ounces) cheese-filled tortellini, cooked

Parmesan cheese

1. Heat margarine in large saucepan until melted. Cook and stir onion, celery and chicken in margarine over medium heat about 8 minutes or until chicken is done.

2. Stir in flour and pepper; gradually add chicken broth. Cook over medium heat, stirring constantly until mixture boils; boil 1 minute.

3. Stir in tortellini; heat until warm. Serve with Parmesan cheese.

1 SERVING: Calories 245 (Calories from Fat 110); Fat 12g (Saturated 3g); Cholesterol 85mg; Sodium 720mg; Carbohydrates 14g (Dietary Fiber 1g); Protein 21g.

Manhattan Clam Chowder

I'll take Manhattan . . . chowder, that is! Rich, tomatoey broth, chock-full of smoky bacon, tender potatoes and sweet fresh clams makes this soup the talk of the town.

1/4 cup finely chopped bacon or salt pork

1 small onion, finely chopped (about 1/4 cup)

1 pint shucked fresh clams with liquor*

2 cups finely chopped potatoes

1/3 cup chopped celery

1 cup water

2 teaspoons chopped fresh parsley

1/2 teaspoon salt

1 teaspoon chopped fresh or 1/4 teaspoon dried thyme leaves

1/8 teaspoon pepper

1 can (16 ounces) whole tomatoes, undrained

1. Cook bacon and onion in Dutch oven, stirring occasionally, until bacon is crisp and onion is tender.

2. Stir clams and clam liquor, potatoes, celery and water into bacon and onion. Heat to boiling; reduce heat. Cover and simmer about 10 minutes or until potatoes are tender.

3. Stir in remaining ingredients. Break up tomatoes. Heat to boiling, stirring occasionally.

1 SERVING: Calories 210 (Calories from Fat 0); Fat 13g (Saturated 0g); Cholesterol 15mg; Sodium 610mg; Carbohydrates 17g (Dietary Fiber 0g); Protein 7g.

*2 cans (6 1/2 ounces each) minced clams, undrained, can be substituted for fresh clams. Stir in clams with remaining ingredients.

Lillian Washington
Steubenville, Ohio

Raising seven children, my mother, Lillian Washington, took pleasure in serving full-course meals and delightful deserts. We ate as a family everyday together. My mother's favorite product is the Betty Crocker (Gold Medal) flour.

My father was the financial provider, my mother, the emotional, the spiritual, the ethical, the educational, and the humanitarian guide to all of us. She would open up our dining room to anyone who was hungry, stranger or acquaintance. Good-hearted cannot begin to describe this person. She made due with very little, stretching our little resources. She is God-fearing and serves our community, constantly baking for families who have lost loved ones or for those who are celebrating a joyful moment. When I think of love, kindness, happiness, food delights, and humanitarians, no one else can top my mother.

New England Clam Chowder

4 SERVINGS

New Englanders claim to have invented this hearty all-white clam chowder. It evolved from a fisherman's dish, made up of layers of salt pork, fish and dough, all cooked up in a large kettle. Then, milk was added to the mixture to make it more of a stew, clams replaced the fish, and potatoes were swapped for the dough to create this soup. To finish off this famous chowder, sprinkle with paprika, fresh chives, parsley, tarragon or dill.

1/4 cup cut-up bacon or lean
    salt pork

1 medium onion, chopped
    (about 1/2 cup)

2 cans (6 1/2 ounces each)
    minced clams, drained and
    liquid reserved

1 medium potatoes, diced (about
    2 cups)

Dash of pepper

2 cups milk

1. Cook and stir bacon and onion in 2-quart saucepan over medium heat until bacon is crisp.

2. Add enough water, if necessary, to reserve clam liquid to measure 1 cup. Stir clams, liquid, potatoes and pepper into onion mixture. Heat to boiling; reduce heat.

3. Cover and boil until potatoes are tender, about 15 minutes. Stir in milk. Heat, stirring occasionally, just until hot (do not boil).

1 SERVING: Calories 215 (Calories from Fat 0); Fat 6g (Saturated 0g); Cholesterol 45mg; Sodium 200mg; Carbohydrates 20g (Dietary Fiber 0g); Protein 20g.

Tomato Vegetable Soup with Yogurt

4 OR 5 SERVINGS

Yogurt adds a nice creaminess to this soup without adding unwanted calories or fat. We added the yogurt at the end so it doesn't boil or become curdled.

1 can (24 ounces) tomato juice (3 cups)

1/4 to 1/2 teaspoon ground red pepper

1/4 teaspoon salt

1 package (10 ounces) frozen whole kernel corn

1 bunch green onions (about 6 with tops), sliced

1 medium red or green pepper, coarsely chopped

1 medium zucchini, coarsely chopped

1 container (18 ounces) plain yogurt

Cilantro or parsley, if desired

1. Heat all ingredients except yogurt to boiling in 4-quart Dutch oven; reduce heat. Simmer uncovered, stirring occasionally, until vegetables are crisp-tender, 7 to 8 minutes. Remove from heat; cool 5 minutes before adding yogurt to prevent curdling.

2. Stir yogurt into soup until smooth. Heat over medium heat, stirring constantly, just until hot (do not boil). Garnish with snipped cilantro or parsley.

1 SERVING: Calories 195 (Calories from Fat 45); Fat 5g (Saturated 3g); Cholesterol 15mg; Sodium 880mg; Carbohydrates 32g (Dietary Fiber 4g); Protein 9g.

Cheesy Cauliflower Soup

5 SERVINGS

Did you know cauliflower comes in three different colors? The most popular and easy to find color is white, but you can also find green and a vibrant purple (which turns pale green when cooked). All three varieties can be used in this recipe, of course, or you could also substitute broccoflower—a hybrid of broccoli and cauliflower.

2 cups water

1 small head cauliflower (about 1 pound), broken into large flowerets, or 2 packages (8 ounces each) frozen cauliflower

1 medium stalk celery, cut into 1/2-inch pieces

1 medium carrot, cut into 1/2-inch pieces

1 small onion, cut into eighths

1 tablespoon instant chicken bouillon (dry)

1/4 teaspoon lemon and pepper seasoning salt

1 can (5 ounces) evaporated milk

1 1/2 cups shredded Harvati or Monterey Jack cheese (6 ounces)

1. Cover and cook all ingredients except milk and cheese in 3-quart saucepan over medium-low heat until vegetables are very tender, about 1 1/2 hours.

2. Carefully pour mixture into work bowl of food processor fitting with steel blade or into blender container. Cover and process until smooth.

3. Return mixture to saucepan; stir in milk and cheese. Heat over medium heat, stirring constantly, until cheese is melted and mixture is hot.

1 SERVING: Calories 200 (Calories from Fat 115); Fat 13g (Saturated 8g); Cholesterol 40mg; Sodium 1110mg; Carbohydrates 10g (Dietary Fiber 2g); Protein 13g.

Golden Onion Soup

This soup is perfect to make when you have a bit of time on your hands and some chores to get done. Just pop it in the oven and come back in a couple hours; this soup bakes in the oven to a rich, golden goodness all on its own. It doesn't get any easier than that.

Parmesan Croutons (right)

1/4 cup margarine or butter

1 tablespoon packed brown sugar

1 teaspoon Worcestershire sauce

4 large onions (3/4 to 1 pound each), cut into
      fourths and sliced

2 cans (10 1/2 ounces each) condensed beef broth

2 soup cans water

1. Prepare Parmesan Croutons; reserve.

2. Reduce oven temperature to 325°.

3. Heat margarine in 4-quart ovenproof Dutch
    oven until melted; stir in brown sugar and
    Worcestershire sauce. Toss onions in margarine
    mixture.

4. Bake uncovered, stirring every hour, until onions
    are deep golden brown, about 2 1/2 hours. Stir
    in broth and water; heat to boiling over high
    heat. Serve with Parmesan Croutons.

PARMESAN CROUTONS

1/4 cup margarine or butter

3 slices bread, cut into 1-inch cubes

Grated Parmesan cheese

1. Heat oven to 400°.

2. Heat margarine in rectangular pan, 13 x 9 x 2
    inches, in oven until melted. Toss bread cubes in
    margarine until evenly coated. Sprinkle with
    cheese. Bake uncovered, stirring occasionally,
    until golden brown and crisp, 10 to 15 minutes.

1 SERVING: Calories 235 (Calories from Fat 155); Fat 17g
(Saturated 4g); Cholesterol 5mg; Sodium 820mg; Carbohydrates 17g (Dietary Fiber 2g); Protein 5g.

Golden Onion Soup

Lisa Brannen
Glenville, Georgia

My daughter, Lisa, graduated in March 1996 with a major in home economics education from Georgia Southern University. Lisa is a member of the National Home Economics Honor Society, Phi Upsilon Omicron. The qualifications for the society are the following: student must maintain a 3.5 G.P.A., excel in

leadership, and demonstrate high morals and good character. Even though Lisa is very bright and innovative and has won many, many honors, she is very humble and unpretentious.

Growing up on a farm lent itself to exposing Lisa to all facets of home-making and helped mold her into the homemaker she is today. Lisa's love for cooking developed at the very early age of six while she stood on a stool and assisted her grandmother in cooking chewy bread and cookies and rolling dough for dumplings. To this day, no one in the family can bake chewy bread like my mother's except Lisa. She still continues to go to Grandma's, who is now eighty-five, and helps her cook whenever possible.

Lisa is a very responsible young lady who sets high ambitions and fulfills those goals. One goal of Lisa's is to one day host her own "cooking show" on public television and share her expertise in the kitchen with the audience. Perhaps, she may even publish her own cookbook! Lisa's favorite Betty Crocker product is the brownie mix. She enjoys baking them for any occasion because they're delicious as well as quick and easy to prepare—and they're always a success!

Cream of Broccoli Soup

For a lighter cream soup, we suggest using half-and-half or milk in place of the whipping cream. Look for broccoli with tight, compact heads and a nice green color throughout. Stay away from broccoli flowerets that are starting to yellow.

1 1/2 pounds broccoli

2 cups water

1 large stalk celery, chopped
   (3/4 cup)

1 medium onion, chopped
   (1/2 cup)

2 tablespoons margarine or
   butter

2 tablespoons all-purpose flour

2 1/2 cups chicken broth

1/2 teaspoon salt

1/8 teaspoon pepper

Dash of ground nutmeg

1/2 cup whipping (heavy) cream

Shredded cheese, if desired

1. Remove flowerets from broccoli; set aside. Cut stalks into 1-inch pieces.

2. Heat water to boiling in 3-quart saucepan. Add broccoli flowerets and stalk pieces, celery and onion. Cover and heat to boiling. Boil about 10 minutes or until broccoli is tender (do not drain).

3. Carefully place broccoli mixture in blender. Cover and blend on medium speed until smooth.

4. Melt margarine in 3-quart saucepan over medium heat. Stir in flour. Cook, stirring constantly, until mixture is smooth and bubbly; remove from heat.

5. Stir broth into flour mixture. Heat to boiling, stirring constantly. Boil and stir 1 minute.

6. Stir in broccoli mixture, salt, pepper and nutmeg. Heat just to boiling. Stir in whipping cream. Heat just until hot (do not boil). Serve with cheese.

1 SERVING: Calories 105 (Calories from Fat 70); Fat 8g (Saturated 4g); Cholesterol 15mg; Sodium 440mg; Carbohydrates 6g (Dietary Fiber 2g); Protein 4g.

Vegetable–Cheddar Cheese Soup

For lunch or dinner, this creamy, colorful cheese soup is popular with adults and kids alike. Warm whole-grain bread or rolls are perfect for sopping up and dunking in the soup.

1/2 cup margarine or butter

1 cup carrot, finely chopped

1/2 cup onion, finely chopped

1/2 cup celery, finely chopped

2 medium zucchini, cut into 2-inch strips

1/2 cup all-purpose flour

1 teaspoon dry mustard

2 cups chicken broth

2 cups half-and-half

3 cups shredded Cheddar cheese

1. Heat margarine in Dutch oven until melted. Cook carrot, onion and celery in margarine until softened. Stir in zucchini and cook about 2 minutes or until crisp-tender. Mix flour and mustard; stir into vegetable mixture.

2. Gradually stir in chicken broth and half-and-half. Cook over medium heat, stirring constantly until mixture boils; boil 1 minute. Slowly stir in cheese until melted.

1 SERVING: Calories 400 (Calories from Fat 295); Fat 33g (Saturated 15g); Cholesterol 65mg; Sodium 710mg; Carbohydrates 13g (Dietary Fiber 2g); Protein 15g.

Minestrone with Pesto

The great thing about minestrone is that you can use whatever vegetables are in season. White cannellini beans can also be used in place of the kidney beans. The swirl of pesto stirred in before serving is a flavorful, fresh-tasting addition to the soup.

4 cups raw vegetable pieces (carrots, celery, zucchini or yellow summer squash, green beans, cut into 1-inch slices, chopped tomatoes or shelled peas)

1 ounce uncooked spaghetti, broken into 2- to 3-inch pieces, or 1/2 cup uncooked macaroni

1/2 teaspoon dried basil leaves

1/8 teaspoon pepper

1 medium onion, chopped

1 clove garlic, finely chopped

1 can (15 ounces) kidney or garbanzo beans, undrained

2 cans (10 1/2 ounces each) condensed beef broth

2 broth cans (10 1/2 ounces each) water

5 ounces spinach, cut crosswise into 1/4-inch strips

Prepared pesto

Grated Parmesan cheese, if desired

1. Heat all ingredients except spinach, pesto and cheese to boiling in 4-quart Dutch oven; reduce heat.

2. Cover and simmer until vegetables and spaghetti are tender, about 10 minutes. Stir in spinach until wilted. Serve with pesto and, if desired, grated Parmesan cheese.

1 SERVING: Calories 200 (Calories from Fat 80); Fat 9g (Saturated 2g); Cholesterol 2mg; Sodium 800mg; Carbohydrates 24g (Dietary Fiber 6g); Protein 12g.

Great-Tasting Gazpacho

Great-Tasting Gazpacho

4 SERVINGS

Gazpacho is a cold tomato-vegetable soup, perfect for sultry summertime weather. Popular garnishes of gazpacho include croutons, a dollop of sour cream or yogurt or chopped hard-boiled eggs.

1 can (28 ounces) whole tomatoes, undrained

1 medium green bell pepper, finely chopped (1 cup)

1 cup finely chopped cucumber

1 medium onion, chopped (1/2 cup)

1 cup croutons

2 tablespoons dry white wine or chicken broth

2 tablespoons olive or vegetable oil

1 tablespoon ground cumin

1 tablespoon white vinegar

1/2 teaspoon salt

1/4 teaspoon pepper

1. Place tomatoes, 1/2 cup of the bell pepper, 1/2 cup of the cucumber, 1/4 cup of the onion, 1/2 cup of the croutons and the remaining ingredients in blender or food processor. Cover and blend on medium speed until smooth.

2. Cover and refrigerate at least 1 hour. Serve remaining vegetables and croutons as accompaniments.

1 SERVING: Calories 150 (Calories from Fat 70); Fat 8g (Saturated 2g); Cholesterol 0mg; Sodium 670mg; Carbohydrates 19g (Dietary Fiber 3g); Protein 4g.

Wild Rice Soup

Native Americans called wild rice mahnomen, *or "precious grain." This delicacy isn't actually rice but is a grain from an aquatic plant. Cooks have used this native plant in many recipes, this creamy, chowderlike soup being one of the more popular creations.*

2 medium stalks celery, slices (about 1 cup)

1 medium carrot, coarsely shredded (about 1/2 cup)

1 medium onion, chopped (about 1/2 cup)

1 small green bell pepper, chopped (about 1/2 cup)

2 tablespoons margarine or butter

3 tablespoons all-purpose flour

1 teaspoon salt

1/4 teaspoon pepper

1 1/2 cups cooked wild rice

1 cup water

1 can (10 1/2 ounces) condensed chicken broth

1 cup half-and-half

1/3 cup slivered almonds, toasted

1/4 cup chopped fresh parsley

1. Cook and stir celery, carrot, onion and bell pepper in margarine in 3-quart saucepan until celery is tender, about 5 minutes.

2. Stir in flour, salt and pepper. Stir in wild rice, water and broth. Heat to boiling; reduce heat. Cover and simmer 15 minutes, stirring occasionally.

3. Stir in remaining ingredients. Heat just until hot (do not boil).

1 SERVING: Calories 200 (Calories from Fat 110); Fat 12g (Saturated 4g); Cholesterol 15mg; Sodium 800mg; Carbohydrates 19g (Dietary Fiber 3g); Protein 7g.

Basil Rice Soup

Fresh basil adds such a nice flavor to this soup. Any aromatic rice, such as basmati or jasmine, can be used for the regular long-grain rice.

2 tablespoons olive or vegetable oil

2 cloves garlic, finely chopped

2 medium stalks celery, chopped (1 cup)

1 medium onion, chopped (1/2 cup)

1 medium carrot, chopped (1/2 cup)

1/4 cup chopped fresh basil leaves

3/4 cup uncooked regular long grain rice

2 medium tomatoes, chopped (1 1/2 cups)

4 cups chicken broth

1 cup water

1 teaspoon salt

1/4 teaspoon pepper

1/4 cup grated Romano cheese

1. Heat oil in Dutch oven over medium-low heat. Cover and cook garlic, celery, onion, carrot and basil in oil 10 minutes, stirring occasionally, until vegetables are crisp-tender. Stir in rice and tomatoes. Cook uncovered over medium heat 5 minutes, stirring occasionally.

2. Stir in remaining ingredients except cheese. Heat to boiling; reduce heat. Cover and simmer bout 20 minutes or until rice is tender. Top each serving with cheese.

1 SERVING: Calories 185 (Calories from Fat 65); Fat 7g (Saturated 2g); Cholesterol 5mg; Sodium 990mg; Carbohydrates 25g (Dietary Fiber 1g); Protein 7g.

Lentil Soup

Vary your lentils. Look for either brown or green lentils to use for this robust soup. Look forward to leftovers, too! This soup tastes even better the second day.

2 tablespoons olive or vegetable oil

2 cloves garlic, finely chopped

1 medium onion, finely chopped

1/2 cup diced prosciutto or fully cooked Virginia
    ham (4 ounces)

1/4 cup diced Genoa salami (2 ounces)

1 bay leaf

4 cups water

2 cups chicken broth

1 1/2 cups dried lentils (8 ounces), sorted and rinsed

1/2 teaspoon pepper

1. Heat oil in Dutch oven over medium-high heat.
   Cook garlic and onion in oil 5 to 7 minutes,
   stirring frequently, until onion is tender. Stir in
   prosciutto and salami. Cook over medium heat
   10 minutes, stirring frequently.

2. Stir in remaining ingredients. Heat to boiling;
   reduce heat. Cover and simmer about 1 hour,
   stirring occasionally, until lentils are tender.
   Remove bay leaf.

1 SERVING: Calories 315 (Calories from Fat 125); Fat 14g
(Saturated 4g); Cholesterol 15mg; Sodium 710mg; Carbohydrates 37g (Dietary Fiber 13g); Protein 23g.

Green Pea Soup

For a beautiful color contrast, you can garnish this bright green soup with a dollop of sour cream or yogurt. If you have any soup left over, reheat it gently over low heat, just until warm. Avoid boiling this soup once the cream is added so it won't curdle.

1 package (16 ounces) frozen green peas

1 cup milk

2 tablespoons margarine or butter

2 tablespoons all-purpose flour

3/4 teaspoon salt

1/8 teaspoon pepper

1/2 cup whipping cream or half-and-half

Mint leaves, if desired

1. Cook peas as directed on package; reserve 1/2
   cup for garnish if desired.

2. Place remaining peas and the milk in work bowl
   of food processor fitted with steel blade or in
   blender container. Cover and process until of
   uniform consistency.

3. Heat margarine in 2-quart saucepan until
   melted. Stir in flour, salt and pepper. Cook, stirring constantly, until smooth and bubbly.
   Remove from heat; stir in pea mixture.

4. Heat to boiling, stirring constantly. Boil and stir
   1 minute. Stir in cream; heat just until hot (do
   not boil). Garnish each serving with reserved
   peas and mint leaves.

1 SERVING: Calories 225 (Calories from Fat 135); Fat 16g
(Saturated 8g); Cholesterol 40mg; Sodium 650mg; Carbohydrates 21g (Dietary Fiber 6g); Protein 8g.

CHAPTER THREE

Sit Down to Dinner

Sit around my table. It is a time for your family to gather and share the day over a home-cooked dinner. Roasted, grilled, baked, broiled, or fried—whatever you might want to satisfy any craving. You'll find succulent and marvelously seasoned beef and pork; curried, creamed, barbecued or fried-to-a-crisp chicken and turkey; fresh and snappy ideas for fish which capture the essence of great seafood, plus a host of sublime entrées for vegetarians.

Meat

Beef Enchiladas
(page 125)

Western Meat Loaf

Rustle up this loaf when you're hankering for something a little different. The horseradish adds a nice little kick.

1 can (8 ounces) tomato sauce

1 1/2 pounds ground beef

1/2 pound ground pork

2 cups soft bread crumbs

2 to 4 tablespoons prepared horseradish

1 teaspoon dry mustard

1/2 teaspoon salt

1/4 teaspoon pepper

1 medium onion, finely chopped (about 1/2 cup)

2 eggs, slightly beaten

1 tablespoon packed brown sugar

1/4 teaspoon dry mustard

1. Heat oven to 350°.

2. Reserve 1/4 cup of the tomato sauce. Mix the remaining tomato sauce and remaining ingredients except brown sugar and 1/4 teaspoon dry mustard.

3. Spread in ungreased loaf pan, 8 1/2 x 4 1/2 x 2 1/2 or 9 x 5 x 3 inches, or shape mixture into loaf in ungreased rectangular pan, 13 x 9 x 2 inches. Mix reserved tomato sauce, brown sugar and 1/4 teaspoon dry mustard; spread over loaf.

4. Bake uncovered until done, 1 to 1 1/4 hours or until mixture is no longer pink in center and juice is clear. Cover loosely with aluminum foil; let stand 10 minutes. Remove from pan.

1 SERVING: Calories 370 (Calories from Fat 170); Fat 19g (Saturated 7g); Cholesterol 120mg; Sodium 625mg; Carbohydrates 25g (Dietary Fiber 1g); Protein 26g.

Favorite Meat Loaf

A family favorite, this meat loaf often does double duty. Once, served up with hot mashed or baked potatoes (check out the wonderful potato sides on pages 249–262), then cold, served on thick slices of bread. For added flavor, spread the top of the meat loaf before baking with ketchup, barbecue sauce or salsa.

1 pound ground beef

1/2 pound ground pork

1 cup milk

1 tablespoon Worcestershire sauce

1/4 teaspoon pepper

1/4 teaspoon celery salt

1/4 teaspoon garlic salt

1/4 teaspoon ground mustard (dry)

1/4 teaspoon ground sage

1 egg, beaten

3 slices white bread, torn into pieces

1 small onion, chopped (1/4 cup)

1. Heat oven to 350°.

2. Mix all ingredients. Spread in ungreased loaf pan, 9 x 5 x 3 inches.

3. Bake 1 1/2 hours or until beef mixture is no longer pink in center and juice is clear.

4. Let stand 5 minutes; remove from pan.

1 SERVING: Calories 340 (Calories from Fat 170); Fat 19g (Saturated 7g); Cholesterol 105mg; Sodium 370mg; Carbohydrates 17g (Dietary Fiber 1g); Protein 26g.

Favorite Meat Loaf

Jo Ann Vincent
Metairie, Louisiana

My best friend and wife, Jo Ann Gautier Vincent, is currently a reading teacher at John Quincy Adams public school. She has taught for fourteen years, but took time out in the middle of her career to be a full-time mom.

This month, Jo Ann was recognized as the Middle School Teacher of The Year for East Jefferson Parish (County). This award was granted for both work within the classroom and in the community.

While Jo Ann is a reading teacher, she believes in encouraging learning across different subjects. The children are motivated to read and usually do not realize how much they are learning. Teachers in other subjects are often surprised when they find out what their students learned in reading.

Jo Ann's spirit of compassion, service, and action did not begin with teaching. When Jo Ann was thirteen years old, her mother became very ill. Responsibilities for operating the home fell on her. She cared for her mother, father, and younger brother. A kind neighbor gave Jo Ann a *Betty Crocker New Picture Cook Book* for Christmas in 1961. By reading and experimenting, Jo Ann learned how to cook. Her favorite Betty Crocker products are the various cake mixes. There are two in the cupboard now, and we hope that we will find a Betty Crocker cake on the table any day.

All of us are amazed at how she keeps such a full schedule and manages to provide such good meals, too. I not only love her (and her cooking), but am proud of her independent spirit and career achievements as well.

Old-Fashioned Meat Loaf

Rolled oats are a cook's secret ingredient of the perfect meat loaf because they bind the meat mixture into a loaf of wonderful texture and juiciness. Tomatoes, tomato sauce and ketchup are often added to contribute moisture as well as flavor. Some cooks also believe using beef alone makes a drier meat loaf, so this meat loaf uses rolled oats and a mixture of ground pork and beef.

1 can (16 ounces) whole
   tomatoes

1 1/4 pounds ground beef

1/4 pound ground pork

3/4 cup regular oats

1/3 cup chopped onion

1 egg

1 teaspoon salt

1/4 teaspoon pepper

1. Heat oven to 375°.

2. Drain tomatoes, reserving 1/4 cup liquid. Cut tomatoes up with fork. Mix reserved liquid, the tomatoes and remaining ingredients thoroughly.

3. Pack in loaf pan, 8 1/2 x 4 1/2 x 2 1/2 inches. Bake uncovered until done, 1 to 1 1/4 hours or until beef mixture is no longer pink in center and juice is clear. Remove from pan.

1 SERVING: Calories 435 (Calories from Fat 250); Fat 28g (Saturated 11g); Cholesterol 150mg; Sodium 600mg; Carbohydrates 11g (Dietary Fiber 2g); Protein 37g.

The First Betty Crocker Cookbook

When *Betty Crocker's Picture Cook Book* was published in 1950, it was called "a new and different cook book for a new age!" Many homemakers had been asking for a book to replace the *Gold Medal Cook Book* that their mothers and grandmothers had used. Betty dedicated her new book "to homemakers everywhere—to all of you who like to minister to your dear ones by serving them good food . . . " This new book used the latest shortcuts, equipment and prepared foods, and it included extra tips and cooking secrets. There were also interesting tidbits about food history. Recipes were written with new and simplified methods and sent out for testing in consumers' homes. Only those recipes that passed home testing were included in this book, designed to bring "more fun in cooking and deeper joy in your homemaking."

Family-Favorite Tacos

6 SERVINGS

Tacos are always family favorites since you get to fix them the way you like them. Don't forget to offer salsa to top off everyone's creation and for those who like a little heat, sliced jalapeños are the perfect trick.

1 pound ground beef

1 large onion, chopped

1 envelope (about 1 1/4 ounces) taco seasoning mix

1 cup water

1 package (12 ounces) tortilla chips

1/2 head lettuce, shredded

2 medium tomatoes, chopped

1 can (2 1/4 ounces) sliced ripe olives, drained

1 cup shredded Cheddar or Monterey Jack cheese (4 ounces)

2/3 cup dairy sour cream

1. Cook and stir ground beef and onion in 10-inch skillet until beef is brown; drain. Stir in seasoning mix (dry) and water.

2. Heat to boiling; reduce heat. Simmer uncovered 10 minutes, stirring occasionally. Spoon beef mixture onto chips. Top with remaining ingredients.

1 SERVING: Calories 575 (Calories from Fat 315); Fat 35g (Saturated 13g); Cholesterol 80mg; Sodium 950mg; Carbohydrates 46g (Dietary Fiber 6g); Protein 25g.

Sloppy Joes with Potatoes and Onion

4 SERVINGS

This version of Sloppy Joes uses potatoes and onions instead of the bun so it's not quite as sloppy, but it's always a favorite of kids.

1 pound lean ground beef

Salt and pepper to taste

1 medium onion, sliced and separated into rings

2 medium potatoes, thinly sliced

1 can (15 1/2 ounces) Sloppy Joe sauce

1. Crumble ground beef into 10-inch skillet; sprinkle with salt and pepper. Layer onion and potatoes on beef; pour sauce over top.

2. Cover and cook over low heat until beef is done and potatoes are tender, about 30 minutes.

1 SERVING: Calories 410 (Calories from Fat 180); Fat 20g (Saturated 7g); Cholesterol 65mg; Sodium 890mg; Carbohydrates 37g (Dietary Fiber 3g); Protein 24g.

Chili

4 SERVINGS

Cocoa in chili? Yes, indeed. It lends a deep, rich flavor to the chili. It will leave your guests wondering what the secret ingredient is.

1 pound ground beef

1 large onion, chopped (1 cup)

2 cloves garlic, crushed

1 tablespoon chili powder

1/2 teaspoon salt

1 teaspoon ground cumin

1 teaspoon dried oregano leaves

1 teaspoon cocoa

1/2 teaspoon red pepper sauce

1 can (16 ounces) whole tomatoes, undrained

1 can (15 to 16 ounces) red kidney beans, undrained

1. Cook beef, onion and garlic in 3-quart saucepan, stirring occasionally, until beef is brown; drain.

2. Stir in remaining ingredients except beans, breaking up tomatoes. Heat to boiling; reduce heat to low. Cover and simmer 1 hour, stirring occasionally.

3. Stir in beans. Heat to boiling; reduce heat to low. Simmer uncovered about 20 minutes, stirring occasionally, until desired thickness.

1 SERVING: Calories 340 (Calories from Fat 155); Fat 17g (Saturated 7g); Cholesterol 65mg; Sodium 890mg; Carbohydrates 27g (Dietary Fiber 9g); Protein 29g.

The Spice of Life

Chili can be a spicy dish. Some folks say, "The hotter, the better." Do you have all the spices you need for a spicy dish in your pantry? The NPD Group, Inc., on behalf of the Betty Crocker Kitchens and other food companies, has actually *asked* consumers what they have in their cupboards. In the spice category (omitting salt and pepper), the top ten dried spices in the average consumer's pantry, in order, are ground cinnamon, garlic powder, oregano, paprika, chili powder, ground nutmeg, parsley, garlic salt, ground ginger and basil. How does *your* cupboard compare?

Marie McKell

Ukiah, California

My sweet wife, Marie McKell, is primarily a homemaker and as such has made our home a place of love and warmth, a place where the kitchen is the hub of activity. Most often we are drawn there as we arrive home by the smell of freshly baked homemade bread. Marie has taught our children the joy of cooking.

Our oldest son, now thirty, bakes a marvelous cheesecake. And now our two youngest love to try out any new, as well as the old favorite, cookie recipes.

In Marie's library of cookbooks are four well-worn Betty Crocker editions: a 1961 first edition of the *New Picture Cook Book*, a 1967 *Betty Crocker Hostess Cook Book*, a 1979 edition (11th printing) of the *Betty Crocker Cook Book*, and the 1989 (6th printing) of the *New and Revised Betty Crocker Cook Book*. Without a doubt, Marie's favorite Betty Crocker recipes are from the sections on quick breads, pies, and cinnamon rolls. How worn the pages are attest to this. It's Betty Crocker she trusts.

Marie has for many years been a devoted friend and frequent visitor to a shut-in, a lady ninety-three years of age, whose closest relatives live in Germany and who has been confined to a convalescent hospital near us.

Outside of family, school, church, and friends, Marie has also extended her influence into the community in her part-time work. She works for the local daily newspaper as an advisor who trains and supervises twenty-four young paper carriers. Her patience and caring help them to model attitudes and behavior that encourages them as they learn responsibility.

Savory Spaghetti

Delicious, moist spaghetti dish that is really simple to do. What's even better is that you don't have to boil the spaghetti separately. The noodles and sauce all cook up in one skillet. Now, that's easy!

1/2 pound ground beef

1/4 pound ground pork

1 small onion, chopped

1 small green pepper, sliced

1/2 cup sliced ripe olives

1 can (2 ounces) mushrooms, drained

1 can (8 ounces) tomato sauce

2 1/2 cups tomatoes (1 lb. 4 oz.)

2 cups water

2 teaspoons salt

1/4 teaspoon pepper

1 teaspoon Worcestershire sauce

6 drops Tabasco

4 ounces long spaghetti or noodles

1. Brown beef and pork in large skillet over medium heat. Add onion, green pepper and cook 5 minutes. Add olives, mushrooms, tomato sauce and mix lightly. Stir mixture of tomatoes, water, salt, pepper, Worcestershire sauce and Tabasco into meat mixture.

2. Add uncooked spaghetti and bring to boil. Cover tightly, reduce heat to low and simmer about 40 minutes, stirring occasionally. Uncover and simmer 15 minutes longer.

1 SERVING: Calories 275 (Calories from Fat 115); Fat 13g (Saturated 4g); Cholesterol 45mg; Sodium 1230mg; Carbohydrates 25g (Dietary Fiber 3g); Protein 18g.

Christine Fotré O'Neill
Chicago, Illinois

Cooking and baking have been a trademark since Chris's childhood. In 1964, Chris was named Home-maker of Tomorrow by none other than Betty Crocker. Chris says creating in her kitchen appeals to all of her senses; she finds great satisfaction in the whole process: planning the meal or special dish, making it, serving it, and seeing how it is enjoyed.

A typical morning starting at 5:30 A.M. has included taking the dog for a brisk walk; making lunch for the kids; feeding the two cats, the gerbils, the turtle, and the two parakeets; planning ahead for dinner; driving five boys in a carpool to school—all of this before meeting her responsibilities as an executive of a major art museum. Chris loves to put on an apron and bake cookies, yet she is a divorced mother who has worked full-time since her very earliest postcollege days.

Among other commitments, she has worked on a Junior League project to combat emotional child abuse and has been an active volunteer for The ARK, a Jewish social service organization, and for environmental causes. She has assisted the local food pantry and thinks nothing of baking at midnight, if need be, for tomorrow's school bake sale or reception. From her earliest working days, she has helped not-for-profit institutions meet their fund-raising, membership, and marketing objectives, currently as a vice president of The Art Institute of Chicago.

Chris has advised that her favorite product is General Mills unbleached Gold Medal flour, which was often endorsed by Betty Crocker. A favorite recipe, among others, is good old-fashioned Apple Pie, as prepared from the recipe on pages 132 33 of *Betty Crocker: Dinner for Two* (Golden Press, New York, 1979). Although she prefers to make recipes from scratch, she is not immune to selective labor-saving products. Betty Crocker's Fruit Roll-Ups are a lunch and snack-time favorite of her daughter and friends.

Meatball Porcupines

2 SERVINGS

Don't worry—these porcupines won't prick you. The combination of rice and ground beef gives these meatballs the appearance of lots of little porcupines.

1/2 pound ground beef

1/4 cup uncooked rice

1/4 cup milk or water

2 tablespoons chopped onion

1/2 teaspoon salt

1/4 teaspoon celery salt

1/8 teaspoon garlic salt

Dash of pepper

1 tablespoon shortening

1 can (8 ounces) tomato sauce

1/2 cup water

1 1/2 teaspoons Worcestershire
  sauce

1. Mix beef, rice, milk, onion, salt, celery salt, garlic salt and pepper. Form into 4 medium balls.

2. Fry in melted shortening, turning frequently, until light brown (but not crusty) on all sides. Add tomato sauce, water and Worcestershire sauce. Mix well.

3. Cover; simmer 45 minutes over low heat. Add a small amount of additional water if liquid cooks down too much.

1 SERVING: Calories 440 (Calories from Fat 215); Fat 24g (Saturated 8g); Cholesterol 65mg; Sodium 1630mg; Carbohydrates 32g (Dietary Fiber 2g); Protein 26g.

Coupon Collecting

Another way that Betty Crocker found to help homemakers provide a gracious lifestyle for their families was through coupons—not just cents-off coupons, but coupons that could be exchanged for flatware! Beginning in 1932, coupons for the flatware pattern Friendship (later renamed Medality to honor Gold Medal) were available in sacks of Gold Medal flour. Even today, coupons redeemable for merchandise in the Betty Crocker catalog appear on every product package.

Barbecued Beef and Beans

6 SERVINGS

This meaty, cheesy meal, complete with savory beans, is made even better with Traditional Corn Bread (page 300) served alongside for sopping up any extra sauce.

1 pound ground beef

1 teaspoon chili powder

1 teaspoon garlic salt

1 can (16 ounces) barbecue beans

1 can (10 3/4 ounces) condensed tomato soup

1 can (4 ounces) chopped green chilies

1 cup shredded American or Monterey Jack cheese
(4 ounces)

1. Mix ground beef, chili powder and garlic salt. Shape into 6 patties, each about 1/2 inch thick.

2. Cook in 10-inch skillet over medium heat, turning frequently, until brown. Remove patties from skillet; drain drippings from skillet.

3. Stir beans, soup and chilies into skillet until well mixed; place patties on top. Heat to boiling; reduce heat. Cover and simmer until patties are of desired doneness, about 5 minutes.

4. Sprinkle with cheese; cover and let stand until cheese is melted, about 2 minutes. Serve over corn bread or toasted hamburger buns if desired.

1 SERVING: Calories 320 (Calories from Fat 160); Fat 18g (Saturated 8g); Cholesterol 60mg; Sodium 1200mg; Carbohydrates 21g (Dietary Fiber 4g); Protein 23g.

Salisbury Steak

4 SERVINGS

This classic dish was named after Dr. Salisbury, who recommended to his patients that they eat plenty of beef for a wide variety of ailments.

1 pound ground beef

1/3 cup dry bread crumbs

1/2 teaspoon salt

1/4 teaspoon pepper

1 egg

1 large onion, sliced and separated into rings

1 can (10 1/2 ounces) condensed beef broth

8 ounces mushrooms, sliced (about 3 cups)*

2 tablespoons cold water

2 teaspoons cornstarch

1. Mix ground beef, bread crumbs, salt, pepper and egg; shape into 4 oval patties, each about 3/4-inch thick.

2. Cook patties in 10-inch skillet over medium heat, turning occasionally, until brown, about 10 minutes; drain. Add onion, broth and mushrooms. Heat to boiling; reduce heat. Cover and simmer until patties are done, about 10 minutes.

3. Remove patties; keep warm. Heat onion mixture to boiling. Mix water and cornstarch; stir into onion mixture. Boil and stir 1 minute. Serve over patties.

1 SERVING: Calories 325 (Calories from Fat 162); Fat 10g (Saturated 7g); Cholesterol 115mg; Sodium 830mg; Carbohydrates 15g (Dietary Fiber 2g); Protein 28g.

*1 can (4 ounces) mushroom stems and pieces, drained, can be substituted for the fresh mushrooms.

Corn Bread Beef Bake

6 SERVINGS

A cast-iron skillet works well for this casserole. For a Spanish twist, substitute 1/2 cup pitted green olives, 1/4 cup raisins and 1/4 cup slivered almonds and leave the whole kernel corn out.

1 pound ground beef

1 can (14 1/2 ounces) Mexican-style stewed tomatoes, undrained

1 can (15 ounces) black beans, rinsed and drained

1 can (8 ounces) tomato sauce

1/2 cup frozen whole kernel corn

2 teaspoons chili powder

1 can (11 1/2 ounces) refrigerated corn bread twists

1. Heat oven to 350°.

2. Cook beef in 10-inch ovenproof skillet over medium heat 8 to 10 minutes, stirring occasionally, until beef is brown; drain. Stir in tomatoes, beans, tomato sauce, corn and chili powder; heat to boiling.

3. Immediately top with corn bread twists left in round shape (do not unwind), pressing down gently.

4. Bake uncovered 35 to 40 minutes or until corn bread is golden brown.

1 SERVING: Calories 450 (Calories from Fat 170); Fat 19g (Saturated 7g); Cholesterol 45mg; Sodium 1050mg; Carbohydrates 51g (Dietary Fiber 6g); Protein 25g.

Impossible Cheeseburger Pie

6 SERVINGS

We've made mealtime impossibly easy! This main-dish pie makes its own crust with the help of Bisquick baking mix. Serve this family favorite with green beans and whole-wheat rolls for a super supper!

1 pound ground beef

1 large onion, chopped (1 cup)

1/4 teaspoon pepper

1 1/2 cups milk

3 eggs

3/4 cup Bisquick Original baking mix

2 medium tomatoes, sliced

4 slices (1 ounce each) Cheddar or process American cheese, cut in half

1. Heat oven to 400°. Grease pie plate, 10 x 1 1/2 inches, or spare baking dish, 8 x 8 x 2 inches, or six 10-ounce custard cups.

2. Cook beef and onion in 10-inch skillet over medium heat 8 to 10 minutes, stirring occasionally, until beef is brown; drain. Stir in pepper. Spread in pie plate.

3. Stir milk, eggs and baking mix with fork until blended. Pour into pie plate.

4. Bake 25 minutes. Top with tomatoes and cheese. Bake 5 to 8 minutes longer or until knife inserted in center comes out clean. Cool 5 minutes.

1 SERVING: Calories 270 (Calories from Fat 135); Fat 15g (Saturated 8g); Cholesterol 145mg; Sodium 570mg; Carbohydrates 18g (Dietary Fiber 1g); Protein 16g.

Katherine Loftus

Lostine, Oregon

I have always enjoyed cooking and baking and found cooking for our family (and then my own) fun and rewarding. My family loves holiday meals. Cookies always have been theirs—and my—favorites: snicker-doodles (Betty Crocker's recipe), old-fashioned ice-box, and, of course, chocolate chip and peanut butter.

I preferred staying home, so I did child care in my home, caring for seventeen children, plus my own two, every day for over five years. I decided at that point I needed more time for myself and the family, so I took a job as Christian education director and youth advisor for twenty-eight teenagers at my church! I thoroughly enjoyed working with the volunteer teaching staff, but my joy was my energetic, winsome, loving "kids." After almost four years I went back to child care, this time with a twist: foster care. Over the next ten years we cared for twenty-one children, mostly long term (two to five years); I cared for friends' children, too.

The children were involved in a myriad of school activities, so somewhere along the line I became involved: room mother, Title I representative, district Boy Scout advisory board, PTA president, and Girl Scout leader (for twelve years).

We were fortunate to be welcomed into a small, friendly Presbyterian church where the kids and I became involved. When my children reached middle school age, I returned to university after twenty-five years.

Today, I am busy with the Women's Association, vacation Bible school, choir, and other activities. Life is good!

Beef Enchiladas

4 SERVINGS

When you chop the chilies, be sure to wear plastic gloves to prevent the oil in the chili from getting on your hands or even under your nails. The gloves give you a disposable protective layer, so later you don't have to worry about skin or eye irritation caused by the oil in the chilies.

1 pound lean ground beef

1 medium onion, chopped
   (1/2 cup)

1/2 cup sour cream

1 cup shredded Cheddar cheese
   (4 ounces)

2 tablespoons chopped fresh
   parsley

1/4 teaspoon pepper

1/3 cup chopped green bell
   pepper

2/3 cup water

1 tablespoon chili powder

1 1/2 teaspoons chopped fresh
   or 1/2 teaspoon dried
   oregano leaves

1/4 teaspoon ground cumin

2 whole green chilies, chopped,
   if desired

1 clove garlic, finely chopped

1 can (15 ounces) tomato sauce

8 corn tortillas (6 inches in
   diameter)

Shredded cheese, sour cream and
   chopped onions, if desired

1. Heat oven to 350°.

2. Cook beef in 10-inch skillet over medium heat 8 to 10 minutes, stirring occasionally, until brown, drain. Stir in onion, sour cream, 1 cup cheese, the parsley and pepper. Cover and set aside.

3. Heat bell pepper, water, chili powder, oregano, cumin, chilies, garlic and tomato sauce to boiling, stirring occasionally; reduce heat to low. Simmer uncovered 5 minutes. Pour into ungreased pie plate, 9 x 1 1/4 inches.

4. Dip each tortilla into sauce to coat both sides. Spoon about 1/4 cup beef mixture onto each tortilla; roll tortilla around filling. Place in ungreased rectangular baking dish, 11 x 7 x 1 1/2 inches. Pour remaining sauce over enchiladas.

5. Bake uncovered about 20 minutes or until bubbly. Garnish with shredded cheese, sour cream and chopped onions.

1 SERVING: Calories 560 (Calories from Fat 295); Fat 33g (Saturated 16g); Cholesterol 115mg; Sodium 980mg; Carbohydrates 37g (Dietary Fiber 5g); Protein 34g.

Beef Goulash

When looking for favorite recipes, we had to make sure this recipe was included. The mixture of macaroni and ground meat is always a family favorite—and it's easy to make. Add a nice tossed salad to round out the meal.

1 1/2 pounds ground beef

1 medium onion, chopped

1 stalk celery, sliced

1 can (16 ounces) stewed tomatoes

1 tomato can (2 cups) water

1 package (7 ounces) uncooked elbow macaroni (1 1/2 cups)

1 can (6 ounces) tomato paste

1 tablespoon Worcestershire sauce

1 teaspoon salt

1/2 teaspoon pepper

1. Cook and stir ground beef, onion and celery in 4-quart ovenproof Dutch oven until beef is brown; drain. Stir in remaining ingredients.

2. Cover and bake in 350° oven until liquid is absorbed and goulash is hot, about 40 minutes; stir.

1 SERVING: Calories 405 (Calories from Fat 155); Fat 17g (Saturated 7g); Cholesterol 65mg; Sodium 910mg; Carbohydrates 39g (Dietary Fiber 3g); Protein 27g.

Fiesta Taco Casserole

Olé! Create your own fiesta when you serve this popular dish. This is a great way to use up the broken tortilla chips.

1 pound ground beef

1 can (15 to 16 ounces) spicy chili beans, undrained

1 cup salsa

2 cups coarsely broken tortilla chips

1/2 cup sour cream

4 medium green onions, sliced (1/2 cup)

1 medium tomato, chopped (3/4 cup)

1 cup shredded Cheddar or Monterey Jack cheese (4 ounces)

Tortilla chips, if desired

Shredded lettuce, if desired

Salsa, if desired

1. Heat oven to 350°.

2. Cook beef in 10-inch skillet over medium heat 8 to 10 minutes, stirring occasionally, until brown; drain. Stir in beans and 1 cup salsa. Heat to boiling, stirring occasionally.

3. Place broken tortilla chips in ungreased 2-quart casserole. Top with beef mixture. Spread with sour cream. Sprinkle with onions, tomato and cheese.

4. Bake uncovered 20 to 30 minutes or until hot and bubbly. Arrange tortilla chips around edge of casserole. Serve with lettuce and salsa.

1 SERVING: Calories 360 (Calories from Fat 205); Fat 23g (Saturated 11g); Cholesterol 75mg; Sodium 590mg; Carbohydrates 19g (Dietary Fiber 4g); Protein 23g.

Fiesta Taco Casserole

Ann Logan
Rutherfordton, North Carolina

Ann was cooking by the time she was seven, filling in for her mother who worked long hours in a garment plant. Even at an early age, Ann often delighted the family with her delicious cakes.

Years later, she's still baking. Rarely does a birthday pass without a cake from Ann's kitchen; and she continues to experiment with mixes, flavors, and textures. Mack, Ann's husband of thirty-four years, says his favorite is Ann's "famous brownies"—brownies she cooks using Betty Crocker brownie mix.

But if cooking is Ann's passion, then hard work, community service, and self-improvement is her calling. Despite the fact she's worked full-time with a major bank in North Carolina for thirty years, she's still managed to serve as president of the local chapter of the American Heart Association, continues to be a Lunch Pal for children in an Adopt-A-School program, and is active in a local school's PTA.

Ann believes strongly in education. She tutored her mother-in-law in math and English, thereby helping her to obtain that long-awaited high school diploma.

When she finds a spare minute, Ann enjoys sewing, counted cross-stitch embroidery, photography, travel, and reading cookbooks. On Halloween, Ann passes out treats dressed as Betty Crocker.

Pepperoni Pizza–Hamburger Pie

6 SERVINGS

We've added a new twist on a family favorite! This pie has the flavors of traditional pizza—but instead of ground beef sprinkled on top, it has a ground beef crust!

1 pound lean ground beef

1/3 cup dry bread crumbs

1 egg

1 1/2 teaspoons chopped fresh
   or 1/2 teaspoon dried
   oregano leaves

1/4 teaspoon salt

1/2 cup sliced mushrooms

1 small green bell pepper

1/3 cup chopped pepperoni
   (2 ounces)

1/4 cup sliced ripe olives

1 cup spaghetti sauce

1 cup shredded mozzarella
   cheese (4 ounces)

1. Heat oven to 400°.

2. Mix beef, bread crumbs, egg, oregano and salt; press evenly against bottom and side of ungreased pie plate, 9 x 1 1/4 inches.

3. Sprinkle mushrooms, bell pepper, pepperoni and olives into meat-lined plate. Pour spaghetti sauce over toppings.

4. Bake uncovered 25 minutes or until beef is no longer pink in center and juice is clear; carefully drain. Sprinkle with cheese. Bake about 5 minutes longer or until cheese is light brown. Let pie stand 5 minutes before cutting.

1 SERVING: Calories 310 (Calories from Fat 180); Fat 20g (Saturated 8g); Cholesterol 95mg; Sodium 740mg; Carbohydrates 10g (Dietary Fiber 1g); Protein 23g.

Cindy Winter-Hartley
Cary, North Carolina

SPIRIT OF BETTY CROCKER CONTEST
Winner

In the midst of my most busy day, the one thing that slows me down and refuels my tired body is cooking. I believe that one of the finest gifts I give my family is a healthful and delicious meal. And perhaps the most important ingredients in all my cooking is the love and care I try to put into it.

I have a college degree, have done graduate study work, and am married with three sons. Professionally, I am a business owner, and my company, Speak Up! Communication Training, conducts courses and consultations on presentation skills, speaking, and dealing with the media.

Personally, I'm a room mother at the elementary school and on the Hospitality Committee. I created and taught a Sunday school class at our church. I've been a career counselor at The Women's Center in downtown Raleigh and on the board of a parent education program.

Currently, I'm a volunteer in Welcome Baby/Safe Child as a parent mentor. This program is designed to help prevent child abuse by pairing up experienced mothers with new or high-need mothers. Right now, I'm working with a young, low-income mother who has three small children.

So today, as a businesswoman, wife, mother, and volunteer, the greatest joy I get is in creating memories for my family. I've finally grown up and now am as comfortable in a client's office as I am in my kitchen. Life can be pretty scrambled at the Winter-Hartley house. Probably the best idea I had was years ago when I found a good husband who respects my commitments and is an equal partner in our family life.

Mexican Beef and Bean Casserole

4 SERVINGS

If you like Mexican food topped with gooey cheese, try using Monterey Jack cheese with jalapeño peppers or one of the shredded pizza cheese mixtures available.

1 pound lean ground beef

2 cans (15 to 16 ounces each)
   pinto beans, drained

1 can (8 ounces) tomato sauce

1/2 cup mild chunky salsa

1 teaspoon chili powder

1 cup shredded Monterey Jack
   cheese (4 ounces)

1. Heat oven to 375°.

2. Cook beef in 10-inch skillet over medium heat 8 to 10 minutes, stirring occasionally, until brown; drain.

3. Mix beef, beans, tomato sauce, salsa and chili powder in ungreased 2-quart casserole.

4. Cover and bake 40 to 45 minutes, stirring once or twice, until hot and bubbly. Sprinkle with cheese. Bake uncovered about 5 minutes or until cheese is melted.

1 SERVING: Calories 565 (Calories from Fat 235; Fat 26g (Saturated 12g); Cholesterol 90mg; Sodium 1230mg; Carbohydrates 54g (Dietary Fiber 15g); Protein 44g.

Betty, Will You Marry Me?

Betty Crocker sounded so appealing on the radio that she began attracting serious suitors. By the mid-forties she had received at least ten marriage proposals, including one from a gentleman who said that if Betty was unavailable, could she recommend someone that she worked with who might be interested? An ad ran in *The Saturday Evening Post* and *American* magazines in 1945 in which General Mills graciously thanked the gentlemen, but politely declined, saying, "when you remember that the Betty Crocker staff already has a full-time job helping millions of American homemakers learn the secrets of fluffy, fine-textured cakes, crisp, flaky piecrust and golden-brown biscuits . . . well, you can see why Betty Crocker just *can't* marry anyone."

Overnight Lasagna

Lasagna is an American favorite, always perfect for family meals, casual get-togethers and potluck suppers.
Even better, you can put this lasagna together the night before and bake it the following day.

1 pound ground beef

1 medium onion, chopped (about 1/2 cup)

1 clove garlic, crushed

1/3 cup chopped fresh or 2 tablespoons dried parsley
  leaves

1 tablespoon sugar

2 tablespoons chopped fresh or 1 1/2 teaspoons dried
  basil leaves

1 teaspoon seasoned salt

1 can (16 ounces) whole tomatoes, undrained

1 can (10 3/4 ounces) condensed tomato soup

1 can (6 ouces) tomato paste

2 1/2 cups water

12 uncooked lasagna noodles (about 12 ounces)

1 container (12 ounces) creamed cottage cheese

2 cups shredded mozzarella cheese (8 ounces)

1/4 cup grated Parmesan cheese

1. Cook, stirring, ground beef, onion and garlic in
   Dutch oven until beef is brown; drain. Stir in
   parsley, sugar, basil, seasoned salt, tomatoes,
   tomato soup, tomato paste and water; break up
   tomatoes.

2. Heat to boiling, stirring occasionally; reduce
   heat. Simmer uncovered 20 minutes.

3. Spread 2 cups of the sauce mixture in ungreased
   rectangular baking dish, 13 x 9 x 2 inches. Top
   with 4 noodles. Spread half of the cottage cheese
   over noodles; spread with 2 cups of the sauce
   mixture. Sprinkle with 1 cup of the mozzarella
   cheese. Repeat with 4 noodles, the remaining
   cottage cheese, 2 cups of the sauce mixture and
   the remaining mozzarella cheese. Top with the
   remaining noodles and sauce mixture; sprinkle
   with Parmesan cheese. Cover and refrigerate up
   to 12 hours.

4. Heat oven to 350°. Bake covered 30 minutes.
   Uncover and bake until hot and bubbly, 30 to
   40 minutes longer. Let stand 15 minutes before
   cutting.

1 SERVING: Calories 425 (Calories from Fat 155); Fat 17g
(Saturated 8g); Cholesterol 55mg; Sodium 1160mg; Carbohydrates 41g (Dietary Fiber 3g); Protein 30g.

New England Pot Roast

8 SERVINGS

A whole jar of horseradish might sound overpowering to you, but we assure you it adds a nice, savory flavor to this dish without overwhelming your tastebuds. The meat and vegetables simmer away in the juices and emerge tender and flavorful. This roast also makes a great gravy.

4 pound beef arm, blade or cross rib pot roast*

1 to 2 teaspoons salt

1 teaspoon pepper

1 jar (8 ounces) prepared horseradish

1 cup water

8 small potatoes, cut in half

8 medium carrots, cut into fourths

8 small onions

Pot Roast Gravy (right)

1. Cook beef in Dutch oven over medium heat until brown on all sides; reduce hear to low.

2. Sprinkle beef with salt and pepper. Spread horseradish over all sides of beef. Add water to Dutch oven. Heat to boiling; reduce heat to low. Cover and simmer 2 1/2 hours.

3. Add potatoes, carrots and onions. Cover and simmer about 1 hour or until beef and vegetables are tender.

4. Remove beef and vegetables to warm platter; keep warm. Prepare Pot Roast Gravy. Serve with beef and vegetables.

POT ROAST GRAVY

Water

1/2 cup cold water

1/4 cup all-purpose flour

Skim excess fat from broth in Dutch oven. Add enough water to broth to measure 2 cups. Shake 1/2 cup cold water and the flour in tightly covered container; gradually stir into broth. Heat to boiling, stirring constantly. Boil and stir 1 minute.

1 SERVING: Calories 365 (Calories from Fat 100); Fat 11g (Saturated 4g); Cholesterol 85mg; Sodium 400mg; Carbohydrates 38g (Dietary Fiber 6g); Protein 35g.

*3 pound beef bottom round, rolled rump, tip or chuck eye roast can be substituted; decrease salt to 3/4 teaspoon.

Carol Weitzman
Cleveland, Ohio

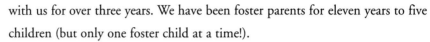

In 1968, I was named Betty Crocker Homemaker of Tomorrow at Nordonia High School. I married my high school sweetheart and worked until my first child was born in 1980. In this family is my husband of twenty-six years, a daughter, a son who is profoundly hearing impaired, and a foster son, who has been with us for over three years. We have been foster parents for eleven years to five children (but only one foster child at a time!).

Besides managing this household, I am a dedicated child advocate. I spend a great deal of time at my children's schools and of a great deal of effort raising money for the Hearing Aid Fund. Over the years, I have spent much time volunteering at church. When it was called for, I taught Sunday School because no one else could begin to teach or understand my son. Today, I am proud to say, that is not the case. He is a wonderfully outgoing, popular boy who speaks quite well.

My love of cooking and entertaining has stood me well! Now I have the pleasure of teaching my sons to cook; my daughter is already quite capable of taking care of herself when she leaves home. I love to cook and no matter what age the children were, I always assumed they would like what I liked. I probably have the only three children in the world who beg for broccoli cheese soup and seafood à la Newburg for dinner! I am proud to be a mother, foster mother, and homemaker. I make the distinction between mother and foster mother only because to be a foster mother, it takes continuous training, a knowledge of psychology, and a willingness to work with the County Department of Children's and Family Resources and the court system.

Fajitas

You'll flip for these fajitas. Remember to allow some time for the meat to marinade—just pop it in before going to work in the morning and it will be ready to cook when you get home!

Fajita Marinade (below)

1 1/2 pound beef boneless top sirloin steak, 1 1/2 inches thick

12 flour tortillas (10 inches in diameter)

2 tablespoons vegetable oil

2 large onions, sliced

2 medium green or red bell peppers, cut into 1/4-inch strips

1 jar (8 ounces) picante sauce (1 cup)

1 cup shredded Cheddar or Monterey Jack cheese (4 ounces)

1 1/2 cups prepared guacamole

3/4 cup sour cream

FAJITA MARINADE

1/4 cup vegetable oil

1/4 cup red wine vinegar

1 teaspoon sugar

1 teaspoon dried oregano leaves

1 teaspoon chili powder

1/2 teaspoon garlic powder

1/2 teaspoon salt

1/4 teaspoon pepper

1. Mix Fajita Marinade ingredients in ungreased, square glass baking dish, 8 x 8 x 2 inches. Set aside.

2. Trim excess fat from beef. Pierce beef with fork in several places. Place beef in marinade, turning to coat both sides. Cover and refrigerate at least 8 hours but no longer than 24 hours, turning beef occasionally.

3. Heat oven to 325°.

4. Wrap tortillas in aluminum foil. Heat in oven about 15 minutes or until warm. Remove tortillas from oven; keep wrapped.

5. Set oven control to Broil.

6. Remove beef from marinade; reserve marinade. Place beef on rack in broiler pan. (For easy cleanup, line broker pan with aluminum foil before placing beef on rack.) Broil beef with top about 3 inches from heat about 8 minutes or until brown. Turn; brush beef with marinade. Broil 7 to 8 minutes longer for medium-rare to medium. Discard any remaining marinade.

7. While beef is broiling, heat oil in 10-inch skillet over medium-high feet. Cook onions and bell peppers in oil 6 to 8 minutes, stirring frequently, until crisp-tender. Cut beef across grain into very thin slices.

8. For each fajita, place a few slices of beef, some of the onion mixture, 1 heaping tablespoonful each picante sauce and cheese, about 2 tablespoons Guacamole and 1 tablespoon sour cream in center of tortilla. Fold 1 end of tortilla up about 1 inch over filling; fold right and left sides over folded end, overlapping. Fold remaining end down.

1 SERVING: Calories 690 (Calories from Fat 325); Fat 36g (Saturated 12g); Cholesterol 90mg; Sodium 1110mg; Carbohydrates 64g (Dietary Fiber 7g); Protein 35g.

Beefy Baked Chili

6 SERVINGS

Instead of ground beef, this hearty chili features chunks of tender beef. It's the perfect chili to make when you want to entertain since you just pop it in the oven and let it slowly cook several hours until it's savory and full of flavor.

1 1/2 cups dried pinto beans

6 cups water

1 1/2 pounds beef boneless chuck, tip or round steak, cut into 1-inch pieces

1 teaspoon chili powder

1 tablespoon cumin seed

1 1/2 teaspoons salt

1 1/2 teaspoons ground red pepper

3 medium onions, chopped

3 cloves garlic, finely chopped

3 cans (8 ounces each) tomato sauce

1. Heat oven to 325°.

2. Heat beans and water to boiling in 4-quart oven-proof Dutch oven. Boil 2 minutes.

3. Stir remaining ingredients into bean mixture. Cover and bake until beef and beans are tender, about 4 hours; stir. Garnish with sour cream, chopped onion and shredded Cheddar cheese, if desired.

1 SERVING: Calories 315 (Calories from Fat 125); Fat 14g (Saturated 5g); Cholesterol 70mg; Sodium 1340mg; Carbohydrates 25g (Dietary Fiber 7g); Protein 29g.

Spicy Pepper Steak Stir-Fry

4 SERVINGS

Chili oil is available in Asian markets or in the Asian foods section of the grocery store. If you don't have chili oil, just add 1/4 teaspoon ground red pepper (cayenne) or a 1/2 teaspoon red pepper sauce to a tablespoon vegetable oil for the same kick and great flavor.

1 tablespoon chili oil or vegetable oil

1 pound cut-up beef for stir-fry

1 medium bell pepper, cut into 3/4-inch squares

1 medium onion, sliced

1/4 cup hoisin sauce

Hot cooked noodles or rice, if desired

1. Heat wok or 12-inch skillet over high heat. Add oil; rotate wok to coat side.

2. Add beef; stir-fry about 2 minutes or until brown. Add bell pepper and onion; stir-fry about 1 minute or until vegetables are crisp-tender. Stir in hoisin sauce; cook and stir about 30 seconds or until hot. Serve with noodles.

1 SERVING: Calories 185 (Calories from Fat 65); Fat 7g (Saturated 2g); Cholesterol 55mg; Sodium 40mg; Carbohydrates 9g (Dietary Fiber 1g); Protein 23g

Spicy Pepper Steak Stir-Fry

Julie Leviner
Wilmington, North Carolina

I love to cook and bake. With a Betty Crocker box cake mix and a can of Betty Crocker frosting, there's a chance to celebrate an event or an accomplishment.

This summer my girls and I had fun making Betty Crocker's recipe for peach pie for our neighbors. It lets our neighbors know we enjoy them in our lives. Cooking helps me teach my girls important values. Several nights a week we share dinner with an elderly neighbor who lives alone. The girls learn a little effort can mean a great deal to someone else.

Being a homemaker gives me not only the time I need to be with my children, but also time to be involved in the community. My biggest volunteer commitments are with Wilmington's Domestic Violence Shelter, Cape Fear Museum, Junior League, and Forest Hills Elementary School. My favorite volunteer activity and Betty Crocker recipe go hand-in-hand. Every holiday I go to Forest Hills Elementary School with some sugar cookies from the *Betty Crocker Cookbook* recipe, some Betty Crocker Frosting, and sprinkles or some other form of decoration, and we decorate cookies in at least two, if not five, classes. Cooking and baking enriches our lives

Classic Beef Stroganoff

8 SERVINGS

This elegant entree, named after a 19th-century Russian diplomat, Count Stroganv, combines a sour cream sauce with tender beef, onions and mushrooms. Don't let the sauce boil once you've added the sour cream or it will curdle.

2 pounds beef sirloin steak,
  1/2-inch thick

8 ounces mushrooms, sliced

2 medium onions, thinly sliced

1 clove garlic, finely chopped

1/4 cup margarine or butter

1 1/2 cups beef broth

1 teaspoon salt

1 teaspoon Worcestershire sauce

1/4 cup all-purpose flour

1 1/2 cups sour cream

4 cups hot cooked egg noodles

1. Cut beef steak across grain into strips, 1 1/2 x 1/2 inch.

2. Cook and stir mushrooms, onions and garlic in margarine in 10-inch skillet until onions are tender; remove from skillet. Cook beef in same skillet until brown. Stir in 1 cup of the broth, the salt and the Worcestershire sauce. Heat to boiling; reduce heat. Cover and simmer 15 minutes.

3. Stir remaining 1/2 cup broth into flour; stir into beef mixture. Add onion mixture; heat to boiling, stirring constantly. Boil and stir 1 minute. Stir in sour cream; heat until hot (do not boil). Serve over noodles.

1 SERVING: Calories 385 (Calories from Fat 170); Fat 19g (Saturated 10g); Cholesterol 125mg; Sodium 300mg; Carbohydrates 28g (Dietary Fiber 2g); Protein 27g.

Wondra®

Drat those lumps in the gravy! Does it happen to you, too? Apparently Betty also was plagued by them, and so she found a way to help get rid of them. In 1963, a revolutionary new flour product was introduced: Gold Medal Wondra instantized flour. It was just like regular all-purpose flour in all respects except one: It was in a granular form that dissolved instantly, even in cold liquids and enabled cooks to make lump-free sauces and gravies. Adding to the convenience is the "Pour 'n Shake" container it comes in. Betty has made sure you'll never have to put up with lumps again!

Pasta with Beef, Broccoli and Tomatoes

6 SERVINGS

If you can't find radiatore pasta, use any large-size pasta such as mostaccioli, penne, rigatoni or ziti instead. Partially frozen beef can be sliced very easily and evenly—give it a try.

3/4 pound beef boneless sirloin steak

3 cups uncooked radiatore (nugget) pasta (9 ounces)

1/2 teaspoon pepper

1 package (16 ounces) fresh or frozen broccoli cuts (6 cups)

1 can (14 1/2 ounces) diced tomatoes with roasted garlic, undrained

1 can (14 1/2 ounces) beef broth

2 tablespoons cornstarch

2 tablespoons Worcestershire sauce

1. Trim fat from beef. Cut beef into 1/4-inch strips.

2. Cook and drain pasta as directed on package. While pasta is cooking, spray 12-inch skillet with cooking spray; heat over medium-high heat. Add beef to skillet; sprinkle with pepper. Cook 2 to 3 minutes, stirring frequently, until brown.

3. Stir in broccoli, tomatoes and broth; reduce heat. Cover and simmer about 10 minutes, stirring occasionally, until broccoli is crisp-tender.

4. Mix cornstarch and Worcestershire sauce; stir into beef mixture. Heat to boiling, stirring constantly. Boil and stir 1 minute. Toss beef mixture and pasta.

1 SERVING: Calories 270 (Calories from Fat 30); Fat 3g (Saturated 1g); Cholesterol 30mg; Sodium 500mg; Carbohydrates 44g (Dietary Fiber 4g); Protein 21g.

Pasta with Beef, Broccoli and Tomatoes

Chicken-Fried Steak

6 SERVINGS

This fried steak and gravy dish, popular in Texas and throughout the Southwest, was invented out of necessity on cattle drives. To feed hungry cowboys, trail cooks would slice beef off a hind quarter, tenderize it by pounding with a meat cleaver, roll it in seasoned coating and fry it in hot sizzling oil like chicken—hence its name. If you'd like to save a bit of time, use tenderized cubed steaks for the round steaks.

1 1/2 pounds beef boneless round steak, about
    1/2 inch thick

1 tablespoon water

1 egg

1 cup soda cracker crumbs (about 28 squares)

1/4 teaspoon pepper

1/4 cup vegetable oil

Milk Gravy (right)

1. Cut beef steak into 6 serving pieces. Pound each piece until 1/4 inch thick to tenderize.

2. Beat water and egg; reserve. Mix cracker crumbs and pepper. Dip beef into egg mixture, then coat with cracker crumbs.

3. Heat oil in 12-inch skillet over medium-high heat until hot. Cook beef in oil, turning once, until brown, 6 to 7 minutes. Remove beef from skillet; keep warm.

4. Reserve drippings for Milk Gravy. Prepare gravy; serve with Chicken-Fried Steak.

MILK GRAVY

1/4 cup all-purpose flour

1/2 teaspoon salt

2 cups milk

Measure reserved drippings (from step 4); add enough vegetable oil to drippings, if necessary, to measure 1/4 cup. Return dripping to skillet. Stir in flour and salt. Cook over low heat, stirring constantly to loosen brown particles from skillet, until smooth and bubbly; remove from heat. Slowly pour milk into skillet, stirring constantly. Heat to boiling over low heat, stirring constantly. Boil and stir 1 minute.

1 SERVING: Calories 325 (Calories from Fat 155); Fat 17g (Saturated 4g); Cholesterol 100mg; Sodium 410mg; Carbohydrates 15g (Dietary Fiber 0g); Protein 28g.

Fran Baldwin
Dublin, Ohio

Twenty-seven years ago, I received my first Betty Crocker cookbook as a bridal shower gift from my mother. In the late 1960s, women strived to acquire Betty's ability of preparing bountiful meals for husbands and family.

Just as Betty's image changed over the years, so did mine. I went from "Susie Homemaker" to "Working Single-Again Mom of Three." That's when I learned to master the art of Betty's ready-made brownie mixes. My motto was "God so loved single parents that He gave us Betty Crocker quick fixes and microwave ovens."

I was able to juggle a demanding career in business, three kids (two of which are twin sons), PTA meetings, Little League games, ballet lessons, car pools, and a host of community service organization positions. My kids never hesitated volunteering me for classroom cookies or brownies because Betty and I were the super women who could whip up these things in the twilight hours.

Although the kids are off to college, a week doesn't go by that I don't whip up a batch of Betty's Snickerdoodles to send to my sons or take the time to show my daughter how to make yummy treats.

I have been a great mother, hardworking woman, community service leader, dedicated friend, accomplished cook, and a true example of a woman who learned how to roll with the punches about as good as she could roll pie dough. Betty has been a part of my life over the years, and now I would like to be a part of hers.

Beef Brisket Barbecue

12 SERVINGS

The slow-cooking brisket emerges tender and succulent. Any leftovers can be transformed into delicious sandwiches the next day. Or, you can shred the brisket and stir in enough warm barbecue sauce to moisten it. It is delicious as a sandwich or spooned over hot mashed potatoes or rice.

4 to 5 pounds well-trimmed fresh beef brisket (not corned)

1 teaspoon salt

1/2 cup ketchup

1/4 cup white vinegar

1 tablespoon Worcestershire sauce

1 1/2 teaspoons liquid smoke

1/4 teaspoon pepper

1 medium onion, finely chopped (1/2 cup)

1 bay leaf

1. Heat oven to 325°.

2. Rub surface of beef with salt. Place in ungreased rectangular pan, 18 x 9 x 2 inches. Mix remaining ingredients; pour over beef.

3. Cover and bake about 3 hours or until beef is tender.

4. Cut thin diagonal slices across grain at an angle from 2 or 3 "faces" of beef. Spoon any remaining pan juices over sliced beef if desired. Remove bay leaf.

1 SERVING: Calories 245 (Calories from Fat 100); Fat 11g (Saturated 4g); Cholesterol 85mg; Sodium 390mg; Carbohydrates 4g (Dietary Fiber 0g); Protein 33g.

Consumer Services Department

Under the leadership of Marjorie Child Husted, the Betty Crocker Home Service Department had responded since the 1920s to the flood of letters asking for cooking advice. Eventually this department evolved into the Betty Crocker Kitchens, which develops and tests new products, recipes and cookbooks, and into the Consumer Services Department, which responds to consumers' inquiries. Staff members use a variety of means to communicate with consumers, including the mail, toll-free phone lines, and, most recently, fax and E-mail. They respond to about 600,000 consumers each year. Some folks have comments about products or recipes, some want advice, some are looking for recipes. As a trusted friend in the kitchen, Betty has always responded quickly and in a friendly way.

Tender Beef Stew with Dumplings

6 SERVINGS

What's better on a cold winter evening than hearty beef stew and fluffy dumplings? Want some company in the kitchen? Recruit family members to help you chop the vegetables!

1 tablespoon vegetable oil or shortening

1 pound beef boneless chuck, tip or round roast, cut into 1-inch cubes

3 cups hot water

1/2 teaspoon salt

1/8 teaspoon pepper

2 medium carrots, cut into 1-inch pieces (1 cup)

1 large potato, cut into 1 1/2-inch pieces (1 1/4 cups)

1 medium turnip, cut into 1-inch pieces (1 cup)

1 medium green bell pepper, cut into 1-inch pieces (1 cup)

1 medium stalk celery, cut into 1-inch pieces (1/2 cup)

1 small onion, chopped (1/4 cup)

1/2 teaspoon browning sauce, if desired

1 teaspoon salt

1 bay leaf

Dumplings (right), if desired

1/2 cup cold water

2 tablespoons all-purpose flour

1. Heat oil in 12-inch skillet or Dutch oven. Cook beef in oil about 15 minutes, stirring occasionally, until beef is brown. Add hot water, 1/2 teaspoon salt and the pepper. Heat to boiling; reduce heat to low. Cover and simmer 2 to 2 1/2 hours or until beef is almost tender.

2. Stir in remaining ingredients except Dumplings, cold water and flour. Cover and simmer about 30 minutes or until vegetables are tender. Remove bay leaf.

3. Prepare Dumplings.

4. Shake cold water and flour in tightly covered container; gradually stir into beef mixture. Heat to boiling, stirring constantly. Boil and stir 1 minute; reduce heat to low.

5. Drop dumpling dough by 10 to 12 spoonfuls onto hot stew (do not drop directly into liquid). Cook uncovered 10 minutes. Cover and cook 10 minutes longer.

DUMPLINGS

3 tablespoons shortening

1 1/2 cups all-purpose flour

1 tablespoon dried parsley flakes, if desired

2 teaspoons baking powder

1/2 teaspoon salt

3/4 cup milk

Cut shortening into flour, parsley, baking powder and salt in medium bowl, using pastry blender or crisscrossing 2 knives, until mixture looks like fine crumbs. Stir in milk.

1 SERVING: Calories 250 (Calories from Fat 145); Fat 16g (Saturated 6g); Cholesterol 45mg; Sodium 590mg; Carbohydrates 14g (Dietary Fiber 2g); Protein 14g.

Beef Burgundy Stew

8 SERVINGS

This is a great dish to make when you are having a crowd over. It feeds a lot of people without much work for you! Grab several loaves of good French bread—this stew makes a wonderfully rich, Burgundy sauce which is oh, so good sopped up with crusty, fresh bread.

2 tablespoons margarine or butter

5 medium onions, sliced

6 cups sliced mushrooms (1 pound)

3 pounds beef stew meat, cut into 1-inch cubes

2 cloves garlic, finely chopped

2 teaspoons salt

1 teaspoon chopped fresh or 1/2 teaspoon dried
  marjoram leaves

1 teaspoon chopped fresh or 1/2 teaspoon dried
  thyme leaves

1/4 teaspoon pepper

3 cups beef broth

3 tablespoons all-purpose flour

3 1/2 cups red Burgundy

French bread, if desired

1. Melt margarine in Dutch oven or 3-quart saucepan over medium heat. Cook onions and mushrooms in margarine about 10 minutes, stirring occasionally, until onions are tender. Remove vegetables from Dutch oven; drain and reserve.

2. Cook beef and garlic in Dutch oven over medium heat, stirring occasionally, until beef is brown; drain. Sprinkle with salt, marjoram, thyme and pepper.

3. Mix broth and flour; pour over beef. Heat to boiling, stirring constantly. Boil and stir 1 minute.

4. Stir in Burgundy. Cover and simmer 1 1/2 to 2 hours, stirring in onions and mushrooms 5 minutes before end of simmer time. Serve in bowls with bread for dipping into sauce.

1 SERVING: Calories 550 (Calories from Fat 315); Fat 35g (Saturated 14g); Cholesterol 100mg; Sodium 890mg; Carbohydrates 13g (Dietary Fiber 2g); Protein 33g.

Joyce Muthig
Parksville, New York

Mom is the entertainer of the neighborhood. She makes kids' birthday cakes, has the men over that dad golfs with, and bakes for my dad's hunt club (his birthday falls in deer season and she sends a sheet cake to the club). She bakes the birthday cakes for four grandchildren, plus sends cupcakes to the classrooms,

most times delivering them herself. I noticed a Betty Crocker box in her closet. I asked Mom how it got there? She very happily said "Good cakes every time, half the preparation time, and the closest thing to "homemade cooking." And always a success! I know that this is true.

Mom bakes for Catholic Daughters local chapter (member forty-five years) and snowmobile club (member since 1973). She works as a volunteer for the needy shop for children, for the Sullivan County Cornell Extension Service member, for the Rosary Society, and, I might add, she is always on the baking committees. In handling everyday tasks, I have seen Mom baby-sit for my children, bake for a club, take calls from the local hospital to put a layette together and deliver, and prepare an old-fashioned meal for dad.

My mom, no matter what else she is involved in, never forgets a few moments of one's time and a nice piece of dessert always make a person feel like a million dollars. Because of this attitude, her friends, of whom there are many, joke about the naming of her house as "The Do Drop Inn."

Country-Style Ribs

These mighty meaty ribs come both bone-in and boneless, so check in the meat department or with your butcher. You'll need about 2 pounds if you prefer boneless. To save clean-up time and elbow grease, we like to line the pan with heavy-duty aluminum foil.

3 pounds pork country-style ribs

2/3 cup chili sauce

1/2 cup grape jelly

1 tablespoon dry red wine

1 teaspoon Dijon mustard

1. Heat oven to 325°.

2. Cut ribs into serving pieces if necessary. Place ribs, meaty sides up, in ungreased rectangular pan, 13 x 9 x 2 inches.

3. Cover and bake about 2 hours or until tender; drain.

4. Heat remaining ingredients, stirring occasionally, until jelly is melted. Pour over ribs.

5. Bake uncovered 30 minutes, spooning sauce over ribs occasionally.

1 SERVING: Calories 340 (Calories from Fat 135); Fat 15g (Saturated 5g); Cholesterol 80mg; Sodium 400mg; Carbohydrates 24g (Dietary Fiber 0g); Protein 27g.

Baked Spareribs with Spicy Barbecue Sauce

8 SERVINGS

Since you don't need a grill, these ribs are great to make in the winter when you want the flavor of summer in your dinner. Serve these with Old-Fashioned Coleslaw (page 267) and Buttermilk Biscuits (page 301).

4 1/2-pound rack fresh pork loin back ribs, cut into serving pieces

Spicy Barbecue Sauce (below)

1. Place pork ribs, meaty sides up, on rack in shallow roasting pan. Roast uncovered in 325° oven 1 1/2 hours.

2. Brush with Spicy Barbecue Sauce. Roast, turning and brushing frequently with sauce, until done, about 45 minutes longer. Serve with remaining sauce.

SPICY BARBECUE SAUCE

1/3 cup margarine or butter

2 tablespoons vinegar

2 tablespoons water

1 teaspoon sugar

1/2 teaspoon garlic powder

1/2 teaspoon onion powder

1/2 teaspoon pepper

Dash of ground red pepper

Heat all ingredients, stirring frequently, until margarine is melted.

1 SERVING: Calories 550 (Calories from Fat 405); Fat 45g (Saturated 15g); Cholesterol 150mg; Sodium 220mg; Carbohydrates 1g (Dietary Fiber 0g); Protein 36g.

Wine-Marinated Country-Style Ribs

6 SERVINGS

Ribs can sometimes be messy, but oh, so good. Have lots of napkins or wet towelettes handy when serving these!

2 tablespoons vegetable oil

1 tablespoon chopped fresh or 1 teaspoon dried rosemary leaves, crushed

1 clove garlic, finely chopped

1/2 cup dry red wine or grape juice

1 teaspoon sugar

1/2 teaspoon salt

1/4 teaspoon pepper

3 pounds pork country-style ribs, cut into serving pieces

1. Heat oil in 1 1/2-quart saucepan over medium heat. Cook rosemary and garlic in oil, stirring frequently, until garlic is golden; remove from heat. Stir in wine, sugar, salt and pepper.

2. Place pork in glass dish. Pour wine mixture over pork; turn to coat. Cover and refrigerate 4 hours, turning pork occasionally.

3. Prepare grill, arranging charcoal around edge of firebox. Place drip pan under grilling area.

4. Remove pork from marinade; reserve marinade. Cover and grill pork over drip pan and 4 to 5 inches from medium coals 1 hour 10 minutes, turning occasionally and brushing with marinade, until pork is tender and no longer pink in center. Discard remaining marinade.

1 SERVING: Calories 280 (Calories from Fat 170); Fat 19g (Saturated 6g); Cholesterol 80mg; Sodium 230mg; Carbohydrates 1g (Dietary Fiber 0g); Protein 26g.

Wine-Marinated Country-Style Ribs

Sheilah Kyburz
Bloomington, Minnesota

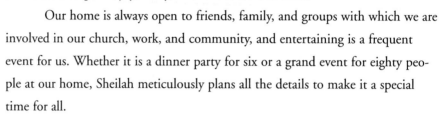

Sheilah, my wife, was awarded the Betty Crocker Future Homemaker of America Award in 1972 and has continued to make that teenage recognition and prediction of her success as an outstanding homemaker a reality over the years. She has created our home to be a place filled with not only delectable daily sustenance but also peace, joy, safety, and love to all who enter.

Our home is always open to friends, family, and groups with which we are involved in our church, work, and community, and entertaining is a frequent event for us. Whether it is a dinner party for six or a grand event for eighty people at our home, Sheilah meticulously plans all the details to make it a special time for all.

She is administrative secretary to the bishop of the Minnesota Area of the United Methodist Church and is an excellent employee, respected by her colleagues and persons of leadership in the church.

She operates a home sewing service for the community, colleagues, and friends, and she enjoys hunting for and restoring antiques, loves to work on cross-stitch projects, is thrilled to travel frequently, explores traditions and art from cultural diverse backgrounds, gardens, and likes to bike and hike. In the past few years, she has learned cake decorating, tap dancing, wood carving, calligraphy, tat, the German language, computer programs, and how to play the harp. Never afraid of putting forth a little extra effort to help people in need, for several years Sheilah has also offered her time to others by ironing for three families in the community who have had difficulty taking care of that household tasks because of health problems, family difficulties, and schooling responsibilities.

We all have the same twenty-four hours in a day, but somehow Sheila seems to accomplish forty-eight-hours' worth in her twenty-four hours available. Sheilah is a woman who knows how to make a house a home, and I am proud to share her story because I know she is a strong, inspiring, motivating role model.

Wild Rice-and Almond-Stuffed Pork Chops

4 SERVINGS

Quick-cooking wild rice is faster to prepare than regular wild rice and is equally delicious. If you can't find wild rice, try a wild rice blend or brown rice instead.

Wild Rice and Almond Stuffing
   (below)

4 pork loin chops, 1 inch thick
   (about 2 1/2 pounds)

1/3 cup apricot preserves

1 tablespoon dry white wine or
   apple juice

1/8 teaspoon ground cinnamon

WILD RICE AND
ALMOND STUFFING

1/3 cup finely chopped celery

1 green onion, finely chopped

1 teaspoon margarine or butter

1 cup cooked wild rice

1 tablespoon sliced almonds

1/4 teaspoon salt

1/8 teaspoon pepper

1. Prepare Wild Rice and Almond Stuffing.

2. Cut a deep pocket in each pork chop on the meatiest side of the bone. Press about 1/3 cup stuffing mixture into each pocket. Secure openings with toothpicks. Mix apricot preserves, wine and cinnamon.

3. Cover and grill pork 4 to 5 inches from medium-low coals 40 to 45 minutes, brushing occasionally with apricot mixture and turning 2 or three times, until pork is no longer pink when cut near bone on the unstuffed sides of chops. Remove toothpicks.

WILD RICE AND ALMOND STUFFING

Cook celery and onion in margarine in 8-inch skillet over medium heat, stirring frequently, until celery is crisp-tender. Stir in remaining ingredients.

1 SERVING: Calories 440 (Calories from Fat 0); Fat 20g (Saturated 0g); Cholesterol 115mg; Sodium 380mg; Carbohydrates 29g (Dietary Fiber 0g); Protein 36g.

Stuffed Pork Chops

This is a must-have for pork lovers—tender, juicy chops filled with savory stuffing.

1/3 cup chopped celery (with leaves)

3 tablespoons finely chopped onion

1/4 cup (1/2 stick) margarine or butter

2 1/4 cups soft bread cubes (about 4 slices bread)

1/2 teaspoon salt

1/4 teaspoon rubbed sage

3/4 teaspoon chopped fresh or 1/4 teaspoon dried
   thyme leaves

1/8 teaspoon pepper

4 pork loin chops, about 1 inch thick (with pockets
   cut into chops)

2 tablespoons vegetable oil

1/4 cup apple cider or juice

1. Cook and stir celery and onion in margarine in
   2-quart saucepan over medium heat, stirring frequently, until celery is tender; remove from heat.
   Stir in bread cubes, salt, sage, thyme and pepper.

2. Stuff each pork chop pocket with about 1/3 cup
   of the bread mixture. Fasten by inserting 2
   toothpicks in **X** shape through edges of pork.

3. Fry in oil in 10-inch skillet over medium heat
   until brown on both sides, about 15 minutes;
   drain. Add apple cider; reduce heat. Cover and
   simmer until pork chops are done, about 1 hour.
   Remove toothpicks before serving.

1 SERVING: Calories 395 (Calories from Fat 245); Fat 28g
(Saturated 6g); Cholesterol 60mg; Sodium 580mg; Carbohydrates 16g (Dietary Fiber 1g); Protein 20g.

Grilled Honey-Mustard Pork Chops

The orange juice sweetens up the nice spicy mustard glaze. This is a great dinner to throw on the grill when you want lots of flavor. Add some slices of fresh pineap-ple on the grill for the perfect accompaniment to these pork chops.

1/4 cup honey

2 tablespoons Dijon mustard

1 tablespoon orange juice

1 teaspoon chopped fresh or 1/4 teaspoon dried
   tarragon leaves

1 teaspoon cider vinegar

1/2 teaspoon white wine or regular Worcestershire
   sauce

Dash of onion powder

4 boneless pork loin chops, 1/2 inch thick
   (about 1 pound)

1. Mix all ingredients except pork.

2. Cover and grill pork 4 to 5 inches from medium
   coals 10 to 12 minutes, brushing occasionally
   with honey mixture and turning once, until
   pork is tender and slightly pink when centers of
   thickest pieces are cut. Discard any remaining
   honey mixture.

1 SERVING: Calories 285 (Calories from Fat 115), Fat 13g
(Saturated 5g); Cholesterol 70mg; Sodium 140mg; Carbohydrates 19g (Dietary Fiber 0g); Protein 23g.

Pork Chop and New Potato Skillet

6 SERVINGS

New potatoes are young potatoes of any variety. If you can't find any new potatoes, use Round Red or Round White instead. If they are large, you might have to cut them into sixths instead of fourths.

6 pork loin or rib chops, 1/2 inch thick (about 1 1/2 pounds)

1 can (10 3/4 ounces) condensed cream of mushroom soup

1 can (4 ounces) mushroom stems and pieces, undrained

1/4 cup water

2 tablespoons dry white wine or apple juice

3/4 teaspoon chopped fresh or 1/4 teaspoon dried thyme leaves

1/2 teaspoon garlic powder

1/2 teaspoon Worcestershire sauce

6 medium new potatoes (about 1 1/2 pounds), cut into fourths

1 tablespoon chopped pimiento

1 package (10 ounces) frozen green peas, rinsed and drained

1. Spray 10-inch nonstick skillet with nonstick cooking spray; heat skillet over medium-high heat. Cook pork in skillet until brown on both sides.

2. Mix soup, mushrooms, water, wine, thyme, garlic powder and Worcestershire sauce; pour over pork. Heat to boiling, stirring occasionally; reduce heat. Cover and simmer 15 minutes.

3. Add potatoes. Cover and simmer 15 minutes. Stir in pimiento and peas. Cover and simmer about 10 minutes, stirring occasionally, until pork is tender and slightly pink when centers of thickest pieces are cut and peas are tender.

1 SERVING: Calories 385 (Calories from Fat 155); Fat 17g (Saturated 6g); Cholesterol 70mg; Sodium 580mg; Carbohydrates 34g (Dietary Fiber 5g); Protein 29g.

Pork Chop and New Potato Skillet

Diann Gordon
Brownsville, Texas

Diann Gordon is a devoted wife and partner, true friend, a reliable volunteer, and a hard worker. However, the first thing that comes to mind when asked about Diann Gordon is her reputation as a cook and hostess. As Diann's husband, I have heard stories dating back to her early childhood in front of the Easy-Bake

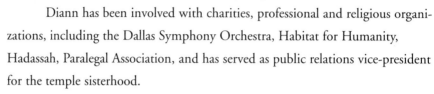

oven when she made cakes and cookies for young friends.

Diann has been involved with charities, professional and religious organizations, including the Dallas Symphony Orchestra, Habitat for Humanity, Hadassah, Paralegal Association, and has served as public relations vice-president for the temple sisterhood.

When friends are in need of assistance, Diann is there to help. When friends have babies, Diann prepares and freezes foods that can be baked in the oven by the "not-so-handy-in-the-kitchen" father. When friends have had a special event, Diann has helped plan the party, prepared and served food, and refused to accept compensation, insisting it was a gift.

Diann is well educated with a degree from Southern Methodist University and a legal education from Pepperdine Law School. In the spring of 1995, Diann made a career change that would allow her to pursue her passion for baking and cooking. She left a career in the legal community to attend a culinary arts program.

Cooking is but one of the many ways Diann demonstrates her creative talents. She buys and refinishes old and antique furniture, decorates our home, and gardens. Her other interests include step aerobics, golf, camping, hiking, and fishing.

Diann demonstrates ideals that typify the nineties. She is smart, dedicated to her beliefs, and willing to pursue her passions because they make her happy.

Zesty Pork Tenderloin

6 SERVINGS

The tenderloin is considered the choicest of pork cuts. It may be a little higher in price per pound than loin roast, but tenderloin is a good value because it is lean and has no waste.

1/4 cup ketchup

1 tablespoon sugar

1 tablespoon dry white wine
   or water

1 tablespoon hoisin sauce

1/2 teaspoon salt

1 clove garlic, finely chopped

2 pork tenderloins (about 3/4
   pound each)

1. Mix all ingredients except pork in shallow glass or plastic dish. Add pork; turn to coat with marinade. Cover and refrigerate at least 1 hour but no longer than 24 hours.

2. Heat oven to 425°. Place pork on rack in shallow roasting pan. Insert meat thermometer horizontally so tip is in thickest part of pork. Roast uncovered 27 to 29 minutes or until thermometer reads 160° (medium doneness).

1 SERVING: Calories 155 (Calories from Fat 35); Fat 4g (Saturated 2g); Cholesterol 70mg; Sodium 340mg; Carbohydrates 6g (Dietary Fiber 0g); Protein 24g.

It's Dinnertime—Do You Know Where Your Fondue Pot Is?

Many people give newlyweds an appliance as a shower or wedding gift. Most of these are ooh'd and aah'd over when opened, but sometimes they end up on a shelf, collecting dust. Ever wonder if your popcorn popper is the only one with a thick dusty coating on it since the advent of microwave popcorn? The NPD Group, Inc.'s recent Pantry Audit, commissioned by the Betty Crocker Kitchens and other food companies, can tell you. You aren't alone! About a third of all popcorn poppers have not been used during the past month. And although nearly 80 percent of America's households own a blender-juicer, nearly half of them sat quietly on the shelf last month. Surprisingly, even though less than one-fourth of all households own an automatic bread machine, most of those are being used at least once a month!

Pecan-Breaded Pork Chops

6 SERVINGS

Add a little sweetness to these savory chops by using a honey-Dijon mustard. Serve rice on the side to sop up all the nice pan juices.

1 egg white, slightly beaten

1 tablespoon Dijon mustard

3/4 cup soft bread crumbs (1 1/2 slices)

1/2 cup finely chopped pecans

1 clove garlic, finely chopped

6 pork loin chops, about 3/4 inch thick

2 tablespoons vegetable oil

1/2 cup dry white wine or chicken broth

1 tablespoon chopped fresh parsley

1 teaspoon Dijon mustard

1. Mix egg white and 1 tablespoon mustard. Mix bread crumbs, pecans and garlic. Dip pork into mustard mixture, then coat with pecan mixture.

2. Heat oil in 10-inch skillet over low heat. Cook pork in oil about 10 minutes on each side or until coating is golden brown and pork is tender and slightly pink when centers of thickest pieces are cut. Remove pork from skillet.

3. Stir wine, parsley and 1 teaspoon mustard into skillet. Heat to boiling over high heat. Cook 3 to 4 minutes, stirring constantly, until sauce is reduced by half. Pour sauce over pork.

1 SERVING: Calories 345 (Calories from Fat 225); Fat 25g (Saturated 6g); Cholesterol 70mg; Sodium 130mg; Carbohydrates 6g (Dietary Fiber 1g); Protein 25g.

Skillet Pork Stew

4 SERVINGS

For a super-quick meal, this one-skillet recipe fits the bill. Serve this stew in hollowed-out small round bread loaves instead of bowls.

1 pound pork boneless loin, cut into 1/2-inch pieces

1 jar (12 ounces) pork gravy

2 tablespoons ketchup

8 unpeeled small red potatoes, cut into fourths

1 cup fresh or frozen cut green beans

1. Spray 12-inch nonstick skillet with cooking spray; heat over medium-high heat. Cook pork in skillet 3 to 5 minutes, stirring frequently, until light brown.

2. Stir in gravy, ketchup and potatoes. Heat to boiling; reduce heat to medium-low. Cover and cook 10 minutes.

3. Stir in green beans. Cover and cook 5 to 10 minutes, stirring occasionally, until vegetables are tender.

1 SERVING: Calories 370 (Calories from Fat 80); Fat 9g (Saturated 4g); Cholesterol 55mg; Sodium 610mg; Carbohydrates 51g (Dietary Fiber 5g); Protein 26g.

Skillet Pork Stew

Ham and Scalloped Potatoes

6 SERVINGS

You might want to make this recipe using unpeeled potatoes for some added nutrition and flavor. The few extra minutes you use scrubbing the potatoes will be worth it!

6 medium boiling or baking potatoes (2 pounds), peeled

3 tablespoons margarine or butter

1 small onion, finely chopped (1/4 cup)

3 tablespoons all-purpose flour

1 teaspoon salt

1/4 teaspoon pepper

2 1/2 cups milk

1 1/2 cups diced fully cooked ham

1 tablespoon margarine or butter

1. Heat oven to 350°. Grease 2-quart casserole.

2. Cut potatoes into enough thin slices to measure about 4 cups.

3. Melt 3 tablespoons margarine in 2-quart saucepan over medium heat. Cook onion in margarine about 2 minutes, stirring occasionally, until tender. Stir in flour, salt and pepper. Cook, stirring constantly, until smooth and bubbly; remove from heat.

4. Stir milk into sauce. Heat to boiling, stirring constantly. Boil and stir 1 minute. Stir in ham.

5. Spread potatoes in casserole. Pour sauce over potatoes. Dot with 1 tablespoon margarine.

6. Cover and bake 30 minutes. Uncover and bake 1 hour to 1 hour 10 minutes longer or until potatoes are tender. Let stand 5 to 10 minutes before serving.

1 SERVING: Calories 295 (Calories from Fat 115); Fat 13g (Saturated 4g); Cholesterol 25mg; Sodium 1040mg; Carbohydrates 33g (Dietary Fiber 2g); Protein 13g.

Honey-Mustard Ham

4 SERVINGS

Dinner doesn't get much easier than this! This satisfying skillet meal with smokey ham in a creamy sauce will be on the table in under 20 minutes. Breadsticks and a quick salad completes the meal without much extra time.

1/4 cup water

2 tablespoons honey

1 tablespoon Dijon mustard

1 pound fully cooked smoked ham sliced (about 1 inch thick), cut into 4 serving pieces

1/2 cup sour cream

1 green onion, sliced

1. Mix water, honey and mustard in 10-inch skillet. Add ham. Cover and heat to boiling; reduce heat to low. Simmer about 15 minutes, turning once, until ham is heated through. Remove ham from skillet; keep warm.

2. Stir sour cream into mixture in skillet; heat 1 minute. Pour over ham. Sprinkle with onion.

1 SERVING: Calories 345 (Calories from Fat 205), Fat 23g (Saturated 9g); Cholesterol 90mg; Sodium 1130mg; Carbohydrates 11g (Dietary Fiber 0g); Protein 24g.

Ham and Scalloped Potatoes

Impossible Ham and Swiss Pie

6 TO 8 SERVINGS

When searching for best-loved recipes, this one ranked right up there. This impossibly good pie is the answer for those leftovers from any holiday dinner.

2 cups cut-up fully cooked smoked ham

1 cup shredded natural Swiss cheese (4 ounces)

1/3 cup sliced green onions or chopped onion

2 cups milk

4 eggs

1 cup Bisquick Original baking mix

1/4 teaspoon salt, if desired

1/8 teaspoon pepper

1. Heat oven to 400°.

2. Grease glass pie plate, 10 x 1 1/2 inches. Sprinkle ham, cheese and onions in pie plate.

3. Stir remaining ingredients with fork until blended. Pour into pie plate.

4. Bake 35 to 40 minutes or until knife inserted in center comes out clean. Cool 5 minutes. Garnish with tomato slices and green bell pepper rings.

1 SERVING: Calories 320 (Calories from Fat 155); Fat 17g (Saturated 8g); Cholesterol 190mg; Sodium 1090mg; Carbohydrates 19g (Dietary Fiber 1g); Protein 24g.

Sausage Pie

6 SERVINGS

Want to make this delicious pie in no time flat? Pick up the ready-made rolled out pastries available in the refrigerated section of the supermarket. Also, check out the variety of sausages—from spicy hot or mild to savory herbs mixed in—found at your local supermarket.

1 1/2 pounds bulk pork sausage

1 medium onion, chopped (about 1/2 cup)

1 tablespoon sugar

1 1/2 teaspoons salt

1 medium head green cabbage (1 3/4 pounds), cut into large chunks and cored

1 can (16 ounces) whole tomatoes, undrained

Pastry for Baked Pie Crust pie crust (see page 349)

2 tablespoons all-purpose flour

1/4 cup cold water

1. Cook and stir sausage and onion in Dutch oven until sausage is done; drain. Stir in sugar, salt, cabbage and tomatoes. Heat to boiling; reduce heat. Cover and simmer 10 minutes.

2. Heat oven to 400°.

3. Prepare pastry on page 349 through step 2. Shape into flattened round on lightly floured cloth-covered board. Roll to fit top of 2-quart casserole. Fold into fourths; cut slits so steam can escape.

4. Mix flour and water; stir into hot sausage mixture. Pour into ungreased casserole. Place pastry over top and unfold; seal pastry to edge of casserole. Bake until crust is brown, 25 to 30 minutes.

1 SERVING: Calories 260 (Calories from Fat 155); Fat 17g (Saturated 6g); Cholesterol 45mg; Sodium 1420mg; Carbohydrates 18g (Dietary Fiber 5g); Protein 4g.

Gloria Solum

Hector, Minnesota

She was born and raised in the small town of Bird Island, Minnesota. She grew up in the days of the Depression, when things were homemade rather than bought. With nine children in the house, needless to say, there was a lot of baking to be done. Gloria has always loved to bake and cook her family's favorites.

While her children were growing up, she always made sure that she had time to help them with their home-work and give them baking tips, teach them to knit or crochet, or give them a caring ear to listen or a shoulder to cry on. She also found time to be an active member of their church, Sunday school teacher/superintendent, district P.T.A. vice-president, Woman's Club vice-president, certified L.P.N., plus she was named the 1977 Minnesota Mother of the Year. She is an unbelievable woman.

The most important things to Gloria are her family and friends. She has always said that her family is like a link in the chain of her life and that friendships are a very special blessing. She's always there to help people out, whether it's driving them to a doctor's appointment, lending an ear, or making someone a cake. Even now, she makes sure that every Friday she drives from Hector to Minneapolis to work at the VA Hospital, and when a new grandchild arrives, she makes sure that they have one of her quilts to come home in.

Still, even after her husband had passed on, she never let her community duties slip because she knew that people were counting on her and she would never let anyone down. When I was a child, I would spend at least two weeks with them every summer, and Grandma would make sure that the time I spent there revolved around me. Her favorite recipe is the Betty Crocker Applesauce Cake, which she made for me a lot when I was a child. Even though now that I am a grown woman with children of my own, she still knows how to make me feel special.

Three-Bean Casserole

Popular at potlucks and other gatherings, this dish conveniently stays hot a good while thanks to the added insulation from the mixture of sausage and beans in a savory tomato sauce.

1 pound bulk pork sausage

2 medium stalks celery, sliced
   (1 cup)

1 medium onion, chopped
   (1/2 cup)

1 large clove garlic, crushed

2 cans (21 ounces each) baked
   beans in tomato sauce

1 can (15 to 16 ounces) lima
   beans, drained

1 can (15 to 16 ounces) kidney
   beans, drained

1 can (8 ounces) tomato sauce

1 tablespoon ground mustard
   (dry)

2 tablespoons honey

1 tablespoon white vinegar

1/4 teaspoon red pepper sauce

1. Heat oven to 400°.

2. Cook sausage, celery, onion and garlic in 10-inch skillet over medium heat about 10 minutes, stirring occasionally, until sausage is no longer pink; drain.

3. Mix sausage mixture and remaining ingredients in ungreased 3-quart casserole. Bake uncovered about 45 minutes, stirring once, until hot and bubbly.

1 SERVING: Calories 340 (Calories from Fat 90); Fat 10g (Saturated 3g); Cholesterol 20mg; Sodium 1670mg; Carbohydrates 54g (Dietary Fiber 14g); Protein 22g.

Search for the Homemaker of Tomorrow

Do you know someone who was chosen as a Betty Crocker Homemaker of Tomorrow? Maybe it was you! This program, which ran for more than twenty years starting in the mid-fifties, was designed to draw attention to "the so-called 'forgotten career' of homemaking, and on the untiring job being done by America's high schools to develop citizens and homemakers of the future." During the '70s, the program was changed to the Betty Crocker Search for Leadership in Family Living, and young men became eligible. Each year, a winner was chosen from each state, based on his or her knowledge of cooking, baking and household management. All were awarded scholarships and a trip to the national awards ceremony. There, a national winner was chosen who was awarded further scholarships and travel opportunities.

Italian Sausage Calzone

A calzone is a stuffed pizza and looks like a large turnover. While this is made with a sausage filling, other fillings may include vegetables, cheese and other meats.

1/2 pound bulk Italian sausage

1/4 cup chopped onion

1/3 cup pizza sauce

1 can (2 ounces) mushroom stems and pieces, drained

2 cups Bisquick Original baking mix

1/3 cup hot water

1 tablespoon vegetable oil

1 cup shredded mozzarella cheese (4 ounces)

1/4 cup grated Parmesan cheese

1 egg white

1. Heat oven to 450°.

2. Cook and stir sausage until brown; drain. Stir in onion, pizza sauce and mushrooms; reserve.

3. Mix baking mix, hot water and oil until dough forms. Roll into 12-inch circle on cloth-covered surface dusted with baking mix. Place on ungreased cookie sheet.

4. Top half of the circle with mozzarella cheese, sausage mixture and Parmesan cheese to within 1 inch of edge. Fold dough over filling; press edge with fork to seal. Brush with egg white. Bake until golden brown, 15 to 20 minutes. Cool 5 minutes; cut into wedges.

1 SERVING: Calories 515 (Calories from Fat 260); Fat 29g (Saturated 10g); Cholesterol 50mg; Sodium 1620mg; Carbohydrate 41g (Dietary Fiber 2g); Protein 24g

Brats over Creamy Potatoes

An easy way to cut the fat is to use turkey bratwurst. Just leave out the oil and cook the bratwurst in a nonstick skillet sprayed with cooking spray. Slice the bratwurst, about 1/4 inch, before cooking it for a pretty presentation.

1 tablespoon vegetable oil

6 fully cooked bratwurst (1 to 1 1/2 pounds)

1 package Betty Crocker® scalloped potatoes

1 3/4 cups hot water

2 to 3 tablespoons white vinegar

Paprika, if desired

1. Heat oil in 10-inch skillet over medium heat. Cook bratwurst in oil, turning occasionally, until brown; drain.

2. Mix potatoes, sauce mix and water in same skillet. Heat to boiling; reduce heat. Cover and simmer about 20 minutes, stirring occasionally, until potatoes are tender.

3. Stir in vinegar; place bratwurst on potatoes. Cover and simmer about 5 minutes or until hot. Sprinkle with paprika.

1 SERVING: Calories 380 (Calories from Fat 250); Fat 28g (Saturated 10g); Cholesterol 60mg; Sodium 1210mg; Carbohydrates 19g (Dietary Fiber 0g); Protein 13g.

Brats over Creamy Potatoes

Susanna Hui
Woodbury, Minnesota

Susanna is a first-generation Asian American coming from Hong Kong. Her upbringing in Hong Kong and her living experience in different continents gave her a new perspective on life. She is genuinely interested in meeting people and visiting places. Besides having a full-time job working as an accountant, she is also a full-time housewife. Susanna keeps in very close touch with her parents and relatives in the Far East.

Susanna loves to cook, especially using the recipes from the Betty Crocker cookbook. Although she cooked a lot of delicious Chinese cuisine, she learned her most delicious dish from the Betty Crocker cookbook—Glazed Lamb Chops. In addition, her favorite dessert that she bakes is "Cheesecake with Strawberry Topping," which is also a Betty Crocker recipe.

Susanna also has been involved with the community. She has been active in the American Cancer Society, serving as a speaker in different community events, educating the public on women's cancer issues.

Susanna possesses all the qualities of Betty Crocker—a good cook, resourceful, dedicated to family and friends, actively involved in community services.

Glazed Lamb Chops

6 SERVINGS

When purchasing lamb, let the color be the guide. For the most tender lamb, look for the color to be pale pink to pinkish-red. Usually, the darker the color, the older the lamb.

6 lamb loin chops, 1 inch thick (about 1 1/2 pounds)

1/4 cup apricot spreadable fruit

2 tablespoons red wine vinegar or cider vinegar

2 tablespoons Dijon mustard

1/2 teaspoon reduced-sodium soy sauce

1/4 teaspoon pepper

1. Trim fat from lamb chops. Mix remaining ingredients. Brush lamb with 1/3 cup apricot mixture; reserve remaining mixture. Let stand 20 minutes at room temperature or cover and refrigerate up to 12 hours.

2. Set oven control to broil. Spray broiler pan rack with nonstick cooking spray.

3. Place lamb on rack in broiler pan. Brush with reserved apricot mixture. Broil with tops 5 inches from heat about 5 minutes or until brown; turn. Brush with pan drippings. Broil 6 to 9 minutes longer for medium doneness (160°).

1 SERVING: Calories 120 (Calories from Fat 35); Fat 4g (Saturated 0g); Cholesterol 40mg; Sodium 115mg; Carbohydrates 9g (Dietary Fiber 1g); Protein 13g.

Greek Pizza

6 SERVINGS

Kasseri cheese is a Greek cheese made from sheep or goat's milk. It has a sharp, salty flavor and melts beautifully. Plus the cheese itself is hard, so it is perfect for shredding. Look for this creamy gold-colored cheese, sold in blocks, in your grocer's refrigerator or at speciality cheese shops.

Crust (right)

1 cup shredded Kasseri or mozzarella cheese
(4 ounces)

1 package (10 ounces) frozen chopped spinach,
thawed and squeezed dry

1/2 pound ground lamb

1 tablespoon snipped fresh oregano leaves or
1 teaspoon dried oregano leaves

1 medium tomato, chopped

1/2 cup crumbled feta cheese

1/2 cup Greek or ripe olives, cut up

1. Place oven rack in lowest position of oven. Heat oven to 425°.

2. Prepare Crust; sprinkle remaining ingredients evenly over top to within 1/2 inch of edge. Bake on lowest oven rack until crust is golden brown, 25 to 30 minutes. Drizzle with 1 tablespoon olive oil if desired.

CRUST

1 package active dry yeast

1 cup warm water (105° to 115°)

2 1/2 cups all-purpose flour

2 tablespoons olive or vegetable oil

1 teaspoon sugar

1 teaspoon salt

1. Dissolve yeast in warm water in 2 1/2-quart bowl. Stir in remaining ingredients; beat vigorously 20 strokes. Let rest 5 minutes.

2. With floured fingers, press dough in greased 12-inch pizza pan or into 11-inch circle on greased cookie sheet

1 SERVING: Calories 415 (Calories from Fat 160); Fat 18g (Saturated 7g); Cholesterol 45mg; Sodium 780mg; Carbohydrates 46g (Dietary Fiber 3g); Protein 20g.

Greek Pizza

Chicken&Turkey

Baked Barbecue Chicken
(page 171)

Baked Chicken and Rice

6 SERVINGS

This hearty favorite is based on a traditional Spanish recipe, Arroz con Pollo, "chicken with rice." A specialty of Mexico and Puerto Rico, this classic dish is especially popular in the southwestern United States.

2 1/2- to 3-pound cut-up broiler-fryer chicken

3/4 teaspoon salt

1/4 to 1/2 teaspoon paprika

1/4 teaspoon pepper

2 1/2 cups chicken broth

1 cup uncooked regular long grain rice

1 medium onion, chopped (about 1/2 cup)

1 clove garlic, finely chopped

1/2 teaspoon salt

1 1/2 teaspoons chopped fresh or 1/2 teaspoon dried oregano leaves

1/8 teaspoon ground turmeric

1 bay leaf

2 cups shelled fresh green peas*

Pimiento strips

Pitted ripe olives

1. Heat oven to 350°.

2. Place chicken, skin sides up, in ungreased rectangular baking dish, 13 x 9 x 2 inches. Sprinkle with salt, paprika and pepper. Bake uncovered 30 minutes.

3. Heat broth to boiling. Remove chicken and drain fat from dish. Mix broth, rice, onion, garlic, salt, oregano, turmeric, bay leaf and peas in baking dish. Top with chicken. Cover with aluminum foil and bake until rice and thickest pieces of chicken are done and liquid is absorbed, about 30 minutes. Remove bay leaf. Top with pimiento strips and olives.

1 SERVING: Calories 355 (Calories from Fat 110); Fat 12g (Saturated 6g); Cholesterol 70mg; Sodium 1030mg; Carbohydrates 36g (Dietary Fiber 3g); Protein 29g.

*1 package (10 ounces) frozen green peas, thawed and drained, can be substituted for the fresh green peas.

Betty's Signature

At about the same time the persona of Betty Crocker was created to respond to the flood of requests for cooking advice from around the country, company officials realized that she would need to sign those letters somehow; a signature was needed! So a contest was held among the female employees of the Washburn Crosby Company (soon to become General Mills). The judges chose what they felt was the most distinctive and appropriate penmanship, and the winner was Florence Lindeberg. Her signature became the basis for the Betty Crocker signature that you see on many General Mills products today.

Baked Barbecued Chicken

6 SERVINGS

Barbecued chicken is a year-round favorite. Serve with a side of mashed pototoes, coleslaw or corn bread to make this best-loved recipe a best-loved meal.

1/4 cup (1/2 stick) margarine or butter

2 1/2- to 3-pound cut-up broiler-fryer chicken

1 cup ketchup

1/2 cup water

1/4 cup lemon juice

1 tablespoon Worcestershire sauce

2 teaspoons paprika

1/2 teaspoon salt

1 medium onion, finely chopped (about 1/2 cup)

1 clove garlic, finely chopped

1. Heat oven to 375°.

2. Heat margarine in rectangular pan, 13 x 9 x 2 inches, in oven. Place chicken in margarine, turning to coat. Arrange skin side down in pan. Bake uncovered 30 minutes.

3. Mix remaining ingredients in 1-quart saucepan. Heat to boiling; remove from heat. Drain fat from chicken; turn skin side up. Spoon sauce over chicken. Bake uncovered until thickest pieces are done and juices of chicken run clear, about 30 minutes longer.

1 SERVING: Calories 315 (Calories from Fat 170); Fat 19g (Saturated 4g); Cholesterol 70mg; Sodium 710mg; Carbohydrates 10g (Dietary Fiber 1g); Protein 23g.

Baked Barbecued Chicken

Samantha DeCerce

· Colts Neck, New Jersey

SPIRIT OF BETTY CROCKER CONTEST **Winner**

My sister, Samantha, is the Betty Crocker of the 1990s, an example of a young person who is focused, generous, and dedicated. "Sam," as she prefers to be called, is a twenty-year-old honors student at New York University's Tisch School of the Arts. She has, for as long as anyone can remember, dreamed of performing on Broadway. It became obvious to everyone who heard her perform at the age of five in the St. Mary's Church Children's Choir that she was destined to fill the world with beautiful music.

Her friends call her "Mom" from her homemaking projects. Sam is the best cook and baker any dormitory has ever seen. She has a dog-eared *Betty Crocker Cookbook* that she uses to delight her roommates and friends. She is known for Old-Fashioned Oatmeal Cookies.

Yet the real Sam that everyone cherishes is the person who is committed to those around her. Every Saturday morning, Sam assists New Yorkers in adopting homeless and abused dogs. She has been involved in environmental efforts, projects for AIDS victims, and performances at nursing homes. Recently, Sam became a volunteer for the "Mighty Mutts" program.

Sam is the ideal daughter, sister, and friend. She has an infectious smile that is sure to help brighten everyone's day. It is a pleasure to have Sam part of anything—just ask anyone who has enjoyed her meals, watched her perform, or helped her with her latest volunteer project.

Cornmeal Chicken with Casera Sauce

7 SERVINGS

If you eat a lot of chicken, this recipe offers a nice change. Casera sauce is a mixture of tomato and spicy peppers and gives the chicken a little kick. Serve Spanish Rice (page 277) on the side to complete the meal.

2 1/2- to 3-pound broiler-fryer
    chicken

2 tablespoons yellow cornmeal

1/8 teaspoon salt

1/2 teaspoon chili powder

1/4 teaspoon dried oregano
    leaves

2 tablespoons margarine or
    butter

2 tablespoons vegetable oil

Casera Sauce (below)

1. Heat oven to 375°.

2. Cut chicken into pieces; cut each breast half into halves and remove skin. Mix cornmeal, salt, chili powder and oregano. Coat chicken with cornmeal mixture.

3. Heat margarine and oil in rectangular pan, 13 x 9 x 2 inches, in oven until margarine is melted. Place chicken, meaty sides down, in pan. Bake uncovered 30 minutes. Turn chicken; cook until brown and thickest pieces are done, 20 to 30 minutes longer.

4. Prepare Casera Sauce; serve with chicken.

CASERA SAUCE

1 medium tomato, finely
    chopped

1 small onion, chopped
    (about 1/4 cup)

1 small clove garlic, crushed

1 canned green chili or jalapeño
    pepper, seeded and finely
    chopped

2 teaspoons finely snipped
    cilantro or parsley

2 teaspoons lemon juice

1/4 teaspoon dried oregano
    leaves

CASERA SAUCE

Mix all ingredients.

1 SERVING: Calories 200 (Calories from Fat 110); Fat 12g (Saturated 2g); Cholesterol 55mg; Sodium 160mg; Carbohydrates 5g (Dietary Fiber 1g); Protein 19g.

Mary Rowell
Kansas City, Missouri

While Mary Rowell was teaching second grade, she worked with her students for four-and-a-half years to get Grandparents' Day, first for the state of Missouri and then for all the grandparents in the United States.

She was willing to give up a twenty-three-year teaching career to take care of her sister, Kathy, after both of their parents died of cancer. Kathy has Downs Syndrome.

She keeps the bowling scores for the handicapped. That is where we met. On August 12, 1989, we were married and she took on the role of wife and mother to my mentally retarded daughter. Mary treats her like she is her own daughter.

She got a traffic light installed in our neighborhood and a streetlight installed on our street. That took a lot of letter writing and stamps.

She is a member of the Care-Giving Ministry at our church. She fixes delicious meals for members who are sick, have a family member die, or have a new baby. It was her idea to adopt a boy at our church as our grandson.

Her favorite product is Betty Crocker's angel food cake mix because our family and friends enjoy the sugarless dessert that she makes with it. Her favorite recipe right now is Strawberry Angel Food Cake.

Chicken Cacciatore

Slash time from the preparation of this dish by using 2 cups of your favorite prepared spaghetti sauce for the whole tomatoes, tomato sauce, oregano, basil and salt.

3- to 3 1/2-pound cut-up
    broiler-fryer chicken

1/2 cup all-purpose flour

1/4 cup vegetable oil

1 medium green bell pepper

2 medium onions

2 cloves garlic, crushed

1 can (16 ounces) whole toma-
    toes, drained

1 can (8 ounces) tomato sauce

1 cup sliced mushrooms
    (3 ounces)*

1 1/2 teaspoons chopped fresh
    or 1/2 teaspoon dried
    oregano leaves

1 teaspoon chopped fresh or
    1/4 teaspoon dried basil
    leaves

1/2 teaspoon salt

Grated Parmesan cheese

1. Coat chicken with flour.

2. Heat oil in 12-inch skillet over medium-high heat. Cook chicken in oil 15 to 20 minutes or until brown on all sides; drain.

3. Cut bell pepper and onions crosswise in half; cut each half into fourths. Stir bell pepper, onions and remaining ingredients except cheese into chicken in skillet, breaking up tomatoes. Heat to boiling; reduce heat. Cover and simmer 30 to 40 minutes or until juice of chicken is no longer pink when centers of thickest pieces are cut. Serve with cheese.

1 SERVING: Calories 330 (Calories from Fat 145); Fat 16g (Saturated 4g); Cholesterol 75mg; Sodium 730mg; Carbohydrates 19g (Dietary Fiber 3g); Protein 30g.

*1 can (4 ounces) sliced mushrooms, drained, can be substituted for the fresh mushrooms.

Country Captain

6 SERVINGS

An American classic, this recipe is said to have gotten its name from a British officer who brought the recipe home from India. It is a mixture of chicken and vegetables, seasoned with curry and other spices, cooked over low heat, then garnished with almonds and served over rice.

1/2 cup all-purpose flour

1 teaspoon salt

1/4 teaspoon pepper

2 1/2- to 3-pound cut-up broiler-fryer chicken

1/4 cup vegetable oil

1 1/2 teaspoons curry powder

1 1/2 teaspoons chopped fresh or 1/2 teaspoon dried thyme leaves

1/4 teaspoon salt

1 large onion, chopped (about 1 cup)

1 large green bell pepper, chopped (about 1 1/2 cups)

1 clove garlic, finely chopped, or 1/8 teaspoon garlic powder

1 can (16 ounces) whole tomatoes, undrained

1/4 cup currants or raisins

1/3 cup slivered almonds, toasted

3 cups hot cooked rice

Grated fresh coconut and chutney, if desired

1. Heat oven to 350°.

2. Mix flour, 1 teaspoon salt and the pepper. Coat chicken with flour mixture. Heat oil in 10-inch skillet until hot. Cook chicken in oil over medium heat until light brown, 15 to 20 minutes. Place chicken in ungreased 2 1/2-quart casserole. Drain oil from skillet.

3. Add curry powder, thyme, 1/4 teaspoon salt, the onion, bell pepper, garlic and tomatoes to skillet. Heat to boiling, stirring frequently to loosen brown particles from skillet. Pour over chicken. Cover and bake until thickest pieces are done and juices of chicken run clear, about 40 minutes. Skim fat from liquid if necessary; add currants. Bake uncovered 5 minutes. Sprinkle with almonds. Serve with rice and, if desired, grated fresh coconut and chutney.

1 SERVING: Calories 490 (Calories from Fat 215); Fat 12g (Saturated 5g); Cholesterol 70mg; Sodium 670mg; Carbohydrates 44g (Dietary Fiber 3g); Protein 28g.

Chicken Pot Pie

Traditionally, whenever fried chicken was made (whether for Sunday dinner, a picnic or a potluck supper), the pan drippings were saved. The next day, the drippings were made into gravy and combined with leftover chicken and vegetables for chicken pot pie. Many cooks liked to personalize their pot pies, some preferring a lattice top and others using small cookie cutters to cut openings for the steam.

1/3 cup margarine or butter

1/3 cup all-purpose flour

1/3 cup chopped onion

1/2 teaspoon salt

1/4 teaspoon pepper

1 3/4 cups chicken or turkey broth

2/3 cup milk

2 1/2 to 3 cups cut-up cooked chicken or turkey

1 cup shelled fresh green peas*

1 cup diced carrots*

Pastry for Two-Crust Pie (page 343)

1. Heat margarine in 2-quart saucepan over low heat until melted. Stir in flour, onion, salt and pepper. Cook, stirring constantly, until mixture is bubbly; remove from heat.

2. Stir in broth and milk. Heat to boiling, stirring constantly. Boil and stir 1 minute. Stir in chicken, peas and carrots.

3. Heat oven to 425°.

4. Prepare Pastry. Roll two-thirds of the pastry into 13-inch square; ease into ungreased square pan, 9 x 9 x 2 inches. Pour chicken mixture into pastry-lined pan. Roll remaining pastry into 11-inch square. Fold pastry in half and cut slits near center so steam can escape. Place square over filling; turn edges under the flute. Bake until golden brown, about 35 minutes.

1 SERVING: Calories 655 (Calories from Fat 385); Fat 43g (Saturated 14g); Cholesterol 65mg; Sodium 1120mg; Carbohydrates 45g (Dietary Fiber 3g); Protein 25g.

*1 package (10 ounces) frozen peas and carrots can be substituted for the fresh peas and carrots. Rinse with cold water to separate; drain.

Sharon White
Durham, North Carolina

My roots stem from a deep southern tradition of cooking and baking. This background provided me with a love and enjoyment for cooking. My home as a child was always filled with a wonderful aroma emanating from the kitchen.

This heritage for cooking continues to embody my spirit into adulthood. Although I have a technical and analytical job requiring long hours at the personal computer, cooking provides an opportunity to use my creative side, thus providing relaxation.

Family and friends are one of the most important gifts God gives us. My family and many friends are scattered throughout the United States; however, my bond runs deep with them. I have reciprocated that love with assistance in their personal and professional lives as well as providing them an unselfish heart, kind words, and a supportive shoulder.

Our involvement in the community is critical and is more important today than ever before. An old African proverb states, "It takes a whole village to raise a child." My employer's motto states, "Build your community and you build your bank." I believe that if both these philosophies are embraced, by building our communities, we essentially strengthen our nation. To that end, I am involved in the following activities: board member and regular member of the National Association of Urban Bankers; member of the YMCA Black Achievers; member of Redeeming Light Center Church and member of the Women's Christian Fellowship.

The daily juggle of work, home, family, friends, and spiritual time leaves little time for the individual. However, I have found that the use of a daily organizer system as well as starting my day with guidance from our Creator assist me in getting it all done and taking care of myself also.

Chicken in Cream

2 SERVINGS

Sophisticated yet easy to make, this recipe is perfect when you want a romantic dinner for two. Just double the recipe if serving four.

2 pounds bone-in chicken pieces
  (thighs, legs, breast)

1 can (10 1/2 ounces) condensed
  cream of chicken soup

1/2 cup apple cider

1 tablespoon plus 2 teaspoon
  Worcestershire sauce

3/4 teaspoon salt

1/3 cup chopped onion

1 clove garlic, minced

1 can (3 ounces) sliced
  mushrooms, drained

Paprika

1. Heat oven to 350°.

2. Place chicken in ungreased baking pan, 9 x 9 x 2 inches. Mix all ingredients except paprika; pour on chicken.

3. Bake uncovered 1 hour, spooning off excess fat and basting once with sauce in pan. Sprinkle with paprika and bake until tender, about 30 minutes.

1 SERVING: Calories 560 (Calories from Fat 290); Fat 32g (Saturated 9g); Cholesterol 175mg; Sodium 1429mg; Carbohydrates 14g (Dietary Fiber 1g); Protein 55g.

The Betty Crocker Kitchens

One of the few professions open to women in the early part of this century was that of home economist. In 1921, the Washburn Crosby Company hired its first home economist, and soon after, the Home Service Department was born. Marjorie Child Husted, who has been widely regarded as the personification of Betty Crocker, managed the department for twenty years. Eventually, as Betty's name became synonymous with sound cooking advice and recipes that always worked, the Home Service Department became the famous Betty Crocker Kitchens. Today, there are seven kitchens and three photography kitchens staffed with about forty people who work together to ensure that only top-quality products, cookbooks and recipes are available to you.

Jill Shannon
Prairie Village, Kansas

Following the diagnosis of an extremely rare form of cancer, my friend Jill Shannon (wife and mother of four) had surgery that left her unable to walk unaided. Another friend and I, hoping to ease Jill's home-coming from the hospital, arranged to take some meals to Jill and her family. Expecting to find Jill resting,

we instead found her in the kitchen, leaning on a pair of crutches, making not one but two different kinds of cookies!

A former labor and delivery nurse, Jill interrupted her career to stay at home to commit herself to her family. Jill's commitment to her family includes driving the children to all of the regular "kid activities" as well as to clinic appointments for the two children who have cystic fibrosis.

Jill loves to bake, cook, and share what she creates. She makes her own noodles, pizza dough, baking mix, and vanilla. She cans apples and tomatoes, dries herbs from her garden. Whether taking lunch to the teachers at school, delivering a steaming homemade chicken pot pie to a sick friend, or relinquishing "just one more" cookie to a shy child, Jill's joy in cooking and sharing is evident. She keeps at least thirty days' worth of meals cooked and in the freezer.

An informal record of Jill's community involvement includes Jill visiting a nursing home resident, providing a home for a pregnant teenager, working with international students, acting as a Boy Scout merit badge counselor, teaching Sunday school, and volunteering at her children's school are just a sample. Jill Shannon embodies the Betty Crocker Spirit!

Chicken and Dumplings

4 TO 6 SERVINGS

Who can resist the classic chicken and dumplings recipe? This is a good meal to make when the wind is blowing outside and you need dinner to warm your body and soul.

3- to 3 1/2-pound stewing
   chicken, cut up

4 celery stalk tops

1 medium carrot, sliced
   (1/2 cup)

1 small onion, sliced

2 sprigs parsley, chopped

1 teaspoon salt

1/8 teaspoon pepper

5 cups water

2 1/2 cups Bisquick Original
   baking mix

2/3 cup milk

1. Remove any excess fat from chicken. Place chicken, giblets (except liver), neck, celery, carrot, onion, parsley, salt, pepper and water in Dutch oven. Cover and heat to boiling; reduce heat to low. Cook over low heat about 2 hours or until juice of chicken is no longer pink when centers of thickest pieces are cut.

2. Remove chicken and vegetables from Dutch oven. Skim 1/2 cup fat from broth; reserve. Remove broth; reserve 4 cups.

3. Heat reserved fat in Dutch oven over low heat. Stir in 1/2 cup of the baking mix. Cook, stirring constantly, until mixture is smooth and bubbly; remove from heat.

4. Stir in reserved broth. Heat to boiling, stirring constantly. Boil and stir 1 minute. Return chicken and vegetables to Dutch oven; heat until hot.

5. Mix remaining 2 cups baking mix and the milk until soft dough forms. Drop dough by spoonfuls onto hot chicken mixture (do not drop directly into liquid). Cook uncovered over low heat 10 minutes. Cover and cook 10 minutes longer.

1 SERVING: Calories 645 (Calories from Fat 260); Fat 29g (Saturated 8g); Cholesterol 130mg; Sodium 1750mg; Carbohydrates 51g (Dietary Fiber 2g); Protein 47g.

Chicken in Red Wine Vinegar

6 SERVINGS

The chicken simmered in red wine vinegar keeps the meat moist and juicy and lends a sophisticated flavor to the dish. Even better, this dish can be done in about 30 minutes. Serve rice and a nice green salad on the side.

2 tablespoons margarine or butter

2 cloves garlic, crushed

3 shallots, chopped

6 boneless, skinless chicken breast halves (about 2 1/4 pounds)

1/2 cup red wine vinegar

2 cups finely chopped tomato (about 2 medium tomatoes)

2 teaspoons chopped fresh or 1/2 teaspoon dried thyme leaves

1/2 teaspoon salt

1/4 teaspoon pepper

1. Melt margarine in 10-inch skillet. Add garlic, shallots and chicken. Cook over medium-high heat 12 to 15 minutes, turning after 6 minutes, until chicken is no longer pink. Reduce heat to low. Add vinegar, cover and cook 5 minutes.

2. Stir in remaining ingredients, turn chicken. Cook over low heat 10 to 12 minutes until chicken is done.

1 SERVING: Calories 195 (Calories from Fat 70); Fat 8g (Saturated 2g); Cholesterol 75mg; Sodium 320mg; Carbohydrates 5g (Dietary Fiber 1g); Protein 27g.

Sweet-and-Sour Chicken

4 SERVINGS

Take advantage of packages of precut vegetables for stir-fry or self-serve bins of cut-up raw vegetables, such as broccoli, cauliflower, carrots and celery, in the produce aisle.

1 tablespoon vegetable oil

1 pound boneless, skinless chicken breast halves, cut into 1-inch pieces

3 cups assorted cut-up vegetables (bell pepper, carrots, tomatoes)

1 can (8 ounces) pineapple chunks in juice, drained

1/2 cup sweet-and-sour sauce

Hot cooked rice or chow mein noodles, if desired

1. Heat wok or 12-inch skillet over high heat. Add oil; rotate wok to coat side.

2. Add chicken; stir-fry about 3 minutes or until no loner pink in center. Add vegetables; stir-fry about 2 minutes or until crisp-tender. Stir in pineapple and sweet-and-sour sauce; cook and stir 1 minute. Serve with rice.

1 SERVING: Calories 215 (Calories from Fat 55); Fat 6g (Saturated 2g); Cholesterol 45mg; Sodium 150mg; Carbohydrates 23g (Dietary Fiber 2g); Protein 19g.

Sweet-and-Sour Chicken

Debbie Hedrick-Pope

Williamsburg, West Virginia

My wife, Debra (Debbie), is the proud mother of two wonderful sons, Brian and Jason, and a fine step-daughter, Trista. Working in the secretarial field for fifteen years, Debbie felt she needed a more fulfilling career. Now a certified home health aid, she works with the elderly. She sees five elderly people daily, taking care of their personal care, cooking, light house work, and errands. But what Debbie feels is most important is what these elderly give to her: wisdom, knowledge, caring, compassion, and LOVE.

Debbie finds time to remain very active in her community. For five years, she has sang alto/lead with a mixed gospel quartet, singing for functions in our community as well as in surrounding areas. She is very active in her church, being one of the churches two pianists and being adult choir director. She also holds a church board office. Sometimes she does small-scale catering for friends and for small get-togethers. Her most extensive use of a Betty Crocker product would be the enormous number of Betty Crocker cake mixes she has used over the years in her wedding cakes.

Debbie's Christian love for family, friends, and community is outwardly visible daily. She is always willing to help anyone who asks and goes the extra mile without being asked.

Stuffed Chicken Breasts

Stuffing chicken breasts is a beautiful way to dress up chicken. Not only do the stuffings add color, they are delicious as well!

4 chicken breast halves (about 1 1/4 pounds)

Apple-Hazelnut Stuffing (below)

1/2 teaspoon salt

1/4 teaspoon pepper

2 teaspoons margarine or butter

1. Heat oven to 375°. Grease square pan, 9 x 9 x 2 inches, with shortening.

2. Remove bones from chicken breasts. Do not remove skin.

3. Loosen skin from chicken breasts.

4. Prepare desired dressing.

5. Spread one-fourth of the stuffing evenly between meat and skin of each chicken breast. Smooth skin over breasts, tucking under loose areas. Place chicken, skin sides up, in pan. Sprinkle with salt and pepper. Drizzle with margarine.

6. Bake uncovered 45 to 55 minutes or until juice of chicken is no longer pink when centers of thickest pieces are cut.

APPLE-HAZELNUT STUFFING

1/4 cup chopped hazelnuts

1 medium apple, chopped (1 cup)

1 package (3 ounces) cream cheese, softened

APPLE-HAZELNUT STUFFING

Mix all ingredients.

1 SERVING: Calories 330 (Calories from Fat 190); Fat 21g (Saturated 7g); Cholesterol 95mg; Sodium 440mg; Carbohydrates 7g (Dietary Fiber 1g); Protein 29g.

Fried Chicken

6 SERVINGS

Fried chicken used to be the Sunday dinner of choice for many Southern families. Most cooks swear by a heavy cast-iron skillet for frying chicken, to make it crisp on the outside, moist and tender on the inside. If you don't have a cast-iron skillet, a heavy enameled Dutch oven will do well, too.

1/2 cup all-purpose flour

1 teaspoon salt

1 teaspoon paprika

1/4 teaspoon pepper

2 1/2- to 3-pound cut-up broiler-fryer chicken

Vegetable oil

Creamy Gravy (right)

1. Mix flour, salt, paprika and pepper. Coat chicken with flour mixture.

2. Heat oil (1/4 inch) in 12-inch skillet over medium-high heat until hot. Cook chicken in oil until light brown on all sides, about 10 minutes; reduce heat. Cover tightly and simmer, turning once or twice, until thickest pieces are done and juices of chicken run clear, about 35 minutes. If skillet cannot be covered tightly, add 1 to 2 tablespoons water.

3. Remove cover during the last 5 minutes of cooking to crisp chicken. Remove chicken; keep warm. Prepare Creamy Gravy; serve with chicken.

CREAMY GRAVY

1 tablespoons all-purpose flour

1/2 cup chicken broth or water

1/2 cup milk

Salt and pepper to taste

1. Pour drippings from skillet into bowl, leaving brown particles in skillet. Return 2 tablespoons drippings to skillet. Stir in flour.

2. Cook over low heat, stirring constantly, until smooth and bubbly; remove from heat. Stir in broth and milk. Heat to boiling, stirring constantly. Boil and stir 1 minute. Stir in a few drops browning sauce, if desired. Stir in salt and pepper.

1 SERVING: Calories 310 (Calories from Fat 170); Fat 19g (Saturated 4g); Cholesterol 70mg; Sodium 710mg; Carbohydrates 10g (Dietary Fiber 0g); Protein 25g.

Pesto Ravioli with Chicken

4 SERVINGS

Looking for something different for dinner? The kids might like this dish topped with a pat of butter and some extra grated cheese. It is a meal everyone will love.

2 teaspoons olive or vegetable oil

1 package (15 ounces) chicken tenders

3/4 cup chicken broth

1 package (9 ounces) refrigerated cheese-filled ravioli

3 small zucchini, cut into 1/4-inch slices

1 large red bell pepper, thinly sliced

1/4 cup refrigerated pesto

Freshly grated Parmesan cheese, if desired

1. Heat oil in 12-inch skillet over medium-high heat. Cook chicken in oil about 4 minutes, turning occasionally, until brown. Remove chicken from skillet.

2. Add broth and ravioli to same skillet. Heat to boiling; reduce heat. Cover and simmer about 4 minutes or until ravioli is tender. Stir in zucchini, bell pepper and chicken. Cook over medium-high heat about 3 minutes, stirring occasionally, until vegetables are crisp-tender and chicken is no longer pink in center. Toss with pesto. Sprinkle with cheese.

1 SERVING: Calories 370 (Calories from Fat 180); Fat 20g (Saturated 6g); Cholesterol 125mg; Sodium 760mg; Carbohydrates 16g (Dietary Fiber 2g); Protein 33g.

Pesto Ravioli with Chicken

Chicken Spaghetti Sauce

Looking for a tasty way to use up leftover chicken? This dish fits the bill and it is popular with the younger set, too, so it is sure to please the entire family!

1 cup water

1 teaspoon salt

1 teaspoon sugar

1 tablespoon snipped fresh oregano leaves or
   1 teaspoon dried oregano leaves

2 teaspoons snipped fresh basil leaves or
   3/4 teaspoon dried basil leaves

1 teaspoon snipped fresh marjoram leaves or
   1/2 teaspoon dried marjoram leaves

1/2 teaspoon snipped fresh rosemary leaves or
   1/4 teaspoon dried rosemary leaves, if desired

1 large onion, chopped

1 clove garlic, crushed

1 bay leaf

1 can (8 ounces) tomato sauce

1 can (6 ounces) tomato paste

1 1/2 cups cut-up cooked chicken

Hot cooked spaghetti

Grated Parmesan cheese, if desired

1. Heat all ingredients except chicken and spaghetti to boiling in 10-inch skillet; reduce heat. Cover and simmer 30 minutes, stirring occasionally.

2. Stir in chicken. Cover and simmer 30 minutes, stirring occasionally. Remove bay leaf. Serve sauce over spaghetti. Sprinkle with Parmesan cheese.

1 SERVING: Calories 125 (Calories from Fat 45); Fat 5g (Saturated 1g); Cholesterol 30mg; Sodium 870mg; Carbohydrates 12g (Dietary Fiber 3g); Protein 11g.

Chicken and Pepper Stir-Fry

Here's the answer for those hectic days when you feel like time is not on your side. Mix up the marinade when you get home and let it sit 15 minutes while you change into comfortable clothes. If you prepare quick-cooking rice, a satisfying dinner will be on the table in no time flat!

2 tablespoons soy sauce

2 tablespoons ketchup

1/2 teaspoon ground ginger

2 cloves garlic, finely chopped

3/4 pound boneless, skinless chicken breast halves, thinly sliced

1 tablespoon vegetable oil

6 medium green onions, cut into 1-inch pieces

2 medium bell peppers, thinly sliced

2 tablespoons vegetable oil

4 cups hot cooked rice

1. Mix soy sauce, ketchup, ginger and garlic in large resealable plastic bag. Add chicken; seal bag. Let stand 15 minutes.

2. Heat 1 tablespoon oil in 10-inch skillet or wok over medium-high heat. Add onions and bell pepper; stir-fry until crisp-tender. Remove mixture from skillet.

3. Heat 2 tablespoons oil in same skillet. Add chicken; stir-fry until no loner pink in center. Stir in pepper mixture. Serve over rice.

1 SERVING: Calories 415 (Calories from Fat 115); Fat 13g (Saturated 3g); Cholesterol 45mg; Sodium 650mg; Carbohydrates 52g (Dietary Fiber 2g); Protein 24g.

Cheesy Chicken Tortellini

5 SERVINGS

To turn this into an interesting meatless meal, omit the chicken and add an additional cup chopped red or yellow bell pepper. Serve with warm crusty bread to dip into the cheesy sauce and, for dessert, slices of cut-up fresh melon.

1 package (7 ounces) dried cheese-filled tortellini

1 tablespoon vegetable oil

1 pound boneless, skinless chicken breast halves, cut into thin slices

1/4 cup margarine or butter

1 small green bell pepper, chopped (1/2 cup)

2 shallots, finely chopped

1 clove garlic, finely chopped

1/4 cup all-purpose flour

1/4 teaspoon pepper

1 3/4 cups milk

1/2 cup shredded mozzarella cheese (2 ounces)

1/2 cup shredded Swiss cheese (2 ounces)

1/4 cup grated Parmesan or Romano cheese

1. Cook and drain tortellini as directed on package.

2. While tortellini is cooking, heat oil in 3-quart saucepan over medium-high heat. Cook chicken in oil, stirring frequently, until no longer pink in center. Remove from saucepan; keep warm.

3. Melt margarine in saucepan over medium-high heat. Cook bell pepper, shallots and garlic in margarine, stirring frequently, until bell pepper is crisp-tender. Stir in flour and pepper. Cook over medium heat, stirring constantly, until mixture is bubbly, remove from heat. Stir in milk. Heat to boiling, stirring constantly. Boil and stir 1 minute; remove from heat.

4. Stir in mozzarella and Swiss cheeses until melted. Stir in tortellini and chicken until coated. Sprinkle with Parmesan cheese.

1 SERVING: Calories 430 (Calories from Fat 225); Fat 25g (Saturated 9g); Cholesterol 110mg; Sodium 400mg; Carbohydrates 18g (Dietary Fiber 1g); Protein 34g.

Cheesy Chicken Tortellini

Marielle Guay

St. Philippe, Argenteuil

I told myself that Betty Crocker is really my sister. She has been married for thirty-four years and is fifty-four years old. She is the mother of six children and a grandmother of four grandchildren. While raising six children on a farm, she also managed to feed all her people, including on some occasions the employees. She even makes her own bread.

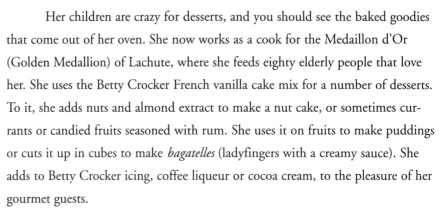

Her children are crazy for desserts, and you should see the baked goodies that come out of her oven. She now works as a cook for the Medaillon d'Or (Golden Medallion) of Lachute, where she feeds eighty elderly people that love her. She uses the Betty Crocker French vanilla cake mix for a number of desserts. To it, she adds nuts and almond extract to make a nut cake, or sometimes currants or candied fruits seasoned with rum. She uses it on fruits to make puddings or cuts it up in cubes to make *bagatelles* (ladyfingers with a creamy sauce). She adds to Betty Crocker icing, coffee liqueur or cocoa cream, to the pleasure of her gourmet guests.

She was involved in the worship and sacrament committee of her church for many years. She was secretary-treasurer of the Women Farmer's Circle of St. Philippe, and has been a member of this group for twelve years. She has volunteered at the local library for ten years and has been involved with the local Church Education Committee. Also, she is the baby-sitter of her four grandchildren.

Savory Chicken and Rice

4 SERVINGS

This same recipe can easily tranform beef and pork into a savory meal. Just use one pound of beef boneless sirloin steak or pork tenderloin, cut into 1-inch pieces, in place of the chicken. Cook the meat in oil about 5 minutes or until beef is brown or pork is no longer pink.

1 pound boneless, skinless
 chicken breast halves

1 1/2 cups sliced mushrooms
 (4 ounces)

1 cup baby-cut carrots

1 1/2 cups water

1 package (4.1 ounces) long
 grain and wild rice mix with
 chicken and herbs

1. Trim fat from chicken. Cut chicken into 1-inch pieces.

2. Spray 10-inch nonstick skillet with cooking spray. Heat over medium heat. Cook chicken in skillet about 5 minutes, stirring occasionally, until no longer pink in center.

3. Stir in remaining ingredients. Heat to boiling; reduce heat. Cover and simmer 15 minutes, stirring occasionally. Uncover and simmer about 3 minutes longer, stirring occasionally, until carrots are tender.

1 SERVING: Calories 255 (Calories from Fat 45); Fat 5g (Saturated 2g); Cholesterol 70mg; Sodium 280mg; Carbohydrates 25g (Dietary Fiber 1g); Protein 29g.

Betty Crocker's Basic Cookbook

Do you have a copy of *Betty Crocker's Cookbook* that you turn to for help with your cooking problems? You aren't alone! When the first one, *Betty Crocker's Picture Cook Book,* came out in 1950, a million copies were sold in the first year! There have been eight revised editions, and altogether, over 27 million have been sold. Many are given as wedding presents! People seem to have their favorite editions, but the 1950 edition remains one of the most popular. The Betty Crocker Kitchens still gets calls wanting to know how to obtain one! Some copies have been found at garage sales or through secondhand book dealers. So in answer to your many requests, we are excited that we will be offering the 1950 cookbook exactly as it was printed in 1950! Check your favorite book store for your copy.

Grilled Lemon Chicken

Lemon and chicken go together so well. The lemon adds a nice flavor to the chicken and keeps the meat juicy and tender.

2 1/2- to 3-pound broiler-fryer chicken, cut up

1/2 cup dry white wine

1/4 cup lemon juice

2 tablespoons vegetable oil

1 teaspoon paprika

1 lemon, thinly sliced

1 clove garlic, crushed

1 lemon, thinly sliced

Paprika

1. Place chicken in glass or plastic bowl. Mix remaining ingredients except 1 lemon and paprika; pour over chicken. Cover and refrigerate at least 3 hours.

2. Remove chicken and lemon slices. Discard lemon slices; reserve marinade. Cover and grill chicken, bone sides down, 5 to 6 inches from medium coals 15 to 20 minutes; turn chicken. Cover and grill, turning and brushing 2 or 3 times with marinade, until chicken is done, 20 to 40 minutes longer.

3. Roll edges of remaining lemon slices in paprika; arrange around chicken. Garnish with celery leaves if desired.

1 SERVING: Calories 240 (Calories from Fat 145); Fat 16g (Saturated 4g); Cholesterol 70mg; Sodium 70mg; Carbohydrates 2g (Dietary Fiber 0g); Protein 22g.

Turkey Tetrazzini

Here's a tasty way to get only 13 grams fat and 390 calories per serving and keep the flavor and creaminess. Use 2 teaspoons chicken bouillon granules and 4 cups evaporated skimmed milk for the chicken broth and half-and-half. Then, decrease the flour to 1/4 cup, the margarine to 2 tablespoons and the almonds to 1/4 cup. Top with reduced-fat Cheddar cheese. Yum!

1 package (7 ounces) spaghetti

2 cups chicken or turkey broth

2 cups half-and-half or milk

1/2 cup all-purpose flour

1/4 cup margarine or butter

1/2 teaspoon salt

1/4 teaspoon pepper

2 cups cut-up cooked turkey or chicken

1 cup sliced ripe olives

1/2 cup slivered almonds

1 cup shredded Cheddar cheese (4 ounces)

1. Heat oven to 350°. Cook and drain spaghetti as directed on package.

2. Mix broth, half-and-half, flour, margarine, salt and pepper in 3-quart saucepan. Heat to boiling over medium heat, stirring constantly. Boil and stir 1 minute.

3. Stir in spaghetti, turkey, olives and almonds. Spread in ungreased 2-quart casserole. Sprinkle with cheese.

4. Bake uncovered 25 to 30 minutes or until hot and bubbly.

1 SERVING: Calories 590 (Calories from Fat 315); Fat 35g (Saturated 13g); Cholesterol 85mg; Sodium 1030mg; Carbohydrates 42g (Dietary Fiber 3g); Protein 30g.

Turkey Tetrazzini

Susana Lewis
Carrabelle, Florida

My wife, Susana, embodies the qualities of a trusted friend that one can come to for a recipe, for help, or to discuss a problem in confidence.

Susana enjoys cooking and baking. She is an excellent cook, blending her traditional foods and seasonings with the international flavors she has experienced since coming to America. Somehow she is able to retain the original flavor of the foods so that they are not lost, but are combined into a new mosaic of sensations. She has recently taught herself to bake, because she grew up in houses without ovens. I often come home to the warm fragrance of bread in the oven.

Susana enjoys her involvement in the community. Two evenings every week she volunteers her time, serving as a teacher of English as a second language to new immigrants at the local high school. She also helps orient young people to some of the problems and complexities of living in America. Susana also has been helping at the elementary school by translating the school's Parent's Handbook into Spanish.

My wife is a loyal and trusted friend and a calm, patient, and caring mother. She encourages the best in all of us, gives support during hard times, and is playful and loving.

Black and White Turkey Chili

6 SERVINGS

Cannellini beans are large, white Italian kidney beans that are quite delicious. Top your chili with some sliced avocado, chopped fresh cilantro or a dollop of sour cream to add a creamy texture and kick of flavor to this chili.

1 tablespoon vegetable oil

1 1/2 pounds turkey breast tenderloins, cut into 1/2-inch cubes

1 medium onion, chopped (1 cup)

1/2 cup chopped Anaheim or poblano chilies

1 clove garlic, finely chopped

3 cups chicken broth

1 tablespoon chili powder

1 large tomato, chopped (1 cup)

1 can (15 ounces) black beans, drained

1 can (15 to 16 ounces) cannellini beans, rinsed and drained

1. Heat oil in 3-quart saucepan over medium-high heat. Cook turkey, onion, chilies and garlic in oil, stirring occasionally, until turkey is no longer pink in center and onion is tender.

2. Stir in remaining ingredients. Heat to boiling; reduce heat. Cover and simmer 30 minutes, stirring occasionally.

1 SERVING: Calories 350 (Calories from Fat 65); Fat 7g (Saturated 2g); Cholesterol 65mg; Sodium 770mg; Carbohydrates 39g (Dietary Fiber 9g); Protein 42g.

Letters, Letters, Letters

Betty Crocker got her start by answering letters requesting advice and recipes. Some requests are humorous, some are touching. Some of the most touching came during the Depression and World War II years. Here are some examples:

"I wonder if you know how much your talks over the radio mean to some of us. I am a young girl who has to stay home and cook for a large family while my parents work. I try to make the home just as pleasant as if Mother were right at home. Now that's a problem in itself, but since I've been listening to your talks, I find some things aren't as puzzling as they used to be. My little sisters are just crazy about nice pretty cakes, and you can imagine how much the *pretty* counts to them, so I will wait anxiously for your booklet on cakes."

"You don't know how much you have helped me. You have opened my eyes and lightened my heart. My husband is just making a living for my four children and myself. He has had his wages cut terribly. I must try and do something. You have told me over the radio, you are so wonderful. Would you please send me a good bread and biscuit recipe, also a cheap cake recipe?"

Kristi Pardue

Boise, Idaho

I grew up on a farm in a remote area in southern Idaho. My responsibilities included cooking for five adults, very burly men, as well as for my little brother and sister. My mother gave me a gift that became a fundamental companion to me for the next several years: *Betty Crocker's Cookbook for Boys and Girls.* The meals were delicious, and I quickly learned to cook with confidence.

I am now forty years old and have two children. I still enjoy cooking and still rely on Betty Crocker's cookbooks and products as much as I did thirty-one years ago. Tuna Chip Casserole is still a favorite family recipe. I still am able to cook nutritious meals with the aid of Betty Crocker's helper meals and other quick-to-prepare products. These products are easy to prepare, and the kids love them.

Along with two children, I have a very challenging full-time job and have been going to college at night for the past eight years. The past four years I have been most involved with United Way, Young Business Professionals of America, numerous civic organizations, and the Christian Children's Ranch. All are very important, but my most rewarding project continues to be the Christian Children's Ranch.

Community service is a more rewarding experience than anything else you will ever do for yourself. It is my mission to let people know that even the smallest deed can change a life.

Turkey Divan

Don't wait until you have Thanksgiving leftovers to make this recipe! Use six large slices of turkey (about 1/4 inch thick) from the deli. This is also wonderful with fresh asparagus spears in place of the broccoli.

1 1/2 pounds broccoli*

1/4 cup margarine or butter

1/4 cup all-purpose flour

1/8 teaspoon ground nutmeg

1 1/2 cups chicken broth

1/2 cup grated Parmesan cheese

2 tablespoons dry white wine or chicken broth

1/2 cup whipping (heavy) cream

6 large slices cooked turkey breast, 1/4 inch thick (3/4 pound)

1/2 cup grated Parmesan cheese

1. Prepare and cook broccoli until crisp-tender. (See step 1, page 242.)

2. Melt margarine in 1-quart saucepan over medium heat. Stir in flour and nutmeg. Cook, stirring constantly, until smooth and bubbly; remove from heat. Stir in broth. Heat to boiling, stirring constantly. Boil and stir 1 minute; remove from heat. Stir in 1/2 cup cheese and the wine.

3. Beat whipping cream in chilled small bowl on high speed until stiff. Fold cheese sauce into whipped cream.

4. Place hot broccoli in ungreased rectangular baking dish, 11 x 7 x 1 1/2 inches. Top with turkey. Pour cheese sauce over turkey. Sprinkle with 1/2 cup cheese.

5. Set oven control to Broil.

6. Broil with top 3 to 5 inches from heat, about 3 minutes, or until cheese is bubbly and light brown.

1 SERVING: Calories 325 (Calories from Fat 190); Fat 21g (Saturated 9g); Cholesterol 75mg; Sodium 600mg; Carbohydrates 9g (Dietary Fiber 2g); Protein 27g.

*2 packages (10 ounces each) frozen broccoli spears, cooked and drained, can be substituted for the fresh broccoli.

Savory Southern Turkey Barbecue

8 SANDWICHES

Tangy and spicy, this is a nice change from Sloppy Joes or burgers. Classic Crunchy Coleslaw (page 267) and a fruit salad would be perfect accompaniments. To trim the fat even more, choose ground turkey breast.

2 tablespoons water

1/4 cup diced onion

1/4 cup diced green bell pepper

1 pound ground turkey

1/4 cup cider vinegar

2 tablespoons packed brown sugar

1 teaspoon ground mustard (dry)

1 teaspoon chili powder

1 teaspoon paprika

1 teaspoon Worcestershire sauce

1/4 teaspoon pepper

1 can (8 ounce) tomato sauce

8 kaiser rolls, split

1. Heat water in 10-inch skillet over medium heat. Cook onion and bell pepper in water about 2 minutes, stirring occasionally, until crisp-tender. Stir in turkey. Cook 4 to 5 minutes, stirring occasionally, until no longer pink.

2. Stir in remaining ingredients except rolls; reduce heat. Cover and simmer about 20 minutes, stirring occasionally, until hot. Fill rolls with turkey mixture.

1 SANDWICH: Calories 265 (Calories from Fat 70); Fat 8g (Saturated 2g); Cholesterol 40mg; Sodium 490mg; Carbohydrates 33g (Dietary Fiber 2g); Protein 17g.

Wild Rice and Turkey Casserole

6 SERVINGS

This wonderful casserole can be put together in a snap. Are you a mushroom lover? Then, stir in a can (4 ounces) sliced mushrooms, drained, in step 2. Complete the meal by serving steamed broccoli on the side.

2 cups cut-up cooked turkey

2 1/4 cups boiling water

1/3 cup milk

1 small onion, chopped (1/4 cup)

1 can (10 3/4 ounces) condensed cream of mushroom soup

1 package (6 ounces) seasoned long grain and wild rice

1. Heat oven to 350°.

2. Mix all ingredients, including seasoning packet from rice mix, in ungreased 2-quart casserole.

3. Cover and bake 45 to 50 minutes or until rice is tender. Uncover and bake 10 to 15 minutes longer or until liquid is absorbed.

1 SERVING: Calories 155 (Calories from Fat 45); Fat 5g (Saturated 2g); Cholesterol 40mg; Sodium 500mg; Carbohydrates 12g (Dietary Fiber 0g); Protein 16g.

Wild Rice and Turkey Casserole

Fish & Seafood

Broiled Salmon with Hazelnut Butter

4 SERVINGS

Salmon and hazelnuts are both native to—and favorites of—the Pacific Northwest. Fresh king salmon, largest of the Pacific salmon, and silver salmon, with its deep coral color, are especially prized. You'll find the delicate Hazelnut Butter a wonderful topping for fish, vegetables and poultry.

Hazelnut Butter (below)

4 salmon fillets (1 to 1 1/2 pounds)

1/2 teaspoon salt

1/8 teaspoon pepper

1. Prepare Hazelnut Butter.

2. Set oven control to broil. Grease shallow roasting pan or jelly roll pan, 15 1/2 x 10 1/2 x 1 inch.

3. Sprinkle both sides of fish with salt and pepper. Place in pan. Broil fish with tops 4 to 6 inches from heat 4 minutes; turn and spread each fillet with about 1 tablespoon Hazelnut Butter. Broil until fish flakes easily with fork, 4 to 8 minutes.

HAZELNUT BUTTER

2 tablespoons finely chopped hazelnuts

3 tablespoons margarine or butter, softened

1 tablespoon chopped fresh parsley

1 teaspoon lemon juice

Heat oven to 350°. Spread hazelnuts on ungreased cookie sheet. Bake until golden brown, 4 to 6 minutes, stirring occasionally; cool. Mix with remaining ingredients.

1 SERVING: Calories 245 (Calories from Fat 160); Fat 18g (Saturated 3g); Cholesterol 55mg; Sodium 450mg; Carbohydrates 1g (Dietary Fiber 0g); Protein 20g.

Broiled Salmon with Hazelnut Butter

Southern-Fried Catfish

Pan-fried catfish used to be a southern secret, but it seems the rest of the country has caught on. Dipped in seasoned cornmeal and quickly fried, catfish served with hush puppies and coleslaw steals the show at southern fish fries. Found naturally in the Mississippi River and southern inland waterways, catfish are also farmed in several states of the Mississippi Delta.

Vegetable oil

1 1/4 cup cornmeal

1 teaspoon salt

1/2 teaspoon ground red pepper (cayenne)

1/4 teaspoon pepper

6 small catfish (about 1/2 pound each), skinned and
   pan dressed

1/2 cup all-purpose flour

2 eggs, slightly beaten

1. Heat oven to 275°.

2. Heat oil (1/2 inch) in 12-inch skillet over medium-high heat until hot. Mix cornmeal, salt, red pepper and pepper; reserve.

3. Coat catfish with flour; dip into eggs. Coat with cornmeal mixture. Fry catfish, 2 at a time, until golden brown, about 6 minutes on each side. Keep warm in oven while frying remaining catfish. Garnish with lemon wedges if desired.

1 SERVING: Calories 340 (Calories from Fat 45); Fat 5g (Saturated 1g); Cholesterol 175mg; Sodium 450mg; Carbohydrates 28g (Dietary Fiber 2g); Protein 48g.

Grilled Tuna with Salsa

To seed tomatoes, cut in half crosswise and squeeze gently—the seeds will slide right out.

3/4 cup finely chopped fresh parsley

1/4 cup finely chopped onion

1/3 cup lemon juice

2 tablespoons vegetable oil

1/4 teaspoon salt

2 medium tomatoes, seeded and chopped

1 clove garlic, crushed

1 can (4 1/4 ounces) chopped black olives, drained

6 tuna or shark steaks (about 5 ounces each)

1. Combine all ingredients except tuna in glass bowl. Cover tightly and refrigerate salsa 2 to 4 hours to blend flavors.

2. Place tuna on oiled grill over medium-hot coals. Cook 3 minutes; turn steaks and cook 4 to 5 minutes or until tuna turns opaque in center. Remove from grill; keep warm. Serve with salsa.

To Broil: Set oven control to broil. Arrange steaks on oiled rack in broiler pan. Broil with steaks about 4 inches from heat 10 to 15 minutes, turning after 6 minutes, until fish flakes easily with fork.

1 SERVING: Calories 280 (Calories from Fat 125); Fat 14g (Saturated 3g); Cholesterol 55mg; Sodium 320mg; Carbohydrates 5g (Dietary Fiber 1g); Protein 34g.

Impossible Tuna and Cheddar Pie

6 TO 8 SERVINGS

The popularity of this recipe makes it a hit with adults and kids alike. Another plus is that it uses ingredients you usually have on hand so it's a snap to put together

2 cups chopped onions

1/4 cup margarine or butter

2 cans (6 ounces each) tuna, drained

2 cups shredded Cheddar cheese (8 ounces)

3 eggs

1 1/4 cups milk

1 cup Bisquick Original baking mix

1/8 teaspoon pepper

2 tomatoes, thinly sliced

1. Heat oven to 400°. Grease glass pie plate, 10 x 1 1/2 inches, or square baking dish, 8 x 8 x 2 inches, or six 10-ounce custard cups.

2. Cook onions in margarine in 10-inch skillet over low heat, stirring occasionally, until onions are light brown. Sprinkle tuna, 1 cup of the cheese and the onions in pie plate.

3. Stir eggs, milk, baking mix and pepper with fork until blended. Pour into pie plate.

4. Bake pie plate or square dish, 25 to 30 minutes, custard cups, 20 to 25 minutes, or until knife inserted in center comes out clean. Top with tomato slices and remaining cheese. Bake 3 to 5 minutes longer or until cheese is melted. Cool 5 minutes.

1 SERVING: Calories 445 (Calories from Fat 245); Fat 27g (Saturated 12g); Cholesterol 165mg; Sodium 850mg; Carbohydrates 22g (Dietary Fiber 1g); Protein 30g.

Impossible Pies

"Impossible Pies" are popular recipes made with Bisquick baking mix. All the ingredients are mixed together, and as the pie bakes, a crust "magically" forms! There are many flavors of Impossible Pies, from savory to sweet. Whole chapters in Bisquick cookbooks are devoted to these tasty and convenient dishes! Among the most requested Impossible Pies are Impossible Cheeseburger Pie (page 123) and Impossible Coconut Pie (page 348). Which is your family's favorite?

Tuna Noodles Romanoff

6 SERVINGS

*You can use crushed croutons or seasoned crackers if
you run short on seasoned bread crumbs.*

4 cups uncooked egg noodles (8 ounces)

2 cans (6 ounces each) tuna, drained

1 cup sliced mushrooms (3 ounces)

2 tablespoons capers

1 1/2 cups sour cream

3/4 cup milk

1 teaspoon salt

1/4 teaspoon pepper

1/4 cup seasoned dry bread crumbs

1/4 cup grated Romano or Parmesan cheese

2 tablespoons margarine or butter, melted

1. Heat oven to 350°.

2. Cook and drain noodles as directed on package.
   Mix noodles, tuna, mushrooms, capers, sour
   cream, milk, salt and pepper in ungreased
   2-quart casserole or square baking dish, 8 x 8 x 2
   inches.

3. Mix bread crumbs, cheese and margarine; sprinkle over tuna mixture. Bake uncovered 35 to 40
   minutes or until hot and bubbly.

1 SERVING: Calories 350 (Calories from Fat 160); Fat 18g
(Saturated 9g); Cholesterol 85mg; Sodium 8500mg; Carbohydrates 26g (Dietary Fiber 1g); Protein 22g.

Linguine with Red Clam Sauce

6 SERVINGS

*No fresh clams? It's easy to use two cans (6 1/2 ounces
each) minced clams, drained and liquid reserved, for
the fresh clams in this recipe. Serve this pasta dish with
a Caesar salad, garlic bread and dry red wine for a
special meal.*

12 ounces uncooked linguine

1/4 cup olive or vegetable oil

3 cloves garlic, finely chopped

1 can (28 ounces) whole Italian-style tomatoes,
   drained and chopped

1 small red chili, seeded and finely chopped

1 pint shucked fresh small clams, drained and liquid
   reserved

1 tablespoon chopped fresh parsley

1 teaspoon salt

1. Cook and drain linguine as directed on package.

2. While linguine is cooking, heat oil in 3-quart
   saucepan over medium high heat. Cook garlic in
   oil, stirring frequently, until golden. Stir in
   tomatoes and chili. Cook 3 minutes, stirring frequently.

3. Stir in clam liquid. Heat to boiling; reduce heat.
   Simmer uncovered 10 minutes.

4. Chop clams. Stir clams, parsley and salt into
   tomato mixture. Cover and simmer about 15
   minutes, stirring occasionally, until clams are
   tender. Serve over linguine.

1 SERVING: Calories 320 (Calories from Fat 100); Fat 11g
(Saturated 1g); Cholesterol 15mg; Sodium 600mg; Carbohydrates 44g (Dietary Fiber 3g); Protein 14g.

Linguine with Red Clam Sauce

Delores (Sis) Manning

Sloatsburg, New York

It seems that cooking has always been a part of my life. I am sixty-one years old and have enjoyed cooking since I was twelve years old. Today it seems that if anyone needs a recipe for any occasion, they call me.

My family has run a mom-and-pop business in our small town for over thirty-three years, and my husband and I worked very closely together in this business as well as taking care of our six children. I was blessed with six children: three normal, healthy boys and three special children (two boys, one girl) that were mentally and physically handicapped. As a family, we were there for our children's football and baseball games, as well as for church and school functions. My friends are also a great part of our lives; usually we entertain friends for dinner once a week.

My favorite Betty Crocker product is mainly the cake mixes. I am famous for making my Crumb Cake, for which I use only the Betty Crocker cake mix and then add the crumbs made from butter, sugar, flour, and cinnamon on top. My second favorite recipe from Betty Crocker is the cheesecake. I mix ricotta cheese and eggs to make a simply delicious cake.

I volunteer two hours each week as a teacher's aid, reading to children and helping them with their daily work. Another organization that occupies a considerable amount of my time is the Ladies Auxiliary of the Sloatsburg Fire Department. I have been a member for forty-three years. I make sure that I find time to knit lap blankets and "stump socks" for the veterans that are in local veteran's hospitals.

Spaghetti with White Clam Sauce

4 SERVINGS

For a flavor twist, add some chopped fresh basil with the parsley.

1 package (7 ounces) spaghetti

1/4 cup margarine or butter

2 cloves garlic, finely chopped

2 tablespoons chopped fresh
   parsley

2 cans (6 1/2 ounces each)
   minced clams, undrained

Chopped fresh parsley

1/2 cup grated Parmesan cheese

1. Cook spaghetti as directed on package.

2. While spaghetti is cooking, melt margarine in 1 1/2-quart
   saucepan over medium heat. Cook garlic in margarine about 3
   minutes, stirring occasionally, until light golden. Stir in 2 tablespoons parsley and the clams. Heat to boiling; reduce heat to low.
   Simmer uncovered 3 to 5 minutes.

3. Drain spaghetti. Pour sauce over spaghetti; toss. Sprinkle with
   parsley and cheese.

1 SERVING: Calories 400 (Calories from Fat 145); Fat 16g (Saturated 5g); Cholesterol 35mg; Sodium 370mg; Carbohydrates 43g (Dietary Fiber 1g); Protein 22g.

Shrimp Pasta Primavera

Shrimp Pasta Primavera

6 SERVINGS

Want to keep your basil fresh? Instead of refrigerating it, place stems of basil in a glass of water, and keep on the counter for up to five days.

1 package (10 ounces) rotini pasta

1 cup vegetable or chicken broth

2 cups broccoli flowerets

1/4 pound mushrooms, cut in half

6 ounces feta cheese, crumbled

1 cup fresh basil leaves, thinly sliced

4 roma (plum) tomatoes, coarsely chopped

3/4 pound cooked, peeled, deveined large shrimp or
    1 package (12 ounces) frozen cooked, peeled,
    deveined shrimp, thawed and drained

1. Cook and drain pasta as directed on package.

2. While pasta is cooking, heat broth to boiling in 2-quart saucepan; reduce heat. Stir in broccoli and mushrooms. Cover and simmer about 6 minutes or until broccoli is crisp-tender; remove from heat.

3. Stir in cheese and basil until cheese is melted. Stir in tomatoes and shrimp. Cook uncovered over medium heat, stirring occasionally, just until heated through. Toss with pasta.

1 SERVING: Calories 330 (Calories from Fat 70); Fat 8g (Saturated 5g); Cholesterol 135mg; Sodium 620mg; Carbohydrates 43g (Dietary Fiber 3g); Protein 24g.

Angel Hair Pasta with Shrimp

4 SERVINGS

This is a great meal to make when you want something a bit fancy but don't have a lot of time. Of course, any long pasta will do—fettuccini, spaghetti or angel hair.

1 package (16 ounces) capellini (angel hair) pasta

1/4 cup olive or vegetable oil

2 tablespoons chopped fresh parsley

2 cloves garlic, finely chopped

1 small red chili, seeded and finely chopped

1/3 cup dry white wine or vegetable broth

1/2 teaspoon freshly grated nutmeg

3/4 pound uncooked, peeled, deveined small shrimp, thawed if frozen

1. Cook and drain pasta as directed on package.

2. While pasta is cooking, heat oil in Dutch oven or 12-inch skillet over medium-high heat. Cook parsley, garlic and chili in oil 1 minute, stirring occasionally. Stir in wine, nutmeg and shrimp; reduce heat. Cover and simmer about 5 minutes or until shrimp are pink and firm.

3. Mix pasta and shrimp mixture in Dutch oven. Cook over medium heat 2 minutes, stirring occasionally.

1 SERVING: Calories 565 (Calories from Fat 170); Fat 19g (Saturated 3g); Cholesterol 215mg; Sodium 160mg; Carbohydrates 75g (Dietary Fiber 3g); Protein 27g.

Marinated Ginger Shrimp

6 SERVINGS

Fresh ginger adds a wonderful flavor kick to these easy-to-make shrimp. It is all the tastes of summer wrapped into one bite.

1 1/2 pounds large raw shrimp, shelled and deveined

1 tablespoon soy sauce

1 tablespoon lemon juice

1 teaspoon vegetable oil

1 teaspoon finely chopped fresh gingerroot

1. Place shrimp in glass baking dish. Mix remaining ingredients; pour over shrimp. Cover and refrigerate at least 30 minutes.

2. Set oven control to broil. Drain shrimp; arrange on rack in broiler pan. Broil 4 inches from heat 5 to 8 minutes, turning once, until shrimp turn pink. Refrigerate shrimp at least 30 minutes until cold.

1 SERVING: Calories 60 (Calories from Fat 10); Fat 1g (Saturated 0g); Cholesterol 0mg; Sodium 270mg; Carbohydrates 1g (Dietary Fiber 0g); Protein 12g.

Marinated Ginger Shrimp

Kathie Kurtz

Carterville, Illinois

Kathie is thirty-one years old and works as a case manager at the Center for Comprehensive Services (CCS) in Carbondale, Illinois. CCS is an adult residential rehabilitation facility for persons with traumatic brain injuries (TBI). From her job title alone, you must know that this is a person with tremen-

dous compassion, patience, and intelligence. When working with clients with TBI, one must always prepare several possible means to an end as well as be a creative problem solver. She always approaches tasks with an open mind and sense of humor.

Her mother passed away when she was just a child. As a result, when Kathie and her two brothers were old enough, they were responsible for preparing the family meals. Kathie got to start cooking regularly at age nine. Now that Kathie has been practicing for many years, she is always at the top of the guest list for potluck dinner parties. Kathie typically brings ten to twelve dishes to potluck dinners. Let there be no doubt that Kathie *loves* cooking and baking, and she is very good at it!

I have never met anyone that is more dedicated to family and friends than Kathie. She is a person that you can *always* depend on for help or guidance no matter how large or small your problem. When Kathie was twenty-six years old, she moved home to Chicago from Colorado when her father was diagnosed with a terminal illness. She took care of him and their household while working full-time.

Kathie has been recognized as an "Unsung Hero" by a local television station for her volunteer work with Southern Illinois Regional Effort for AIDS (SIREA). She wrote a grant indicating the need for assistance with AIDS-related problems in the southern Illinois region and secured approximately $120,000 in funds from the Ryan White Consortium. Kathie also is very much involved in reintegrating TBI clients back into the community. She continuously works toward promoting head injury prevention and public acceptance of the TBI population and persons with disabilities. Kathie also volunteers periodically for several organizations such as serving Thanksgiving dinner to the needy at her church.

Shrimp Fajitas

Try these fajitas for fun and variety. They're easy to assemble and delicious to consume! After you peel the shrimp, rub your hands with some fresh-cut lemon and then wash as usual. The lemon leaves your hands fresh-smelling and odor-free.

1 pound uncooked medium
   shrimp in shells

8 flour tortillas (7 or 8 inches in
   diameter)

1 tablespoon vegetable oil

1 tablespoon lime juice

1 1/2 teaspoons chopped fresh
   or 1/2 teaspoon dried
   oregano leaves

1/4 teaspoon ground cumin

1 clove garlic, finely chopped

1 cup salsa

1 cup guacamole

1. Peel shrimp. (If shrimp are frozen, do not thaw; peel in cold water.) Make a shallow cut lengthwise down back of each shrimp; wash out vein.

2. Heat oven to 250°.

3. Wrap tortillas in aluminum foil, or place on heatproof serving plate and cover with aluminum foil. Heat in oven about 15 minutes or until warm.

4. Heat oil in 10-inch skillet over medium heat. Cook shrimp, lime juice, oregano, cumin and garlic in oil about 5 minutes, stirring constantly, until shrimp are pink and firm.

5. Divide shrimp evenly among tortillas. Top with salsa and guacamole. Fold one end of each tortilla up about 1 inch over shrimp mixture. Fold right and left sides over folded end, overlapping. Fold down remaining end. Serve fajitas with additional salsa and guacamole if desired.

1 SERVING: Calories 475 (Calories from Fat 160); Fat 18g (Saturated 3g); Cholesterol 160mg; Sodium 1060mg; Carbohydrates 58g (Dietary Fiber 7g); Protein 27g.

Seafood à la Newburg

6 SERVINGS

You can enjoy this rich creamy dish by using imitation crab and lobster pieces if fresh seafood isn't readily available. You may want to try an updated version served over spinach fettuccine or ladled into flaky pastry shells instead of the traditional biscuits or toast points.

2 egg yolks

1/4 cup margarine or butter

1/4 cup all-purpose flour

1/2 teaspoon salt

1/4 teaspoon pepper

2 cups milk

1 tablespoon sherry or lemon juice

2 cups cut-up cooked seafood

Baking Powder Biscuits (page 304) or toast points

1. Beat egg yolks with fork in small bowl. Melt margarine in 2-quart saucepan over low heat. Stir in flour, salt and pepper. Cook over medium heat, stirring constantly, until smooth and bubbly; remove from heat. Gradually stir in milk. Heat to boiling, stirring constantly. Boil and stir 1 minute.

2. Immediately stir at least half of the hot mixture into egg yolks; stir back into hot mixture in saucepan. Boil and stir 1 minute; remove from heat. Stir in lemon juice and seafood. Heat until seafood is hot.

3. Serve over hot biscuits.

1 SERVING: Calories 220 (Calories from Fat 110); Fat 12g (Saturated 3g); Cholesterol 135mg; Sodium 490mg; Carbohydrates 10g (Dietary Fiber 0g); Protein 18g.

Scallop Stir-Fry

4 SERVINGS

The different between bay scallops and sea scallops is their size. Bay scallops are smaller than sea scallops. If you are using whole bay scallops, you can skip cutting them into smaller pieces.

1 package (3 ounces) Oriental flavor ramen noodles

1 tablespoon olive oil or vegetable oil

3/4 pound asparagus, cut into 1-inch pieces

1 large red bell pepper, cut into thin strips

1 small onion, chopped (1/4 cup)

2 cloves garlic, finely chopped

3/4 pound sea scallops, cut into 1-inch pieces

1 tablespoon soy sauce

2 tablespoons lemon juice

1 teaspoon sesame oil

1/4 teaspoon red pepper sauce

1. Reserve seasoning packet from noodles. Cook and drain noodles as directed on package.

2. While noodles are cooking, heat olive oil in 12-inch skillet over high heat. Add asparagus, bell pepper, onion and garlic; stir-fry 2 to 3 minutes or until vegetables are crisp-tender. Add scallops; stir-fry until white.

3. Mix contents of reserved seasoning packet, the soy sauce, lemon juice, sesame oil and pepper sauce; stir into scallop mixture. Stir in noodles; heat through.

1 SERVING: Calories 185 (Calories from Fat 65); Fat 7g (Saturated 1g); Cholesterol 25mg; Sodium 580mg; Carbohydrate 12g (Dietary Fiber 2g); Protein 21g

Scallop Stir-Fry

Shrimp Creole

4 SERVINGS

Overcooking shrimp makes them tough, so cook shrimp just until pink and firm. Hot corn bread muffins served with honey would taste great with this spicy dish.

2 cups frozen stir-fry bell peppers and onions (from 16-ounce package)

1 pound uncooked peeled deveined medium shrimp, thawed if frozen

1 can (14 1/2 ounces) chunky tomatoes with crushed red pepper, undrained

1 teaspoon chopped fresh or 1/4 teaspoon dried thyme leaves

1/8 teaspoon garlic powder

Hot cooked rice, if desired

1. Spray 12-inch nonstick skillet with cooking spray; heat over medium-high heat. Cook stir-fry vegetables in skillet about 3 minutes, stirring occasionally, until crisp-tender.

2. Stir in remaining ingredients, except rice. Heat to boiling; reduce heat. Cover and simmer 8 to 10 minutes, stirring occasionally, until shrimp are pink and firm. Serve with rice.

1 SERVING: Calories 110 (Calories from Fat 10); Fat 1g (Saturated 0g); Cholesterol 160mg; Sodium 350mg; Carbohydrates 8g (Dietary Fiber 2g); Protein 19g.

Shrimp Creole

Savory Seafood Gumbo

Gumbo is a perfect example of why America is "the Great Melting Pot." Back in the eighteenth century, French Canadians who settled in the bayou country southwest of New Orleans became known as Cajuns. They made a hearty soup-stew. Creoles, locals of Spanish and/or French descent, added hot red pepper to the stew. And African Americans contributed okra, a native African vegetable, to thicken it.

1 large onion, chopped (about 1 cup)

1 medium green bell pepper, chopped (about 1 cup)

2 medium stalks celery, chopped (about 1 cup)

1 1/2 pounds fresh okra, cut into 1/2-inch pieces*

2 cloves garlic, crushed

1/4 cup (1/2 stick) plus 2 tablespoons margarine or
   butter

1/2 cup all-purpose flour

1 can (16 ounces) whole tomatoes, undrained

5 cups chicken broth, clam juice or water

2 teaspoons salt

1/2 teaspoon white pepper

1/2 teaspoon black pepper

1/2 teaspoon ground red pepper (cayenne)

2 bay leaves

1 pound raw medium shrimp, peeled and deveined

3/4 pound cooked lump crabmeat

3 cups hot cooked rice

1. Mix onion, bell pepper, celery, okra and garlic; reserve.

2. Heat margarine in 6- to 8-quart Dutch oven over medium heat until hot. Gradually stir in flour. Cook, stirring constantly, until caramel colored, about 7 minutes.

3. Add half of reserved onion mixture. Cook, stirring constantly, about 1 minute. Stir in remaining onion mixture. Cook until celery is crisp-tender, about 4 minutes. Stir in and break up tomatoes. Stir in chicken broth, salt, white pepper, black pepper, red pepper and bay leaves. Heat to boiling; reduce heat. Simmer uncovered, stirring occasionally, 1 hour.

4. Add shrimp and crabmeat to Dutch oven. Heat to boiling. Boil uncovered 1 1/2 minutes; remove from heat. Cover and let stand 15 minutes. Stir and remove bay leaves. Serve over rice.

1 SERVING: Calories 345 (Calories from Fat 0); Fat 11g (Saturated 0g); Cholesterol 95mg; Sodium 1690mg; Carbohydrates 40g (Dietary Fiber 0g); Protein 22g.

*2 packages (10 ounces each) frozen cut okra, thawed and drained, can be substituted for the fresh okra.

Hearty
Meatless Meals

Cheesy Lasagna

12 SERVINGS

It's easy to sing the praises of lasagna—it's cheesy, filling and loved by all ages. And a good lasagna recipe is invaluable when you have to feed a crowd, want a make-ahead meal or need to supply a covered dish.

1/2 cup margarine or butter

1/2 cup all-purpose flour

1/2 teaspoon salt

4 cups milk

1 cup shredded Swiss cheese (4 ounces)

1 cup shredded mozzarella cheese (4 ounces)

1/2 cup grated Parmesan cheese

2 cups small curd cottage cheese

1/4 cup snipped parsley

1 tablespoon snipped fresh or 1 teaspoon dried
    basil leaves

1/2 teaspoon salt

1 teaspoon snipped fresh or 1/2 teaspoon dried
    oregano leaves

2 cloves garlic, crushed

12 uncooked lasagna noodles

1/2 cup grated Parmesan cheese

1. Heat oven to 350°.

2. Heat margarine in 2-quart saucepan over low heat until melted. Stir in flour and 1/2 teaspoon salt. Cook, stirring constantly, until smooth and bubbly. Remove from heat; stir in milk. Heat to boiling, stirring constantly. Boil and stir 1 minute.

3. Stir in Swiss cheese, mozzarella cheese and 1/2 cup Parmesan cheese. Cook and stir over low heat until cheeses are melted. Mix remaining ingredients except noodles and remaining Parmesan cheese.

4. Spread 1/4 of the cheese sauce mixture in ungreased rectangular baking dish, 13 x 9 x 2 inches; top with 4 uncooked noodles. Spread 1 cup of the cottage cheese mixture over noodles; spread with 1/4 of the cheese sauce mixture. Repeat with 4 noodles, the remaining cottage cheese mixture, 1/4 of the cheese sauce mixture, the remaining noodles and remaining cheese sauce mixture. Sprinkle with 1/2 cup Parmesan cheese.

5. Bake uncovered until noodles are done, 35 to 40 minutes. Let stand 10 minutes before cutting.

1 SERVING: Calories 325 (Calories from Fat 155); Fat 17g (Saturated 7g); Cholesterol 30mg; Sodium 680mg; Carbohydrates 26g (Dietary Fiber 1g); Protein 18g.

Rose McBrien
Staten Island, New York

Mom is one of the greatest cooks I know. She can turn a fridge full of "nothing" into a delicious curry, pasta dish, or stew. And I can honestly say Betty Crocker was there behind her.

My grandparents get a Betty Crocker gift package every Christmas, so we always got the updated cookbook. The early sixties cookbook is the finest cookbook we have ever used. That book is what my mother cooked from, and the one we all learned to cook with.

Aside from food, glorious food, Mom is supportive and giving—we have all moved back in for various periods of hard times, and she has helped raise two out of her seven grandchildren. She's extremely intelligent, listens, and even elicits their problems and concerns and comes up with creative answers for them.

My mother is a New York City judge. She has sat on the family court and criminal court and now is acting supreme court. Mom's sixty-two now and has slowed down a bit. She was in the forefront of women becoming lawyers and became a judge when it was rare for women to do so. And she never stopped being a very traditional wife and mother. Thanks!

Macaroni and Cheese

6 SERVINGS

Add extra pep to this favorite recipe by using pizza-flavored or jalapeño pepper cheese.

2 cups uncooked elbow
macaroni (7 ounces)

1/4 cup margarine or butter

1/4 cup all-purpose flour

1/2 teaspoon salt

1/4 teaspoon pepper

1/4 teaspoon ground mustard
(dry)

1/4 teaspoon Worcestershire
sauce

2 cups milk

2 cups shredded or cubed sharp
Cheddar cheese (8 ounces)

1. Heat oven to 350°.

2. Cook macaroni as directed on package.

3. While macaroni is cooking, melt margarine in 3-quart saucepan over low heat. Stir in flour, salt, pepper, mustard and Worcestershire sauce. Cook over low heat, stirring constantly, until mixture is smooth and bubbly; remove from heat. Stir in milk. Heat to boiling, stirring constantly. Boil and stir 1 minute. Stir in cheese. Cook, stirring occasionally, until cheese is melted.

4. Drain macaroni. Gently stir macaroni into cheese sauce. Pour into ungreased 2-quart casserole. Bake uncovered 20 to 25 minutes or until bubbly.

1 SERVING: Calories 445 (Calories from Fat 205); Fat 23g (Saturated 11g); Cholesterol 45mg; Sodium 540mg; Carbohydrates 42g (Dietary Fiber 1g); Protein 18g.

Vegetable Lasagna

8 SERVINGS

You can also add some shredded carrots, chopped broccoli or sliced mushrooms to this cheesy lasagna to make it even more chock-full of vegetables.

3 cups chunky-style spaghetti sauce

1 medium zucchini, shredded

6 uncooked lasagna noodles

1 cup ricotta or small curd creamed cottage cheese

1/4 cup grated Parmesan cheese

1 tablespoon snipped fresh oregano leaves or
  1 teaspoon dried oregano leaves

2 cups shredded mozzarella cheese (8 ounces)

1. Heat oven to 350°.

2. Mix spaghetti sauce and zucchini. Spread 1 cup mixture in ungreased rectangular baking dish, 11 x 7 x 1 1/2 inches; top with 3 uncooked noodles.

3. Mix ricotta cheese, Parmesan cheese and oregano; spread over noodles in dish. Spread with 1 cup of the sauce mixture.

4. Top with remaining noodles, sauce mixture and the mozzarella cheese. Bake uncovered until hot and bubbly, about 45 minutes. Let stand 15 minutes before cutting.

1 SERVING: Calories 290 (Calories from Fat 110); Fat 12g (Saturated 6g); Cholesterol 25mg; Sodium 700mg; Carbohydrates 32g (Dietary Fiber 2g); Protein 16g.

Manicotti

7 SERVINGS

This dish offers a great way to get your kids to eat their spinach. Wrapped in cheese and topped in tomato sauce, there's no wonder manicotti is a best-loved recipe by the whole family.

1 jar (32 ounces) chunky-style spaghetti sauce

2 packages (10 ounces each) frozen chopped spinach, thawed and well drained

1 container (12 ounces) small curd creamed cottage cheese (1 1/2 cups)

1 cup grated Parmesan cheese

1 tablespoon snipped fresh or 1 teaspoon dried oregano leaves

1/4 teaspoon pepper

14 uncooked manicotti shells (about 8 ounces)

2 cups shredded mozzarella cheese (8 ounces)

1. Heat oven to 350°.

2. Spread 1/3 of the spaghetti sauce in ungreased rectangular baking dish, 13 x 9 x 2 inches. Mix spinach, cottage cheese, Parmesan cheese, oregano and pepper. Fill uncooked manicotti shells with spinach mixture; arrange on spaghetti sauce in dish.

3. Pour remaining spaghetti sauce evenly over shells, covering completely; sprinkle with mozzarella cheese. Cover and bake until shells are tender, about 1 1/2 hours.

1 SERVING: Calories 450 (Calories from Fat 145); Fat 16g (Saturated 8g); Cholesterol 35mg; Sodium 1270mg; Carbohydrates 55g (Dietary Fiber 5g); Protein 27g.

Penne with Roasted Tomatoes and Garlic

4 SERVINGS

Garlic has long been associated with health and vitality. With that in mind, this recipe provides a wealth of health! A bulb of garlic may seem like a whole lot, but when it's roasted, as we've done, garlic becomes mellow and sweet with a butter-soft texture.

1/4 cup olive or vegetable oil

8 to 10 roma (plum) tomatoes, cut in half

1 teaspoon sugar

1/4 teaspoon salt

Freshly ground pepper

1 bulb garlic, unpeeled

2 cups uncooked penne pasta (8 ounces)

1/4 cup chopped fresh or 1 tablespoon dried basil leaves

4 ounces feta cheese, crumbled

1. Heat oven to 300°. Cover cookie sheet with aluminum foil; generously brush with 1 tablespoon of the oil.

2. Arrange tomato halves, cut sides up, in single layer on cookie sheet; brush with 4 teaspoons of the oil. Sprinkle with sugar, salt and pepper. Cut 1/2 inch off top of garlic bulb; drizzle 2 teaspoons of the oil over garlic bulb. Wrap in aluminum foil; place on cookie sheet with tomatoes.

3. Bake 55 to 60 minutes or until garlic is soft when pierced with a knife and tomatoes have begun to shrivel; cool slightly.

4. Cook and drain pasta as directed on package.

5. Squeeze garlic into remaining 1 tablespoon oil and mash until smooth; toss with pasta. Add tomato halves and basil; toss. Top with cheese. Serve immediately.

1 SERVING: Calories 450 (Calories from Fat 190); Fat 21g (Saturated 6g); Cholesterol 25mg; Sodium 470mg; Carbohydrates 55g (Dietary Fiber 3g); Protein 13g.

The Red Spoon

For many years, the Red Spoon has been associated with Betty Crocker and her vast line of products. Maybe you can remember when the packages didn't have this trusted symbol; if so, your memory goes back more than forty years. The spoon was designed for General Mills by Lippincott & Margulies, Inc., and first appeared on packages in 1954. Together with Betty's signature, it remains one of the most recognizable symbols of Betty Crocker today.

Margot M. Segura
El Sobrante, California

Growing up a Chicana from East Los Angeles, Betty Crocker and her recipes made her way into our kitchen, especially around Christmas time. In between the *tamales, posole,* and *empanaditas* and *biscochitos,* there would be one of my favorites: coconut-orange tartlets.

Cooking big dinners and baking extra goodies in our family was a very special occasion. It meant that there was a little more money in the house. It was also a time when we kids got to lick the frosting or batter from the pots and pans, dust cookies with powdered sugar, and just make a righteous mess. More importantly, it was a time to get to know my mother and auntie. They were hard working women with six children between them, and we hardly ever saw them.

Those memories remained with me and I passed them down to my own family. The best time we have is at Christmas, where we have a traditional *tamalada* (tamale making party), and somehow those coconut-orange tartlets sneak in.

For thirteen years, I have taught bilingual elementary education. My community involvement comes from a long time of activism. I cannot stand for anyone to be discriminated against. I have been a county human relations commissioner helping to register people to vote. More importantly, the California Hispanic High School Dropout Prevention Project is our creation. It will be released nationally this November. My passionate drive to create more positive visual images and role models for the Hispanic community has given me hope for a better future.

Creamy Fettuccine Alfredo

For a creative touch, top with toasted walnuts, roasted red bell pepper strips, or chopped Kalamata olives instead of the parsley.

8 ounces uncooked fettuccine

1/2 cup margarine or butter

1/2 cup whipping (heavy) cream

3/4 cup grated Parmesan cheese

1/2 teaspoon salt

Dash of pepper

Chopped fresh parsley

1. Cook and drain fettuccine as directed on package.

2. While fettuccine is cooking, heat margarine and whipping cream in 2-quart saucepan over low heat, stirring constantly, until margarine is melted. Stir in cheese, salt and pepper.

3. Pour sauce over fettuccine; stir until fettuccine is well coated. Sprinkle with parsley.

1 SERVING: Calories 380 (Calories from Fat 235); Fat 26g (Saturated 9g); Cholesterol 65mg; Sodium 600mg; Carbohydrates 26g (Dietary Fiber 1g); Protein 9g.

Electric Appliances

Betty has had to adapt to a lot of changes in America's kitchens during her reign as a food expert. In the 1920s when she began dispensing advice, relatively few electric appliances were available to make homemakers' lives easier. There were coffeemakers, toasters and mixers. Electric frypans, waffle irons and can openers came later. It's hard to believe, but the first microwave oven was introduced in the 1960s! The seventies produced slow cookers, food processors and electric deep-fryers, to name a few. And today, the scent of fresh-baked bread wafts through homes more often with the convenience of automatic bread machines. Betty has always tried to keep up with these advances, developing and testing new products and recipes that will help consumers get the most from their appliance investments.

Pasta with Lemon and Basil

Pasta with Lemon and Basil

6 SERVINGS

Chop your fresh basil at the last possible moment so the leaves will stay beautiful bright green.

6 ounces angel hair pasta

1/4 cup chopped fresh basil leaves

1/4 cup lemon juice

1 tablespoon grated lemon peel

3 tablespoons olive oil

1/2 teaspoon black pepper

Grated Parmesan cheese

1. Cook pasta in boiling water 3 to 5 minutes or just until tender; drain.

2. Toss with remaining ingredients except cheese. Serve with cheese.

1 SERVING: Calories 170 (Calories from Fat 65); Fat 7g (Saturated 1g); Cholesterol 0mg; Sodium 5mg; Carbohydrates 24g (Dietary Fiber 1g); Protein 4g.

Black Bean Chili

6 SERVINGS

The flavor of cilantro is distinctive and pungent, but it quickly disappears when cooked, so that's why we stir the cilantro in to the chili after cooking is complete. Serve with flour tortillas and a fresh fruit salad.

2 cups water

2 cups apple juice

1 tablespoon chopped fresh or 1 teaspoon dried oregano leaves

2 tablespoons tomato paste

1 teaspoon ground cumin

1/8 teaspoon ground red pepper (cayenne)

1 large onion, chopped (1 cup)

2 cans (4 ounces each) chopped mild green chilies, drained

3 cans (15 ounces each) black beans, rinsed and drained

1 medium red bell pepper, chopped (1 cup)

3 tablespoons chopped fresh cilantro

1 cup shredded reduced-fat Cheddar cheese (4 ounces)

1. Heat water, apple juice, oregano, tomato paste, cumin, red pepper, onion and chilies to boiling in Dutch oven; reduce heat. Cover and simmer 30 minutes.

2. Stir in beans and bell pepper. Cover and simmer about 10 minutes or until beans are hot. Stir in cilantro. Top each serving with cheese.

1 SERVING: Calories 335 (Calories from Fat 45); Fat 5g (Saturated 3g); Cholesterol 10mg; Sodium 920mg; Carbohydrates 65g (Dietary Fiber 14g); Protein 22g.

Black Bean Chili

Camille Kettel
Algonac, Michigan

One of my clearest memories includes the excitement of the Senior Awards Assembly, May 1967. I had been given the Betty Crocker Homemaker's Award, and I can't say which one of us was more proud, my mother or myself. From the time I was able to stand on a chair at her side at her kitchen counter, she and

I had shared moments together poring over recipes from the Betty Crocker cookbook. I have grown since then into an accomplished woman in my own right. I count along the way as most important those earliest days with my mother in her kitchen, sharing our thoughts and dreams.

I have had a full-time career in the field of education, publishing both academic work and personal books of poetry. I was blessed to have my own family and gave them every bit of love and attention that I could, raising a son who is now a second-year student at the University of Michigan.

I also volunteer in my community in various capacities, most recently as a member of the St. Clair County Comprehensive Community Health Model's (CCHM's) group, which is comprised of caring, committed individuals, countywide, who have come together as a group to work on health care reform. In the past I have served on the local library board of directors and have worked in the local hospital as a volunteer in working with patients. I feel that part of my good fortune in living in beautiful St. Clair County, Michigan, is in my mission to give back to the world much of the goodness with which I have been blessed.

Spinach Phyllo Pie

For best results, be sure the phyllo is completely thawed so each thin layer will easily separate from one another. Also, phyllo dough can dry out easily, so be sure to keep any unused dough wrapped tightly.

1 tablespoon olive or vegetable
   oil

1 medium onion, chopped
   (1/2 cup)

1 medium red bell pepper,
   chopped (1 cup)

1 clove garlic, finely chopped

2 packages (9 ounces each)
   frozen chopped spinach,
   thawed and squeezed to
   drain

1 package (8 ounces) cream
   cheese, softened

1/2 cup crumbled feta or
   Gorgonzola cheese
   (2 ounces)

2 eggs

1 tablespoon chopped fresh or
   1 teaspoon dried dill weed

1/2 teaspoon salt

1/4 teaspoon pepper

8 sheets frozen phyllo (18 x 14
   inches), thawed

2 tablespoons stick margarine or
   butter, melted*

1. Heat oven to 375°. Grease bottom and side of pie plate, 9 x 1 1/2 inches, with margarine.

2. Heat oil in 10-inch skillet, over medium-high heat. Cook onion, bell pepper and garlic in oil, stirring frequently, until vegetables are crisp-tender; remove from heat.

3. Stir in spinach, cream cheese, feta cheese, eggs, dill weed, salt and pepper.

4. Cut stack of phyllo sheets into 12-inch squares; discard extra phyllo. Cover with waxed paper, then with damp towel to prevent them from drying out. Brush each of 4 phyllo squares with margarine and layer in pie plate. Gently press into pie plate, allowing corners to drape over edge.

5. Spread spinach mixture evenly over phyllo. Fold ends of phyllo up and over filling so corners overlap on top. Brush with margarine and layer remaining 4 phyllo sheets over pie, allowing corners to drape over edge.

6. Gently tuck phyllo draping over top inside edge of pie plate. Cut through top phyllo layers into 6 wedges using sharp knife or scissors.

7. Bake 35 to 45 minutes or until crust is golden brown and filling is hot. Let stand 10 minutes before serving.

1 SERVING: Calories 320 (Calories from Fat 190); Fat 21g (Saturated 11g); Cholesterol 120mg; Sodium 610mg; Carbohydrates 25g (Dietary Fiber 2g); Protein 10g.

*We do not recommend using vegetable oil spreads.

Bean and Cheese Pie

Serve this "chili in a pie" in its delicious cheesy crust. You'll just need a simple salad to round out the meal—try slices of mandarin oranges and avocado drizzled with your favorite vinaigrette.

3/4 cup all-purpose flour

1 1/2 cups shredded Cheddar cheese (6 ounces)

1 1/2 teaspoons baking powder

1/2 teaspoon salt

1/3 cup milk

1 egg, slightly beaten

1 can (15 to 16 ounces) garbanzo beans, drained

1 can (15 to 16 ounces) kidney beans, drained

1 can (8 ounces) tomato sauce

1 small green bell pepper, chopped (1/2 cup)

1 small onion, chopped (1/4 cup)

2 teaspoons chili powder

2 teaspoons chopped fresh or 1/2 teaspoon dried
   oregano leaves

1/4 teaspoon garlic powder

1. Heat oven to 375°. Spray pie plate, 10 x 1 1/2 inches, with nonstick cooking spray.

2. Mix flour, 1/2 cup of the cheese, the baking powder and salt in medium bowl. Stir in milk and egg until blended. Spread over bottom and up side of pie plate.

3. Mix 1/2 cup of the remaining cheese and the remaining ingredients. Spoon into pie plate. Sprinkle with remaining 1/2 cup cheese. Bake uncovered about 25 minutes or until edge is puffy and light brown. Let stand 10 minutes before cutting.

1 SERVING: Calories 260 (Calories from Fat 90); Fat 10g (Saturated 5g); Cholesterol 50mg; Sodium 840mg; Carbohydrates 34g (Dietary Fiber 6g); Protein 15g.

With a Sift, Sift Here . . .

Do you remember sifting flour before measuring it for use in a recipe? Do you know why you did that, other than the fact that your mother told you to? It was to ensure consistent measurement of flour from person to person so that the recipes would work the way they were supposed to. In 1961, General Mills announced, after extensive research into the ways consumers measured flour and the impact the different measuring approaches had on the prepared recipe, that sifting flour was no longer necessary. Just one more example of the ways Betty has made baking easier.

228   SIT DOWN TO DINNER

Classic Cheese Soufflé

4 SERVINGS

This fluffy golden soufflé only needs asparagus spears and a fresh, colorful fruit for a delicious meal.

1/4 cup margarine or butter

1/4 cup all-purpose flour

1/2 teaspoon salt

1/4 teaspoon ground mustard (dry)

Dash of ground red pepper (cayenne)

1 cup milk

1 cup shredded Cheddar cheese (4 ounces)

3 eggs, separated

1/4 teaspoon cream of tartar

1. Heat oven to 350°.

2. Butter 1-quart soufflé dish or casserole. Make a 4-inch band of triple-thickness aluminum foil 2 inches longer than circumference of dish. Butter one side of foil. Secure foil band, buttered side in, around top edge of dish.

3. Melt margarine in 2-quart saucepan over medium heat. Stir in flour, salt, mustard and red pepper. Cook over medium heat, stirring constantly, until smooth and bubbly; remove from heat. Stir in milk. Heat to boiling, stirring constantly. Boil and stir 1 minute. Stir in cheese until melted; remove from heat.

4. Beat egg whites and cream of tartar in medium bowl with electric mixer on high speed until stiff but not dry. Beat egg yolks on high speed about 3 minutes or until very thick and lemon-colored; stir into cheese mixture. Stir about one-fourth of the egg whites into cheese mixture. Fold cheese mixture into remaining egg whites. Carefully pour into soufflé dish.

5. Bake 50 to 60 minutes or until knife inserted halfway between center and edge comes out clean. Carefully remove foil band and quickly divide soufflé into sections with 2 forks. Serve immediately.

1 SERVING: Calories 335 (Calories from Fat 235); Fat 26g (Saturated 10g); Cholesterol 195mg; Sodium 650mg; Carbohydrates 10g (Dietary Fiber 0g); Protein 15g.

Whole Wheat Vegetable Calzone

6 SERVINGS

The whole wheat dough adds a nice nutty flavor and denser texture to this calzone. Warmed tomato sauce makes a nice accompaniment for dipping.

Whole Wheat Calzone Dough (right)

1 package (10 ounces) frozen chopped broccoli

1/3 cup creamy Italian dressing

1/2 teaspoon salt

1 package (3 ounces) cream cheese, softened

1 cup sliced mushrooms, or 1 jar (4.5 ounces) sliced mushrooms, drained

2 carrots, shredded

1 medium tomato, chopped

1/2 small green pepper, chopped

1 egg, beaten

1. Heat oven to 375°.

2. Prepare Whole Wheat Calzone Dough. Divide into 6 equal pieces. Pat each into 7-inch circle on lightly floured surface, turning dough over occasionally to coat with flour.

3. Rinse frozen broccoli in cold water to separate; drain. Mix dressing, salt and cream cheese until well blended (mixture will appear curdled). Stir in broccoli and remaining vegetables.

4. Top half of each circle with 2/3 cup vegetable mixture to within 1 inch of edge. Fold dough over filling; fold edge up and pinch securely to seal. Place on greased cookie sheet; brush with egg. Sprinkle with coarse salt if desired. Bake until golden brown, 25 to 30 minutes.

WHOLE WHEAT CALZONE DOUGH

1 package active dry yeast

1 cup warm water (105° to 115°)

1 tablespoon sugar

2 tablespoons vegetable oil

1 teaspoon salt

2 1/2 to 3 cups whole wheat flour

1. Dissolve yeast in warm water in large bowl. Stir in sugar, oil, salt and 1 cup of the flour. Beat until smooth. Mix in enough remaining flour to make dough easy to handle.

2. Turn dough onto lightly floured surface; knead until smooth and elastic, about 5 minutes. Cover with bowl and let rest 5 minutes.

1 SERVING: Calories 350 (Calories from Fat 155); Fat 17g (Saturated 5g); Cholesterol 50mg; Sodium 770mg; Carbohydrates 47g (Dietary Fiber 9g); Protein 11g.

Roxyanne Young
San Diego, California

For me "Spirit of Betty Crocker" conjures images of the heavenly aroma of devil's food cake baking in my grandmother's kitchen—my traditional choice for birthday cake—and me sticky-faced with whatever batter is left on the beaters while my two younger brothers clean the mixing bowl and spatula with grubby

little hands. It's me busily chopping pecans in an old wooden bowl and learning how to crack eggs into a cup so as not to get shell bits in the batter and dropping them one at a time into the dry mix, breathing in the chocolate dust, then helping my great grandmother count three hundred strokes by hand while she mixes the brownie batter in her favorite blue stoneware bowl.

It's me thumbing through the yellowed pages of my mother's familiar, worn cookbook as a teenager preparing my first family meal and finding that favorite fried chicken recipe—comfort food if ever there was such a thing.

It's me and my college girlfriends at a sorority sleepover, after hearing that Betty Crocker had been a member of our beloved Delta Zeta, pinky-swearing over chocolate cake (devil's food again, no doubt, with sour cream frosting) never to buy a cake mix from anyone else, like there would be another choice, and it's the tub of frosting that we always seemed to have left over and would eat by the spoonful, or the fingerful if no one was looking.

It's Impossible Broccoli Pie baked in two pie plates so I can share one with my mother-in-law, and happily so since the tomato wedges arranged carefully on top originated in her backyard garden. It's my aunt, showing me how substituting applesauce for oil cuts the fat in cake and that baking it in a scalloped-edge tiara cake pan allows you to pour cherry pie filling in the top so you don't need frosting, and it's me laughing and saying, "But that's half the fun of cake," so we spread fat-free chocolate pudding on top instead.

It's the smell of made-from-scratch sourdough bread and cinnamon rolls baking in my oven every Thursday morning whose recipes call specifically for Betty Crocker Potato Buds® because, according to my grandmother who gave me the liquid dough starter, no other flake does the trick, and it's that same dough that, with sauce that's been simmering all afternoon and whatever toppings are at hand, becomes Pizza Art on Friday nights when my husband and I steal some quality time away from busy work schedules to cook dinner together and then snuggle in front of the television.

Even though it's not spelled out on the box, I think that's the best part of the recipe, the reminiscing about dear friends and family, I mean, because that's the Spirit of Betty Crocker. It's not about cake mixes, fried chicken, pecan brownies, or dried potatoes. It's about long-standing family traditions, lifelong friendships, passing down things like recipes and blue stoneware mixing bowls from one generation to another, laughing together over memories like birthday candles that won't blow out and finding more uses for wooden spoons than mixing cake batter.

Impossible Broccoli 'n Cheddar Pie

6 SERVINGS

It takes only minutes to prepare this cheesy broccoli pie. Quickly thaw the broccoli by removing the outer wrapper from the package and then piercing the package with a knife. Microwave on high 1 1/2 to 2 1/2 minutes or until partially thawed. Break up broccoli with fork and drain thoroughly. Terrific served with coleslaw and assorted fruits.

2 packages (10 ounces each)
   frozen chopped broccoli,
   thawed and drained

2 cups shredded Cheddar cheese
   (8 ounces)

2/3 cup chopped onion

1 1/3 cups milk

3 eggs

3/4 cup Bisquick Original
   baking mix

1/2 teaspoon salt

1/4 teaspoon pepper

1. Heat oven to 400°. Grease pie plate, 10 x 1 1/2 inches.

2. Mix broccoli, 1 1/3 cups of the cheese and the onion in pie plate.

3. Stir milk, eggs, baking mix, salt and pepper with fork until blended. Pour into pie plate.

4. Bake 30 to 35 minutes or until knife inserted in center comes out clean. Sprinkle with remaining cheese. Bake 1 to 2 minutes longer or until cheese is melted. Cool 5 minutes.

1 SERVING: Calories 300 (Calories from Fat 160); Fat 18g (Saturated 10g); Cholesterol 150mg; Sodium 720mg; Carbohydrates 19g (Dietary Fiber 3g); Protein 18g.

Bisquick Baking Mix

Nearly all the cake, muffin, pancake and all-purpose baking mixes we use today are descended from Bisquick. Introduced in the early 1930s, this convenience product was an instant hit with consumers. But how did it happen? Carl Smith, a General Mills executive, boarded a train late one night in 1930. He hungrily headed for the dining car, expecting that only cold food would be available at that hour. To his surprise and delight, a piping-hot meal was served, including freshly baked biscuits! The delicious hot biscuits piqued his curiosity, and he pleaded with the chef to reveal his secret: a mix of lard, flour, baking powder and salt kept ready for use in the refrigerator. Smith brought the idea back to General Mills, where food scientists figured out how to keep the ingredients fresh in a box. Within the first seven months on the market, five hundred thousand cases of the mix were sold! Within a year, there were ninety-five competing mixes from which consumers could choose.

Thin-Crust Pizza

6 SERVINGS

If you like a thin, delicate crust, this is the pizza for you. Since this crust is not yeast-risen, it will just take a few moments to put together. If you are looking for a thicker crust, check out the Chicago Deep-Dish Pizza on page 235.

Thin Crust (below)

Sauce (right)

Meat Toppings (right)

Vegetable Toppings (right)

1 1/2 cups shredded mozzarella cheese (6 ounces)

1. Place oven rack in lowest position of oven. Heat oven to 450°.

2. Prepare Thin Crust; spread with Sauce. Top with one of the Meat Toppings and desired Vegetable Toppings. Sprinkle with mozzarella cheese. Bake on lowest oven rack until crust is brown and cheese is melted and bubbly, 12 to 15 minutes.

THIN CRUST

1 1/2 cups Bisquick Original baking mix

1/3 cup very hot water

1. Mix baking mix and water; beat vigorously 20 strokes. Turn dough onto surface generously dusted with baking mix. Knead until smooth and no longer sticky, about 60 times.

2. Press dough into 13-inch circle on greased cooking sheet or press in greased 12-inch pizza pan with hands dipped in baking mix. Pinch edge, forming 1/2-inch rim.

SAUCE

1 can (8 ounces) tomato sauce

1 teaspoon Italian seasoning

1/8 teaspoon garlic powder

Mix all ingredients.

MEAT TOPPINGS

1/2 to 1 pound ground beef, cooked and drained

1/2 to 1 pound bulk Italian sausage, cooked and drained

1 package (3 1/2 ounces) sliced pepperoni

1 package (6 ounces) sliced Canadian-style bacon

VEGETABLE TOPPINGS

Sliced mushrooms

Chopped green pepper

Sliced green onions or chopped onion

Sliced ripe olives

1 SERVING: Calories 295 (Calories from Fat 135); Fat 15g (Saturated 7g); Cholesterol 35mg; Sodium 870mg; Carbohydrates 24g (Dietary Fiber 1g); Protein 17g.

Chicago Deep-Dish Pizza

8 SERVINGS

You'll get cheers when you serve this hearty, thick-crusted pizza. The make-it-your-way style pleases kids and adults alike.

Chicago Deep-Dish Crust (below)

4 cups shredded mozzarella cheese (16 ounces)

Meat Toppings (right)

Vegetable Toppings (right)

1 can (28 ounces) Italian plum tomatoes, chopped and well drained

1 tablespoon snipped fresh or 1 to 2 teaspoons dried oregano leaves or Italian herb seasoning

1/4 to 1/2 cup grated Parmesan cheese

1. Place oven rack in lowest position of oven. Heat oven to 425°. Prepare Deep-Dish Crust; sprinkle with mozzarella cheese.

2. Top with one of the Meat Toppings, desired Vegetable Toppings and tomatoes; sprinkle with oregano and Parmesan cheese.

3. Bake on lowest oven rack until crust is brown and cheese is melted and bubbly, 20 to 25 minutes.

CHICAGO DEEP-DISH CRUST

1 package active dry yeast

3/4 cup warm water (105° to 115°)

3 cups Bisquick Original baking mix

2 tablespoons olive oil

1. Dissolve yeast in warm water in large bowl. Stir in baking mix and olive oil; beat vigorously 20 strokes. Turn dough onto surface generously dusted with baking mix. Knead dough until smooth and no longer sticky, about 60 times. Let rest 5 minutes.

2. Press in bottom and up sides of jelly roll pan, 15 1/2 x 10 1/2 x 1 inch, greased with olive oil if desired. Or divide dough into halves and press in bottom and up sides of 2 round pans, 9 x 1 1/2 inches, greased with olive oil if desired.

MEAT TOPPINGS

1/2 to 1 pound bulk Italian sausage, cooked and drained

1 package (3 1/2 ounces) sliced pepperoni

VEGETABLE TOPPINGS

Sliced mushrooms

Chopped green or red pepper

Chopped onion

Sliced ripe olives

Sliced pimiento-stuffed olives

Coarsely chopped sun-dried tomatoes in oil

1 SERVING: Calories 565 (Calories from Fat 305); Fat 24g (Saturated 13g); Cholesterol 60mg; Sodium 1890mg; Carbohydrates 39g (Dietary Fiber 3g); Protein 29g.

CHAPTER FOUR

Super Sides, Smaller Bites, & Bread

Turn through the pages for the market's freshest offerings for vegetables and other side dishes. There are scrumptious recipes for every occasion—from tender vegetables and savory salads to spicy rices and side dishes—we've included a complement for every meal you make. Looking for a little something to whet your appetite? Your family will flock to the kitchen to devour the appetizers offered here. And we didn't forget fresh breads and biscuits. Nothing welcomes you to the table faster than the fragrance of baking bread.

Sides&Smaller Bites

Loretta Ivory
Denver, Colorado

In 1987, my mother won the Queen of the Kitchen award for the most ribbons won at the Colorado State Fair. My mom entered sixteen and placed in all sixteen, winning more points (ribbons) than any other contestant in the history of the fair. But that was no surprise to me, I've known that she was the best all my life.

My mom volunteers for the March of Dimes—mother marches and especially donates a lot of time to the Denver Museum of Natural History when it has special exhibits. These special exhibits required that she attend special classes (including tests and essays!) for several months before the exhibits even open.

My mom always bakes for the bake sales at her office and for her Women's Group (The Women's Spiritual Leadership Alliance—they raise money for a battered woman's shelter), and usually people ask, "What did Loretta bring? I'll buy that." She works twenty hours a week at an inner-city health clinic, attends the University of Denver as a special student, edits cookbooks, grows an organic garden, produces TV shows for the local community access channel, sews many of her own clothes (and some award-winning quilts), and patches my jeans. As if that weren't enough, she is passionate in her support of her worship group and volunteers to help put together all its statewide meetings. That sounds like a pretty busy schedule doesn't it? But you know, the most important thing my mom does is always be there for me.

Golden Corn Pudding

8 SERVINGS

Bake in a pretty oven-proof dish and serve it for company-best. The delicate custard is so good! Fresh, frozen or drained, canned corn can be used to make this creamy savory dish.

2 cups frozen whole kernel corn, thawed

1 tablespoon margarine or butter

1 teaspoon sugar

1 teaspoon salt

1/4 teaspoon pepper

2 eggs, well beaten

1 cup milk

1 tablespoon cracker crumbs

1. Heat oven to 350°. Grease 1-quart baking dish.

2. Mix all ingredients together thoroughly. Pour into baking dish. Set baking dish in pan of hot water 1 inch deep. Bake 60 to 70 minutes, or until silver knife inserted 1 inch from edge comes out clean.

1 SERVING: Calories 90 (Calories from Fat 35); Fat 4g (Saturated 2g); Cholesterol 60mg; Sodium 430mg; Carbohydrates 10g (Dietary Fiber 1g); Protein 4g.

How Do You Measure Up?

Many consumers turn to Betty Crocker for recipes. You can get recipes in many places, including books, product packages, booklets, newspapers and even the Internet. But how many of us actually use recipes when we cook? The Betty Crocker Kitchens commissioned a study by the NPD Group, Inc., and discovered that on the average 40 percent of households in America use a recipe at least once a week. These recipes are most often for main dishes or entrées. Dessert recipes are second, followed closely by side-dish recipes. It appears most of us know how to make our own beverages—that category doesn't see much recipe usage at all. This book contains many of Betty's favorite recipes. What's yours?

Broccoli with Pine Nuts

4 SERVINGS

This broccoli tastes as good as it is for you because it is chock-full of vitamins and anti-oxidants. The pine nuts, little tear-drop shaped nuts, add a toasted buttery flavor to the broccoli.

1 cup water

1 1/2 pounds fresh broccoli, cut into spears

2 tablespoons margarine or butter

1/4 cup pine nuts

1. Heat water to boiling in medium saucepan; add broccoli. Cook about 10 minutes until stems are crisp-tender; drain.

2. Melt margarine in 8-inch skillet; add pine nuts. Cook over medium heat 5 minutes until nuts are golden brown, stirring frequently. Sprinkle nuts over broccoli.

1 SERVING: Calories 135 (Calories from Fat 100); Fat 11g (Saturated 2g); Cholesterol 0mg; Sodium 110mg; Carbohydrates 7g (Dietary Fiber 4g); Protein 4g.

Marinated Tomato Slices

4 SERVINGS

Tomatoes go with just about everything! For a richer flavor, cover the tomatoes and marinate in the refrigerator overnight.

1/4 cup chopped fresh or 2 tablespoons dried basil leaves

6 tablespoons olive oil

2 tablespoons red wine vinegar

2 large tomatoes, sliced

Mix all ingredients except tomatoes. Pour mixture over tomatoes in glass bowl; chill for at least 30 minutes.

1 SERVING: Calories 60 (Calories from Fat 45); Fat 5g (Saturated 1g); Cholesterol 0mg; Sodium 10mg; Carbohydrates 4g (Dietary Fiber 1g); Protein 1g.

Marinated Tomato Slices

Roasted Autumn Vegetables

When the crisp, cool evenings of autumn arrive, delight your family with the sweetness of this dish. The slow-roasting of the vegetables helps develop their rich flavor. It makes a perfect partner for roasted chicken.

1/4 cup margarine or butter

1 tablespoon fresh or 1 teaspoon dried sage leaves

1 clove garlic, crushed

1/2 pound Brussels sprouts, cut into halves

1/2 pound parsnips, peeled and cut into 2-inch pieces

1/4 pound baby carrots, peeled

1 small butternut squash, peeled, seeded and cut into 1-inch pieces

1. Heat oven to 375°.

2. Melt margarine in small saucepan; stir in sage and garlic. Place vegetables in rectangular pan, 13 x 9 x 2 inches. Pour margarine mixture over vegetables; stir to coat.

3. Cover; bake 25 to 30 minutes, stirring occasionally, until vegetables are crisp-tender.

1 SERVING: Calories 170 (Calories from Fat 110); Fat 12g (Saturated 2g); Cholesterol 0mg; Sodium 210mg; Carbohydrates 17g (Dietary Fiber 6g); Protein 5g.

Vegetables with Lemon Butter

The tart lemon butter adds just the right zip to the vegetables. Serve this colorful, tasty side with some broiled fresh fish.

3 packages (10 ounces each) frozen whole green beans

1 1/2 pounds Brussels sprouts, cut into halves

1 pound carrots, peeled and cut into julienne strips

1/2 cup margarine or butter, melted

1 tablespoon grated lemon peel

1 tablespoon lemon juice

1. Cook green beans according to package directions; keep warm.

2. Heat 1 inch water to boiling in large saucepan. Add Brussels sprouts. Cover and heat to boiling; reduce heat. Cook 8 to 10 minutes or until stems are tender; keep warm.

3. Heat 1 inch water to boiling in large saucepan. Add carrots. Cover and heat to boiling; reduce heat. Cook 6 to 8 minutes or until tender; keep warm.

4. Combine margarine, lemon peel and lemon juice. Arrange cooked vegetables on platter; pour margarine mixture over vegetables.

1 SERVING: Calories 110 (Calories from Fat 70); Fat 8g (Saturated 1g); Cholesterol 0mg; Sodium 130mg; Carbohydrates 12g (Dietary Fiber 5g); Protein 3g.

Cottie Wright

Gainesville, Florida

My wife, Cottie A. Wright, has developed a passion for cooking. However, when I first met Cottie in the early 1970s, cooking was not her greatest strength. Our first Thanksgiving meal resulted in near disaster. The turkey was far from being juicy, and the kitchen nearly burned. With the help of family members and her Betty Crocker cookbook and a genuine desire to learn how to cook, she has become an exceptionally talented cook. I tell her often, "You've come a long way, baby." She spends many hours gazing through her Betty Crocker cookbooks, selecting dishes and planning meals.

Special occasions are especially grand and festive, with family and friends enjoying a variety of great foods. Cottie's great cooking seems to attract them all. Cottie's favorite recipes are from *Betty Crocker's Dinner For Two Cookbook*. She has tried many of them because they fit into our daily life and busy schedule. Cottie has found them to be very convenient and easy to prepare.

In addition to being a great wife, mother, teacher, and cook, Cottie is also involved in community activities. She is an active member of the marriage and family ministry of our church that emphasizes strong family values. Cottie is a member of the Visionaries, a community service organization with major emphasis on developing leadership potentials in young people and providing greatly needed academic scholarship.

Cottie is a loving wife, devoted mother, and dedicated teacher who strongly upholds family life. We have been married for twenty-two years and are the parents of two sons, Phil, Jr., and Patrick. She is Cottie Ann Wright, my sweetheart.

Spinach Gourmet

Impress your guests when you serve this creamy side. Swiss chard, with tender leaves and firm crisp stalks, can also be used in place of spinach. This succulent side goes perfect with slices of steak.

1 pound fresh spinach* or other
   fresh greens

1 can (4 ounces) button mushrooms, drained

1 teaspoon instant minced onion

1 small clove garlic, crushed

1/2 teaspoon salt

1/3 cup sour cream

1 tablespoon light cream or milk

1. Remove imperfect spinach leaves and root ends. Wash greens several times in water, lifting out of water each time so sand sinks to bottom. Drain.

2. Place greens with just the water that clings to leaves in saucepan. Cover and cook 3 to 10 minutes for spinach; 5 to 15 minutes for beet tops; 15 to 20 minutes for chicory, escarole and lettuce; 10 to 15 minutes for collards; 15 to 20 minutes for Swiss chard and mustard greens; 15 to 25 minutes for turnip greens and kale. Drain.

3. Prepare and cook fresh spinach or Swiss chard as directed above; chop and drain thoroughly.

4. Stir together spinach, mushrooms and seasonings in saucepan. Blend sour cream and light cream; pour over spinach mixture. Heat just to boiling.

1 SERVING: Calories 75 (Calories from Fat 45); Fat 5g (Saturated 3g); Cholesterol 15mg; Sodium 490mg; Carbohydrates 6g (Dietary Fiber 3g); Protein 4g.

*With frozen spinach: Use 1 package (10 ounces) frozen chopped spinach, cooked and drained; add 2 tablespoons butter to ingredients in saucepan.

Stuffed Zucchini

8 SERVINGS

Summertime is the perfect time to use up the pounds of zucchini growing in your garden. This goes well with any chicken recipe.

4 medium zucchini (about 2 pounds)

1 medium onion, chopped (about 1/2 cup)

1/4 cup (1/2 stick) margarine or butter

1 can (4 ounces) chopped green chilies, drained

1 jar (2 ounces) diced pimientos, drained

1 1/2 cups herb-seasoned stuffing mix (dry)

3/4 cup shredded mozzarella or Monterey Jack cheese

1. Heat 2 inches water (salted if desired) to boiling. Add zucchini. Heat to boiling; reduce heat. Cover and simmer just until tender, 8 to 10 minutes; drain. Cool slightly; cut each zucchini lengthwise in half.

2. Spoon out pulp; chop coarsely. Place zucchini, cut sides up, in ungreased baking dish, 13 x 9 x 2 inches.

3. Heat oven to 350°.

4. Cook and stir onion in margarine in 10-inch skillet until onion is tender. Stir in chopped pulp, chilies, pimientos and stuffing mix.

5. Divide stuffing mixture among zucchini halves. Sprinkle each with about 1 tablespoon cheese. Bake uncovered until hot, 30 to 35 minutes.

1 SERVING: Calories 145 (Calories from Fat 70); Fat 8g (Saturated 2g); Cholesterol 5mg; Sodium 330mg; Carbohydrates 14g (Dietary Fiber 2g); Protein 6g.

Betty Helps Out

If you lived through the Depression, perhaps you were one of the many housewives who wrote to Betty Crocker to ask for help in making nutritious meals for the family even as incomes were getting smaller by the week. Betty responded with recipes specifically developed to be low in cost but high in nutrition and appeal, so folks could feel they were eating well. Those families that had access to radios could hear Betty devote two programs a week to menus and recipes specifically for helping them use their rations wisely. Betty heard a need and responded quickly and efficiently. She truly became the best friend in the Depression kitchen.

Stuffed Zucchini

Susan Molzan
Houston, Texas

Susan graduated from James Madison University in Virginia. It was there that she met her husband, Bruce Molzan, and together with his culinary skills they opened the Ruggles Grill in 1986. Susan reigns over the monumental desserts made fresh each day at the restaurant. Her style is big, all-American desserts that simply taste good. Despite the success of the restaurant, the Molzans still found time to start their family. Susan always finds time to spend with the girls, and customers always enjoy seeing them at the restaurant.

Susan's bright smile and contagious laugh make seeing her a high point of anyone's visit to the restaurant. To the employees, she's a mother figure, a great shoulder to lean on, and someone who cares.

Susan's extended family in Houston include the End Hunger Network and Citizen's for Animal protection as well as numerous AIDS organizations. Susan and Bruce were also instrumental in helping the Taste of the NFL raise over $200,000 for food banks and hunger organizations all over the country last year.

And with all this, she is still on hand at the restaurant, either in the kitchen or at the door, with her trademarks—a smile and a hug.

Garlic Smashed Potatoes

Looking for a delicious twist on mashed potatoes. The Yukon Gold potatoes are a beautiful golden color and the roasted garlic adds a subtle sweet flavor to the potatoes. We're sure you'll find them delicious.

6 medium Yukon Gold or russet
  potatoes (2 pounds)

1 bulb garlic

2 tablespoons olive or vegetable
  oil

1 teaspoon chopped fresh or
  1/4 teaspoon dried oregano
  leaves

1/2 teaspoon salt

1/3 to 1/2 cup milk

1/4 cup chopped fresh chives

1. Heat oven to 375°.

2. Pierce potatoes with fork to allow steam to escape. Cut 1/4-inch slice from top of garlic bulb to expose cloves. Carefully remove most of the paperlike skin, leaving the bulb intact and the cloves unpeeled. Wrap garlic in aluminum foil. Bake potatoes and garlic about 1 hour or until potatoes are tender.

3. Heat oil and oregano over medium heat 2 to 3 minutes or until oregano is fragrant.

4. Open garlic pack to cool. Cut potatoes in half; carefully spoon potatoes in large bowl. Save skins for another use or discard. Separate garlic cloves and press the cloves slightly to squeeze the garlic out; discard skin. Place garlic in bowl; add oil mixture and salt.

5. Mash potatoes until no lumps remain. Beat in milk in small amounts (amount of milk needed to make potatoes smooth and fluffy depends on kind of potatoes). Beat vigorously until potatoes are light and fluffy. Stir in chives.

1 SERVING: Calories 155 (Calories from Fat 45); Fat 5g (Saturated 1g); Cholesterol 2mg; Sodium 190mg; Carbohydrates 26g (Dietary Fiber 2g); Protein 3g.

Crispy Potato Pancakes

12 PANCAKES

A dollop of sour cream or applesauce is all you need to top these tasty pancakes. Grilled kielbasa or sausage makes this meal just perfect.

4 large baking potatoes (about 1 pound), peeled and shredded

1/2 cup beer or milk

1/4 cup all-purpose flour

1/4 cup finely chopped onion

2 tablespoons finely chopped parsley

1/2 teaspoon salt

1/4 teaspoon pepper

1 egg

2 to 3 tablespoons vegetable oil

1. Mix all ingredients except oil until well blended.

2. Heat oil on griddle or in large skillet until hot. Spread about 1/4 cup batter on griddle for each pancake. Cook on medium-high heat 2 minutes on each side until crispy; keep warm. Add more oil to griddle, if necessary. Serve with applesauce if desired.

1 SERVING: Calories 90 (Calories from Fat 25); Fat 3g (Saturated 1g); Cholesterol 15mg; Sodium 105mg; Carbohydrates 15g (Dietary Fiber 1g); Protein 2g.

Roasted Rosemary-Onion Potatoes

4 SERVINGS

Instead of French fries, try this as a side. Roasted potatoes, redolent with rosemary and sweet onion, this dish is a great partner for any sandwich, burger or even breakfast eggs!

4 medium potatoes (1 1/3 pounds)

1 small onion, finely chopped (1/4 cup)

2 tablespoons olive or vegetable oil

2 tablespoons chopped fresh or 2 teaspoons dried rosemary leaves

1 teaspoon chopped fresh or 1/4 teaspoon dried thyme leaves

1/4 teaspoon salt

1/8 teaspoon pepper

1. Heat oven to 450°. Grease jelly roll pan, 15 1/2 x 10 1/2 x 1 inch.

2. Cut potatoes into 1-inch chunks. Mix onion, oil, rosemary, thyme, salt and pepper in large bowl. Add potatoes; toss to coat. Spread potatoes in single layer in pan.

3. Bake uncovered 20 to 25 minutes, turning occasionally, until potatoes are light brown and tender when pierced with fork.

1 SERVING: Calories 150 (Calories from Fat 65); Fat 7g (Saturated 1g); Cholesterol 0mg; Sodium 140mg; Carbohydrates 22g (Dietary Fiber 2g); Protein 2g.

Roasted Rosemary-Onion Potatoes

Laurie Peterson
New Richmond, Wisconsin

Our daughter, Laurie Peterson, is a dedicated homemaker, wife, and mother with a very strong spirit that just seems to spread to everyone and everything she touches. Whether it is baking and frosting cut-out cookies for her son's kindergarten class or working on a project for her Sunday school committee, she gives

willingly of her time and talents without expecting anything in return—just the joy she receives from doing it.

She spends countless hours in her children's school and classrooms, assisting teachers with a variety of projects and hands-on help with children who need it. She is an adult leader for the gifted and talented program and works with the remedial reading program. She also is involved in education through her church as a devotional leader and substitute Sunday school teacher. She recently has volunteered to provide care, support, and counseling for a nine-year-old neighbor girl whose mother was killed in an auto accident last winter.

Three years ago, Laurie met her biggest challenge yet. At age thirty-two, with her children just ages two and five, she was diagnosed with breast cancer. With the same determination and positive attitude she exhibits in everything she does, she has fought this disease with courage and grace. She is now in her third year of remission.

Along with her busy schedule, she still finds the time to exercise several times a week. Laurie has four brothers and sisters who are all especially close and dear to her.

Although she continues to keep up her hectic pace with all of the things to which she has committed herself, her home, husband, and children continue to be her number one priority. Her credo is "Always live each day to its fullest."

Creamy Scalloped Potatoes

6 SERVINGS

Make it your way with either peeled or unpeeled potatoes. This creamy side is the perfect partner for pork chops.

6 medium boiling or baking
   potatoes (2 pounds)
3 tablespoons margarine or
   butter
1 small onion, finely chopped
   (1/4 cup)
3 tablespoons all-purpose flour
1 teaspoon salt
1/4 teaspoon pepper
2 1/2 cups milk
1 tablespoon margarine or
   butter

1. Heat oven to 350°. Grease bottom and side of 2-quart casserole with shortening.

2. Scrub potatoes; peel if desired. Cut into enough thin slices to measure about 4 cups.

3. Melt 3 tablespoons margarine in 2-quart saucepan over medium heat. Cook onion in margarine about 2 minutes, stirring occasionally, until tender. Stir in flour, salt and pepper. Cook, stirring constantly, until smooth and bubbly; remove from heat.

4. Stir in milk. Heat to boiling, stirring constantly. Boil and stir 1 minute.

5. Spread potatoes in casserole. Pour sauce over potatoes. Dot with 1 tablespoon margarine.

6. Cover and bake 50 minutes. Uncover and bake 1 hour to 1 hour 10 minutes longer or until potatoes are tender. Let stand 5 to 10 minutes before serving.

1 SERVING: Calories 240 (Calories from Fat 90); Fat 10g (Saturated 8g); Cholesterol 10mg; Sodium 5000mg; Carbohydrates 33g (Dietary Fiber 2g); Protein 6g.

Duchess Potatoes

These potatoes are as elegant as they are delicious—delicate pillows of baked, golden mashed potatoes. Think of this side dish the next time you are having a roast. And if company is coming, these beauties can be made ahead of time. Just pop them in the oven before serving.

12 medium potatoes (4 pounds), peeled

2/3 to 1 cup milk

1/2 cup margarine, butter or spread, softened

1/2 teaspoon salt

Dash of pepper

4 eggs, beaten

Margarine, butter or spread, melted

1. Cut potatoes into large pieces if desired. Heat 1 inch water (salted if desired) to boiling in Dutch oven. Add potatoes. Cover and heat to boiling; reduce heat. Cook whole potatoes 30 to 35 minutes, pieces 20 to 25 minutes, or until tender; drain. Shake pan gently over low heat to dry potatoes.

2. Heat oven to 425°. Grease cookie sheet.

3. Mash potatoes until no lumps remain. Beat in milk in small amounts (amount of milk needed to make potatoes smooth and fluffy depends on kind of potatoes). Add 1/2 cup margarine, the salt and pepper. Beat vigorously until potatoes are light and fluffy. Add eggs; beat until blended.

4. Drop potato mixture by 12 spoonfuls into mounds onto cookie sheet. Or place in decorating bag with star tip and form rosettes or pipe a border around meat or fish. Brush with melted margarine. Bake about 15 minutes or until light brown.

1 SERVING: Calories 240 (Calories from Fat 115); Fat 13g (Saturated 3g); Cholesterol 70mg; Sodium 260mg; Carbohydrates 28g (Dietary Fiber 2g); Protein 5g.

Say Cheese!

Don't some of those photographs in cookbooks and on food packages really make your mouth water? They don't just happen—a lot of work goes into each one! Betty Crocker has three kitchens designed especially for the preparation of food that will be immortalized on film. Betty has strict guidelines about these pictures—all the food is real! In order for the food to look its best in the photo, "stand-in" foods are used during the preparation process. When everything is ready, the actual food is freshly prepared and rushed into the studio, and the photo is snapped! What happens to the leftovers? Although some have to be discarded due to the excessive handling they endure, other leftovers are donated to local food banks.

Basil-Baked New Potatoes

Keep the skins on! The potato peel has lots of flavor and nutrients so don't remove them if you don't have to.

14 to 18 new potatoes (2 1/4 pounds)

1/4 cup finely chopped green onions (3 medium)

2 tablespoons chopped fresh or 2 teaspoons dried
 basil leaves

2 tablespoons olive or vegetable oil

1. Heat oven to 350°. Spray rectangular pan,
   13 x 9 x 2 inches, with nonstick cooking spray.

2. Place potatoes in pan. Sprinkle with onions and
   basil. Drizzle with oil; stir to coat.

3. Bake uncovered about 1 1/4 hours, stirring
   occasionally, until potato skins are crispy and
   potatoes are tender.

1 SERVING: Calories 185 (Calories from Fat 45); Fat 5g (Saturated 1g); Cholesterol 0mg; Sodium 10mg; Carbohydrates 35g (Dietary Fiber 3g); Protein 3g.

Farm-Fried Potatoes

Crispy on the outside, soft and flaky potato on the inside—these potatoes are hard to beat. Try using olive oil in place of the shortening for a deeper, richer flavored potato.

2 tablespoons shortening or vegetable oil

2 pounds potatoes (about 6 medium), thinly sliced
 (about 4 cups)

1 large onion, thinly sliced, if desired

1 1/2 teaspoons salt

Dash of pepper

2 tablespoons margarine or butter

1. Heat shortening in 10-inch skillet until melted.
   Layer one-third of the potatoes and onion in
   skillet; sprinkle with 1/2 teaspoon of the salt and
   dash of pepper. Repeat 2 times. Dot with margarine.

2. Cover and cook over medium heat 20 minutes.
   Uncover and cook, turning once, until potatoes
   are brown.

1 SERVING: Calories 300 (Calories from Fat 110); Fat 12g (Saturated 4g); Cholesterol 5mg; Sodium 1000mg; Carbohydrates 49g (Dietary Fiber 5g); Protein 5g.

Sandi Work
St. Louis, Missouri

I was born in 1942, six years after the first Betty Crocker took her place in my mother's kitchen. Mom had a true love for cooking, baking, and candy making and at a very early age started sharing that passion with me, her only daughter.

I am a busy person and involved with my family, my business, my horses, and the community. I have raised three sons of my own as well as two stepsons. I have four grandsons and two granddaughters of which one fondly calls me, "the cupcake and gingerbread house grandma!" My lovely mother is now greatly debilitated as the result of numerous strokes and is no longer able to bake and cook. I am passing her legacy on by teaching my grandchildren to enjoy cooking as much as Mother and I enjoyed cooking together all those years.

I do know, without a doubt, that Betty's cake mixes are my favorite and most often used product. Everyone in my family loves cake, especially me! With your cake mixes, I can make a wide variety of baked goods in addition to cakes. For example, I frequently use the mix for cookies, cupcakes, dumpcakes, cheesecakes, crumb cakes, bundt and pound cakes, fruitcakes, breads, even my holiday gingerbread houses with all of my grandchildren. I have used Betty Crocker products all my cooking years. I always have felt like I was providing my family with a distinctive, first-class meal that Betty Crocker recipes and products had provided for me.

Bountiful Twice-Baked Potatoes

8 SERVINGS

These potatoes can be ready when you are! Once made, you can refrigerate these potatoes for up to 24 hours; just increase the baking time to 30 minutes. You can freeze them too, then pop them in the oven, uncovered, for about 40 minutes.

4 large baking potatoes (8 to 10 ounces each)

1/4 to 1/2 cup milk

1/4 cup margarine or butter, softened

1/4 teaspoon salt

Dash of pepper

1 cup shredded Cheddar cheese (4 ounces)

1 tablespoon chopped fresh chives

1. Prepare and cook whole potatoes as directed.

2. Cut potatoes lengthwise in half; scoop out inside, leaving a thin shell. Mash potato in medium bowl until no lumps remain. Add milk in small amounts, beating after each addition (amount of milk needed to make potatoes smooth and fluffy depends on kind of potatoes used).

3. Add margarine, salt and pepper; beat vigorously until potato is light and fluffy. Stir in cheese and chives. Fill potato shells with mashed potato. Place on ungreased cookie sheet.

4. Heat oven to 400°.

5. Bake about 20 minutes or until hot.

1 SERVING: Calories 180 (Calories from Fat 100); Fat 11g (Saturated 4g); Cholesterol 15mg; Sodium 280mg; Carbohydrates 16g (Dietary Fiber 1g); Protein 5g.

Marbled Potatoes and Carrots

4 TO 5 SERVINGS

Comfort food at its tastiest—homemade mashed potatoes swirled with sweet cooked carrots flavored with dill weed.

2 medium potatoes (2/3 pound), peeled and cut into
    pieces

4 medium carrots, sliced (2 cups)

2 to 3 tablespoons milk

2 teaspoons margarine, butter or spread

1/4 teaspoon salt

2 to 3 tablespoons milk

1 teaspoon margarine, butter or spread

1/4 teaspoon dried dill weed

1. Heat 1 inch water (salted if desired) to boiling in 1-quart saucepan. Add potatoes. Cover and heat to boiling; reduce heat. Cook 20 to 25 minutes or until tender; drain. Shake pan gently over low heat to dry potatoes.

2. While potatoes are cooking, heat 1 inch water (salted if desired) to boiling in 1-quart saucepan. Add carrots. Cover and heat to boiling; reduce heat. Cook about 15 minutes or until very tender; drain.

3. Mash potatoes until no lumps remain. Beat in 2 to 3 tablespoons milk in small amounts. Add 2 tablespoons margarine and 1/4 teaspoon salt. Beat vigorously until potatoes are light and fluffy. Cover to keep warm.

4. Mash carrots until no lumps remain. Beat in 2 to 3 tablespoons milk in small amounts. Beat in 1 teaspoon margarine and the dill weed.

5. Spoon potato mixture into half of small serving bowl; spoon carrot mixture into other half. Pull a small rubber spatula through mixtures to create a marbled design.

1 SERVING: Calories 105 (Calories from Fat 25); Fat 3g (Saturated 1g); Cholesterol 2mg; Sodium 200mg; Carbohydrates 20g (Dietary Fiber 3g); Protein 2g.

Marbled Potatoes and Carrots

Marie Gilbert
London, Ontario

Marie's focus is her family and community. She is the mother of three daughters, Susan, Pat, and Kate, grandmother of two granddaughters, and wife of Murray Gilbert.

Marie is a very community-oriented person. She gets involved in her community of Hyde Park and her church and supports local business. Marie has always been concerned about her environment and about conserving our natural resources. She has done clean up in Hyde Park area for many years. She supports her local church with enthusiasm and dedication. Presently, she is president of the Hyde Park United Church Women's Group. She has been a volunteer at University Hospital in London, Ontario, for eighteen years. She has collected for the Cancer Society for many years and is a past member of the Women's Institute. Marie is always reliable, supportive, and full of energy.

Marie finds baking relaxing and enjoyable and enjoys good food, especially desserts. She is always available to assist with an unexpected funeral luncheon, and she assists with planning annual services dinners, strawberry teas, barbecues, Christmas bazaar's, and was a model for our local fashion show. Marie's favorite Betty Crocker product is Betty Crocker butter pecan cake mix topped with maple fudge icing. Marie has been involved with the publishing of three community cookbooks.

Marie Gilbert's energy, enthusiasm, and cheerful disposition are truly contagious, and she is a pillar of her community.

Cranberry-Raspberry Salad

The tang of the cranberry and the fruity coolness of the lemon gelatin makes this salad a hit at any meal. We also think it will become a favorite of yours on the Thanksgiving table.

2 packages (12 ounces each) cranberry-orange sauce

1 package (12 ounces) cranberry-raspberry sauce

1 package (6 ounces) lemon gelatin

2 cups boiling water

1. Lightly oil 6 1/2-cup ring mold.

2. Mix cranberry sauces together in large bowl. Dissolve gelatin in boiling water; stir into cranberry sauces. Pour into mold. Cover and refrigerate overnight.

3. Unmold salad. Garnish with watercress and cranberries if desired.

1 SERVING: Calories 190 (Calories from Fat 0); Fat 0g (Saturated 0g); Cholesterol 0mg; Sodium 60mg; Carbohydrates 49g (Dietary Fiber 2g); Protein 1g.

Betty's Gadgets

"What's Betty's name doing on my potato peeler? Wait a minute, Betty's name is on a lot of stuff in my kitchen!" Betty Crocker has been such a trusted expert in all matters of the kitchen that her name has been applied to a wide variety of products, from cheese slicers to recipe cards and note pads, to bakeware and even to small kitchen appliances. It all began in 1946 when her name was applied to the Tru-Heat iron, which was actually manufactured by General Mills. The company eventually expanded the line to about seven appliances before discontinuing its manufacturing venture in 1954. But Betty's name continues to be licensed today. Of course, her name doesn't go on a product until it has been thoroughly tested by experts in the Betty Crocker Kitchens and declared worthy of such an honor.

Classic Creamy Potato Salad

10 SERVINGS

Create a picnic anywhere, anytime, with this creamy potato salad. For a summery flavor and a cool crunch, we stir in 1/2 cup each thinly sliced radishes, chopped cucumber and chopped bell pepper.

6 medium boiling potatoes (2 pounds)

1 1/2 cups mayonnaise or salad dressing

1 tablespoon vinegar

1 tablespoon mustard

1 teaspoon salt

1/4 teaspoon pepper

2 medium stalks celery, chopped (about 1 cup)

1 medium onion, chopped (about 1/2 cup)

4 hard-cooked eggs, chopped

1. Heat 1 inch water (salted, if desired) to boiling. Add potatoes. Cover and heat to boiling; reduce heat to low. Boil gently 30 to 35 minutes or until potatoes are tender; cool slightly. Cut into cubes (about 6 cups).

2. Mix mayonnaise, vinegar, mustard, salt and pepper in large glass or plastic bowl. Add potatoes, celery and onion; toss. Stir in eggs. Cover and refrigerate at least 4 hours. Cover and refrigerate any remaining salad.

1 SERVING: Calories 350 (Calories from Fat 250); Fat 28g (Saturated 5g); Cholesterol 105mg; Sodium 480mg; Carbohydrates 21g (Dietary Fiber 2g); Protein 5g.

Cold Cucumber Salad

12 SERVINGS

When the temperature is too hot to handle, try whipping up this cool salad. Even better, you can make it a day ahead of time. This is the perfect side for deli subs or anything hot off the grill.

1/2 cup sugar

1/3 cup water

1 teaspoon white pepper

1/2 teaspoon salt

1 1/2 cups cider vinegar

4 large cucumbers, peeled and thinly sliced

1/4 cup chopped fresh parsley

1. Mix sugar, water, white pepper and salt in medium saucepan. Heat mixture over medium-high heat to boiling and boil until sugar is dissolved; remove from heat and cool. Stir in vinegar.

2. Pour mixture over cucumber slices; sprinkle with parsley. Cover and refrigerate until ready to serve.

1 SERVING: Calories 50 (Calories from Fat 0); Fat 0g (Saturated 0g); Cholesterol 0mg; Sodium 100mg; Carbohydrates 13g (Dietary Fiber 1g); Protein 1g.

Country Potato Salad

Marinating the potatoes in the dressing beforehand makes this a flavorful potato salad and one of the most requested favorites. Instead of the Cooked Salad Dressing, 1 cup of mayonnaise or salad dressing can be mixed in.

6 medium potatoes (about 2 pounds)

1/4 cup Italian dressing

Cooked Salad Dressing (below) or 1 cup mayonnaise

2 medium stalks celery, sliced (about 1 cup)

1 medium cucumber, chopped (about 1 cup)

1 large onion, chopped (about 3/4 cup)

6 radishes, thinly sliced (about 1/2 cup)

4 hard-cooked eggs, chopped

1. Heat 1 inch water (salted if desired) to boiling. Add potatoes. Cover and heat to boiling; reduce heat. Cook until tender, 30 to 35 minutes. Drain and cool slightly.

2. Peel potatoes; cut into cubes (about 6 cups). Toss warm potatoes with Italian dressing in 4-quart glass or plastic bowl. Cover and refrigerate at least 4 hours. Prepare Cooked Salad Dressing.

3. Add celery, cucumber, onion, radishes and eggs to potatoes. Pour Cooked Salad Dressing over top; toss. Refrigerate until chilled. Immediately refrigerate any remaining salad.

COOKED SALAD DRESSING

2 tablespoons all-purpose flour

1 tablespoon sugar

1 teaspoon dry mustard

3/4 teaspoon salt

1/4 teaspoon pepper

1 egg yolk, slightly beaten

3/4 cup milk

2 tablespoons vinegar

1 tablespoon margarine or butter

1. Mix flour, sugar, mustard, salt and pepper in 1-quart saucepan. Mix egg yolk and milk; slowly stir into flour mixture. Cook over medium heat, stirring constantly, until mixture thickens and boils. Boil and stir 1 minute; remove from heat.

2. Stir in vinegar and margarine. Place plastic wrap directly on surface; refrigerate until cool, at least 1 hour.

1 SERVING: Calories 290 (Calories from Fat 200); Fat 22g (Saturated 4g); Cholesterol 100mg; Sodium 210mg; Carbohydrates 20g (Dietary Fiber 2g); Protein 5g.

Country Potato Salad, Heartland Three-Bean Salad (page 269)

Emily Drake

West Jordan, Utah

I am eighty-three years old and I still make bread, rolls, cakes, cookies, and pastries, besides cooking for my husband. I do enjoy the Betty Crocker cake, muffin, cookie, and frosting mixes. I love to share all these goodies with my family, neighbors, and friends and at church functions. My husband and I live on a

ten-acre farm and have five children, all married, with twenty-nine grandchildren and thirty-seven great grandchildren.

Ever since I was small child, I have always loved to cook and bake. My mother taught my four sisters and me how to cook and be good homemakers. I have made cake, cookies, pastries, and candy since I was six years old.

I have been a 4-H supervisor and leader for fifty-nine years. I have taught many, many boys and girls to cook, sew, finish furniture, garden, preserve food, and raise animals. These children have won countless blue ribbons and medals with their 4-H projects. Through the 4-H program, my clubs have completed numerous community projects, which include planting trees, shrubs, and flowers in the city park and cemetery, painting fences in the city park, and raising funds to build a drinking fountain.

I love to share my vegetables from my garden with my family, friends, and neighbors, and I give away the eggs from my fifteen laying hens so others may have fresh eggs to use in their baking with Betty Crocker. My favorite product is the Betty Crocker German chocolate cake mix. I have made German chocolate cakes for birthdays, funerals, family parties, church activities, and I still make them for Sunday dinners.

I was named Citizen of the Year in West Jordan, and I was also named Vital Volunteer for dedicated service to youth in Salt Lake County. I have served in church organizations for most of my life. I have been involved in the children, youth, and adult programs, being the president many times. Through the years, all these organizations have enjoyed the desserts I have made using Betty Crocker mixes and recipes.

Seven-Layer Salad

6 SERVINGS

This salad is a little mix of everything: crunchy, sweet, smoky and tangy. For less fat and fewer calories but still great flavor, use turkey bacon and low-fat or non-fat salad dressing.

6 cups bite-size pieces mixed
    salad greens

2 medium stalks celery, thinly
    sliced (1 cup)

1 cup thinly sliced radishes

1/2 cup sliced green onions
    (5 medium)

12 slices bacon, crisply cooked
    and crumbled

1 package (10 ounce) frozen
    green peas, thawed

1 1/2 cups mayonnaise or salad
    dressing

1/2 cup grated Parmesan cheese
    or shredded Cheddar cheese
    (2 ounces)

1. Place salad greens in large glass bowl. Layer celery, radishes, onions, bacon and peas on salad greens.

2. Spread mayonnaise over peas, covering top completely and sealing to edge of bowl. Sprinkle with cheese. Cover and refrigerate at least 2 hours to blend flavors but no longer than 12 hours. Toss before serving if desired. Cover and refrigerate any remaining salad.

1 SERVING: Calories 550 (Calories from Fat 480); Fat 53g (Saturated 10g); Cholesterol 50mg; Sodium 720mg; Carbohydrates 11g (Dietary Fiber 3g); Protein 10g.

Mandarin Salad

Enjoy one of our most requested salads, especially by men. The nutty almonds and the sweet mandarin slices blend perfectly together in this salad. Even better, add some grilled chicken pieces or cooked shrimp.

1/4 cup sliced almonds

1 tablespoon plus 1 teaspoon sugar

Sweet-Sour Dressing (below)

1/2 small head lettuce, torn into bite-size pieces (3 cups)

1/2 bunch romaine, torn into bite-size pieces (3 cups)

2 medium stalks celery, chopped (1 cup)

2 tablespoons thinly sliced green onions

1 can (11 ounces) mandarin orange segments, drained

1. Cook almonds and sugar in 1-quart saucepan over low heat, stirring constantly, until sugar is melted and almonds are coated; cool and break apart.

2. Prepare Sweet-Sour Dressing.

3. Toss almonds, dressing and remaining ingredients.

SWEET-SOUR DRESSING

1/4 cup vegetable oil

2 tablespoons sugar

2 tablespoons white vinegar

1 tablespoon chopped fresh parsley

1/2 teaspoon salt

Dash of pepper

Dash of red pepper sauce

Shake all ingredients in tightly covered container. Refrigerate until serving.

1 SERVING: Calories 165 (Calories from Fat 100); Fat 11g (Saturated 2g); Cholesterol 0mg; Sodium 200mg; Carbohydrates 16g (Dietary Fiber 1g); Protein 1g.

Antipasto Salad

Have fun choosing different sausages, cheese, olives and peppers for this salad. Look for different varieties at a neighborhood Italian market, specialty store or deli.

1/4 cup Italian olives

8 ounces fresh mozzarella cheese, drained and cubed

4 ounces sliced Italian salami

4 ounces sliced Italian capicolla, prosciutto or fully cooked smoked Virginia ham

4 ounces marinated Italian peppers

1 jar (8 ounces) marinated mushrooms, drained

1/4 cup chopped fresh basil leaves

Vinaigrette (below)

Arrange all ingredients except basil on 6 salad plates. Sprinkle with fresh basil. Serve with Vinaigrette.

VINAIGRETTE

1/3 cup olive oil

3 tablespoons red wine vinegar

1 clove garlic, crushed

Mix all ingredients.

1 SERVING: Calories 345 (Calories from Fat 245); Fat 27g (Saturated 9g); Cholesterol 45mg; Sodium 1080mg; Carbohydrates 6g (Dietary Fiber 1g); Protein 20g.

Old-Fashioned Coleslaw

8 SERVINGS

Coleslaw is not an American invention. It is thought to have been brought to this country by either German or Dutch immigrants. The Dutch called their salad koolsla *(cabbage salad). Our recipe blends sweet-and-tangy flavor with the richness of sour cream. If you prefer, you can leave out the carrot and bell pepper and toss in a chopped tart apple, and 1/4 cup crumbled blue cheese for an apple-cheese slaw.*

3 tablespoons sugar

2 tablespoons all-purpose flour

1 teaspoon dry mustard

1/2 teaspoon salt

1/8 teaspoon ground red pepper (cayenne)

1 egg

3/4 cup water

1/4 cup lemon juice

1 tablespoon margarine or butter

1/4 cup sour cream

1 pound green cabbage, shredded or finely chopped
(about 6 cups)

1 medium carrot, shredded (about 1 cup)

1 small bell pepper, finely chopped (about 1/2 cup)

1. Mix sugar, flour, mustard, salt and red pepper in heavy 1-quart saucepan; beat in egg. Stir in water and lemon juice gradually until well blended. Cook over low heat 13 to 15 minutes, stirring constantly, until thick and smooth; remove from heat.

2. Stir in margarine until melted. Place plastic wrap directly on surface of dressing; refrigerate about 2 hours or until cool. Stir in sour cream.

3. Mix dressing, cabbage, carrot and bell pepper; toss well. Refrigerate at least 1 hour but no longer than 24 hours.

1 SERVING: Calories 85 (Calories from Fat 35); Fat 4g (Saturated 1g); Cholesterol 30mg; Sodium 190mg; Carbohydrates 12g (Dietary Fiber 2g); Protein 2g.

Linda Smith
Shorewood, Illinois

There's been a standing joke in my family for years that my mother really is Betty Crocker in disguise! My mom doesn't just enjoy cooking and baking; to her there are few pleasures in life more wonderful than having family and friends together to delight in one of her feasts.

Some of my favorite memories of my youth involve the hours my mother spent teaching my friends and me to bake. Before the Christmas season, we would bake breads, cookies, and coffee cakes and make candies, all the while singing round after round of Christmas carols.

Mom's love of cooking, coupled with her strong desire to help the underprivileged, led her to the Nutri Net Agency in Independence, Missouri. There my mom became certified to teach balanced food preparation to low-income families and single parents. Since her certification, she has taught food preparation to single mothers at Joliet (Illinois) Junior College, children through the Salvation Army programs, and assisted in a course for low-income families in Bolingbrook, Illinois.

In addition to being an elder in our church, she has served as the pastor for the past five years. My mom has held elected positions at the district level and has participated in the World Conference as a delegate for many years.

Although she works forty hours a week and spends many, many more in her community service projects, she always has time to give to her family and friends. My mom is also a wonderful role model to me as a wife. Married thirty-one years, my mom and dad believe it's important to have time off just for themselves. This past summer, my parents traveled on their Goldwing motorcycle from the Atlantic coast to the Pacific.

I'd like to say just how very proud I am of my mother. She will always be a winner to me. I am thankful for having had this opportunity to say, "I am proud of you, and I thank God for blessing me with a mother like you."

Heartland Three-Bean Salad

Three-bean salads are picnic favorites in the heartland. But not everyone agrees on which three beans to include in this hearty salad. You can count on finding green beans and wax beans in most recipes. While many recipes—including ours—use kidney beans, there are some that call for lima beans instead. Of course, you can add lima beans to this recipe and enjoy a four-bean salad!

1 can (16 ounces) cut green
  beans, drained

1 can (16 ounces) cut wax beans,
  drained

1 can (15 ounces) kidney beans,
  drained

1 cup thinly sliced onion rings,
  cut in half

1 small bell pepper, finely
  chopped (about 1/2 cup)

2 tablespoons chopped fresh
  parsley

2/3 cup vinegar

1/2 cup sugar

1/3 cup vegetable oil

1/2 teaspoon pepper

1/2 teaspoon salt

2 slices bacon, crisply cooked
  and crumbled

1. Mix beans, onion, bell pepper and parsley in 3-quart bowl.

2. Mix remaining ingredients in 1 1/2-quart saucepan. Heat vinegar mixture to boiling, stirring occasionally. Pour over beans; stir.

3. Cover and refrigerate, stirring occasionally, at least 3 hours or until chilled. Just before serving, sprinkle with bacon.

1 SERVING: Calories 160 (Calories from Fat 65); Fat 7g (Saturated 1g); Cholesterol 0mg; Sodium 400mg; Carbohydrates 23g (Dietary Fiber 4g); Protein 5g.

Sweet-Sour Coleslaw

6 SERVINGS

The Pennsylvania Dutch, originally from southern Germany, use a boiled sweet-sour dressing on both coleslaw and potato salad to give them a nice, tangy flavor that goes with the crunch of the cabbage. The secret to their classic boiled dressing was to cook the dressing quickly and not let the eggs clump. For the best flavor, this coleslaw should be covered and refrigerated for 2 to 4 hours before serving.

1 egg

1/4 cup sugar

1/4 cup vinegar

2 tablespoons water

2 tablespoons margarine or butter

1 teaspoon salt

1/2 teaspoon dry mustard

1 pound green cabbage, finely shredded or chopped (about 4 cups)

1 small bell pepper, chopped (about 1/2 cup)

1. Beat egg until thick and lemon-colored.

2. Heat sugar, vinegar, water, margarine, salt and mustard to boiling, stirring constantly. Gradually stir at least half of the hot mixture into egg; then stir into hot mixture in saucepan.

3. Cook over low heat, stirring constantly, until thickened, about 5 minutes. Pour over cabbage and bell pepper; toss.

1 SERVING: Calories 80 (Calories from Fat 35); Fat 4g (Saturated 1g); Cholesterol 2mg; Sodium 350mg; Carbohydrates 10g (Dietary Fiber 1g); Protein 2g.

Classic Crunchy Coleslaw

8 SERVINGS

Our mayonnaise and sour cream–based recipe for coleslaw is creamy, crunchy and not too sweet. The coleslaw keeps well for several days in the refrigerator; just keep it tightly covered.

1/2 cup sour cream or plain yogurt

1/4 cup mayonnaise or salad dressing

1 teaspoon sugar

1/2 teaspoon dry mustard

1/2 teaspoon seasoned salt

1/8 teaspoon pepper

1 pound green cabbage, finely shredded or chopped (about 4 cups)

1 small onion, chopped (about 1/4 cup)

Paprika, if desired

Dill weed, if desired

Mix sour cream, mayonnaise, sugar, mustard, seasoned salt and pepper; toss with cabbage and onion. Sprinkle with paprika or dried dill weed, if desired.

1 SERVING: Calories 125 (Calories from Fat 100); Fat 11g (Saturated 3g); Cholesterol 20mg; Sodium 180mg; Carbohydrates 6g (Dietary Fiber 2g); Protein 2g.

Spinach Dip

ABOUT 4 1/2 CUPS DIP

Often, this dip is served in the hollowed-out shell of a 1-pound round bread loaf. Cut to tear the soft, inside part of the bread into pieces and use for dipping. When the dip is gone, you can enjoy eating the shell!

2 packages (10 ounces each) frozen chopped spinach, thawed

1 can (8 ounces) water chestnuts, drained and finely chopped

1 cup sour cream

1 cup plain yogurt

1 cup finely chopped green onions (9 medium)

2 teaspoons chopped fresh or 1/2 teaspoon dried tarragon leaves

1/2 teaspoon salt

1/2 teaspoon ground mustard (dry)

1/4 teaspoon pepper

1 clove garlic, crushed

Rye crackers, rice crackers or raw vegetables for dipping, if desired

1. Squeeze excess moisture from spinach until it is dry. Mix spinach with remaining ingredients except crackers in glass or plastic bowl.

2. Cover and refrigerate 1 hour to blend flavors. Serve with crackers.

1 TABLESPOON: Calories 15 (Calories from Fat 10); Fat 1g (Saturated 0g); Cholesterol 5mg; Sodium 25mg; Carbohydrates 1g (Dietary Fiber 0g); Protein 0g.

Spinach Dip

Jeanne Megel
Colorado Springs, Colorado

Jeanne is a wonderful wife (seventeen years) and mother (ten years), but her love and care extend well beyond the family into the community in many ways. Since Jeanne has multiple sclerosis, many things that are normal, everyday events for the rest of us may be impossible for her. So she invents ways to handle them and remain as self-sufficient as possible.

Jeanne's love for cooking was obvious from the start. But one of her crowning achievements is the 550 dozen cookies she baked, in one week, for the cadets studying for final exams at the United States Air Force Academy and for the residents at the Red Cross homeless shelter.

One of Jeanne's greatest "sacrifices" was to take up scuba diving for me. Even though she was so terrified of water, she would not let go of the side of the pool. She did so well, she has also assisted in scuba classes and does particularly well with students who are afraid of the water.

Jeanne is a master gardener. She is a retired registered nurse (the multiple sclerosis forced a permanent, total disability retirement) and has been a Red Cross first-aid and CPR instructor as well as a much requested spokesperson for our United Way campaigns. She also does educational presentations in the elementary schools pertaining to plants, the ocean, and preserving the reefs. Jeanne also does special educational events for our adopted Chinese daughter's class, including Chinese New Year and Moon Festival parties complete with lo mein and other treats.

Hummus

ABOUT 2 CUPS DIP

This is the most famous of all Middle Eastern appetizers! Serve as a dip, a spread, a sandwich filling or a salad.

1 can (15 to 16 ounces)
    garbanzo beans, drained and
    liquid reserved

1/2 cup sesame seeds

1 clove garlic, cut in half

3 tablespoons lemon juice

1 teaspoon salt

Chopped fresh parsley

Pita bread wedges, crackers or
    raw vegetables for dipping, if
    desired

1. Place reserved bean liquid, the sesame seeds and garlic in blender or food processor. Cover and blend on high speed until mixed.

2. Add beans, lemon juice and salt. Cover and blend on high speed, stopping blender occasionally to scrape sides if necessary, until uniform consistency.

3. Spoon dip into serving dish. Garnish with parsley. Serve with pita bread wedges, crackers or raw vegetables.

1 TABLESPOON: Calories 25 (Calories from Fat 10); Fat 1g (Saturated 0g); Cholesterol 0mg; Sodium 90mg; Carbohydrates 3g (Dietary Fiber 0g); Protein 1g.

Corn and Pepper Cakes

6 SERVINGS

If you don't have fresh corn on hand, one 10-ounce package of frozen whole-kernel corn, cooked, can be substituted. That makes it easy to enjoy these yummy cakes all year long.

4 medium ears corn

1/2 cup all-purpose flour

1/4 cup milk

1 tablespoon sugar

1/2 teaspoon salt

1/8 teaspoon pepper

2 egg yolks

1 small bell pepper, finely chopped (about 1/2 cup)

2 egg whites

1/2 cup vegetable oil

1. Cut enough kernels from corn to measure 2 cups (scrape ears with knife to extract all pulp and milk). Beat flour, milk, sugar, salt, pepper and egg yolks in medium bowl. Stir in corn and bell pepper. Beat egg whites until stiff and glossy. Fold corn mixture into egg whites.

2. Heat oil in 10-inch skillet. Drop corn mixture by tablespoonfuls into hot oil. Fry about 30 seconds on each side or until golden brown. Serve with sour cream if desired.

1 SERVING: Calories 220 (Calories from Fat 100); Fat 11g (Saturated 2g); Cholesterol 70mg; Sodium 230mg; Carbohydrates 22g (Dietary Fiber 2g); Protein 5g.

Hoppin' Johns

6 SERVINGS

In South Carolina and neighboring states, it just wouldn't be a proper New Year's Day without a serving of Hoppin' Johns. This southern favorite is said to bring good luck for the coming year. Some believe Hoppin' Johns got its name because hungry children used to hop impatiently around the table as they waited for supper; others contend that it was named after the custom of inviting a guest to eat by saying, "Hop in, John."

1/2 pound dried black-eyed peas (about 1 cup)

3 1/2 cups water

1/4 pound slab bacon, lean salt pork or smoked pork

1 onion, sliced

1/4 to 1/2 teaspoon very finely chopped fresh hot chili or 1/8 to 1/4 teaspoon crushed red pepper

1/2 cup uncooked regular long grain rice

1 teaspoon salt

Pepper

1. Heat peas and water to boiling in 2-quart saucepan; boil 2 minutes. Remove from heat; cover and let stand 1 hour.

2. Cut bacon into 8 pieces. Stir bacon, onion and hot chili pepper into peas. Heat to boiling; reduce heat. Cover and simmer until peas are tender, 1 to 1 1/2 hours.

3. Stir in rice, salt and pepper. Cover and simmer, stirring occasionally, until rice is tender, about 25 minutes. Stir in additional water, if necessary, to cook rice.

1 SERVING: Calories 130 (Calories from Fat 25); Fat 3g (Saturated 1g); Cholesterol 5mg; Sodium 480mg; Carbohydrates 23g (Dietary Fiber 3g); Protein 6g.

Cheesy Grits

Hominy is corn that has its hulls removed, so it cooks up soft with a little texture. You will find it in the hot cereal aisle, near the oatmeal. For a cheesier flavor, select a sharp Cheddar instead of mild.

2 cups milk

2 cups water

1 teaspoon salt

1/4 teaspoon pepper

1 cup hominy quick grits

1 1/2 cups shredded Cheddar cheese (6 ounces)

1/4 cup sliced green onions

2 eggs, slightly beaten

1 tablespoon margarine or butter

1/4 teaspoon paprika

1. Heat oven to 350°. Grease 1 1/2-quart casserole.

2. Heat milk, water, salt and pepper to boiling in 2-quart saucepan. Gradually add grits, stirring constantly; reduce heat. Simmer uncovered, stirring frequently, until thick, about 5 minutes. Stir in cheese and onions. Stir 1 cup of the hot mixture into eggs; stir egg mixture into remaining hot mixture in saucepan.

3. Pour hot mixture into casserole. Dot with margarine; sprinkle with paprika. Bake uncovered until set, 35 to 40 minutes. Let stand 10 minutes.

1 SERVING: Calories 220 (Calories from Fat 100); Fat 11g (Saturated 6g); Cholesterol 80mg; Sodium 490mg; Carbohydrates 19g (Dietary Fiber 0g); Protein 11g.

Hush Puppies

Southern-Fried Catfish (page 202) and hush puppies are a great combination. Use a frying thermometer to make sure the oil is the right temperature so your pups are golden and light.

Vegetable oil

1 1/2 cups cornmeal

1/2 cup all-purpose flour

1/4 cup shortening

1 cup milk

2 tablespoons finely chopped onion

2 teaspoons baking powder

1 teaspoon sugar

1 teaspoon salt

1/2 teaspoon baking soda

1/4 to 1/2 teaspoon ground red pepper (cayenne)

1 egg

1. Heat oil (1 inch) in Dutch oven to 375°.

2. Mix remaining ingredients. Drop by teaspoonfuls into hot oil. Fry, turning once, until golden brown, about 1 minute; drain.

1 HUSH PUPPY: Calories 50 (Calories from Fat 25); Fat 3g (Saturated 1g); Cholesterol 5mg; Sodium 85mg; Carbohydrates 5g (Dietary Fiber 0g); Protein 1g.

Dawn Nemitz

Minooka, Illinois

SPIRIT OF BETTY CROCKER CONTEST
Winner

For my wife, cooking and baking are a complete labor of love. Dawn has a gift that can transform a typical meal into an extraspecial dinner, and the more the better! Some people cringe when guests need to be fed—Dawn thrives on it! No one ever left our home hungry. Ask Dawn to attend a party, and the first thing she wants to know is "What can I make?"

Dawn has an energy that people want to be around, from her youngest niece to her eighty-two-year-old father-in-law. She enjoys having fun and she wants others to have fun, too. Family and friends hold a very special place in the heart of Dawn Nemitz.

To work full time, take care of two boys (ages nine and three), keep house and home in order, and still have time for her husband is way beyond the call of duty. She gives freely of her time and talents and expects nothing in return.

Dawn has unselfishly volunteered her time for many causes. She has been a volunteer fund-raiser for United Cerebral Palsy, as well as a board member for the friends of United Cerebral Palsy. Dawn is a regular donor to the Heartland Blood Center and has helped raise money for Misericordia Homes (homes for developmentally disabled children). When the First Presbyterian Church wanted a cake walk for the kid's Fun Fair—Dawn baked, frosted, and delivered two dozen cakes, plus cupcakes and cookies. Dawn Nemitz is very much involved with bettering the lives of others.

Spanish Rice

6 SERVINGS

Looking for a flavor fiesta? Instead of regular tomato sauce, add even more excitement to your rice by using an herbed or other specially flavored tomato sauce.

2 tablespoons vegetable oil

1 cup uncooked regular long
    grain rice

1 medium onion, chopped
    (1/2 cup)

2 1/2 cups water

1 1/2 teaspoons salt

3/4 teaspoon chili powder

1/8 teaspoon garlic powder

1 small green bell pepper,
    chopped (1/2 cup)

1 can (8 ounces) tomato sauce

1. Heat oil in 10-inch skillet over medium heat. Cook rice and onion in oil about 5 minutes, stirring frequently, until rice is golden brown and onion is tender.

2. Stir in remaining ingredients. Heat to boiling; reduce heat to low. Cover and simmer about 30 minutes, stirring occasionally, until rice is tender.

1 SERVING: Calories 180 (Calories from Fat 45); Fat 5g (Saturated 1g); Cholesterol 0mg; Sodium 770mg; Carbohydrates 32g (Dietary Fiber 1g); Protein 3g.

Mary Lou Weiner
Meridian, Idaho

Mary Lou is a registered dietitian who has spent the majority of her professional life in the field of maternal, child and infant nutrition. Never have we worked with anyone who went the second and third mile so consistently for every one of her clients. When an infant had to be switched to formula, because finances forced the mom back to work, Mary Lou would be working after hours to find a formula the infant could tolerate. When there was an infant who could tolerate only one formula and the formula was being reformulated, Mary Lou would call every store in the valley to save the cans for her until the mom could come collect them.

Mary Lou runs an ecumenical soup kitchen and can turn out low-cost healthful menus revolving around any products or produce donated to this soup kitchen. She was also on the board of Turning Point, a group home for families and children, which shelters them until they can obtain permanent housing. Mary Lou is an ordained deacon in her church. She is very active in the spiritual care of the parishioners. When an acquaintance was jailed, Mary Lou rearranged her lunch schedule so she could offer spiritual comfort. She went beyond the listening ear, she carted loads of laundry home and provided soap, soup packets, etc.

At her most recent job with the local Veterans' Hospital, Mary Lou discovered there were no recipes for low-protein desserts. So Mary Lou set about to create recipes so the veterans on low-protein diets could enjoy one dessert a week. Mary Lou's favorite Betty Crocker product is angel food cake mix. She likes it because it is low-fat and so versatile.

Cranberry–Wild Rice Bake

8 SERVINGS

Ruby red dried cranberries enhance this robust rice dish that complements pork, turkey or game. It's also a nice change from, or addition to, Thanksgiving stuffing.

1 cup uncooked wild rice

2 1/2 cups water

1 tablespoon margarine or
   butter

1 medium onion, chopped
   (1/2 cup)

3 ounces mushrooms, sliced
   (1 cup)

2 1/2 cups chicken broth, heated

1/4 teaspoon salt

2 cloves garlic, finely chopped

1 cup dried cranberries

1. Heat oven to 350°. Grease square baking dish, 8 x 8 x 2 inches, with shortening.

2. Place wild rice in wire strainer. Run cold water through rice, lifting rice with fingers to clean thoroughly. Heat rice and water to boiling in 2-quart saucepan, stirring occasionally; reduce heat to low. Cover and simmer 30 minutes; drain.

3. Melt margarine in 10-inch skillet over medium heat. Cook onion and mushrooms in margarine, stirring occasionally, until onion is tender.

4. Combine rice and onion mixture in baking dish. Mix broth, salt and garlic; pour over rice mixture.

5. Cover and bake 1 1/4 hours. Stir in cranberries. Cover and bake 15 to 20 minutes longer or until liquid is absorbed.

1 SERVING: Calories 120 (Calories from Fat 20); Fat 2g (Saturated 0g); Cholesterol 0mg; Sodium 85mg; Carbohydrates 24g (Dietary Fiber 2g); Protein 4g.

Oven Hash Browns

6 SERVINGS

Hot sauce or salsa is a nice change from ketchup when serving these crisp, brown potatoes. For a real treat, sprinkle some sharp cheddar cheese over the potatoes after removing them from the oven, or top them with a dollop of sour cream.

2 pounds baking potatoes (about 5 medium), peeled and shredded

1/2 cup finely chopped onion

1 teaspoon salt

1/2 teaspoon pepper

2 tablespoons margarine or butter, melted

2 tablespoons vegetable oil

1. Heat oven to 400°.

2. Toss potatoes with onion, salt and pepper in large bowl. Pour margarine and oil into rectangular pan, 13 x 9 x 2 inches; add potato mixture. Bake 20 to 25 minutes, turning once, until golden brown.

1 SERVING: Calories 160 (Calories from Fat 70); Fat 8g (Saturated 1g); Cholesterol 0mg; Sodium 450mg; Carbohydrates 22g (Dietary Fiber 2g); Protein 2g.

Sausage-Cheese Balls

ABOUT 8 1/2 DOZEN

Searching for an appetizer that everyone will flip over? Look no further! This is one of our most requested Bisquick recipe. No only are these easy to whip up, they are a big crowd pleaser, too!

3 cups Bisquick Original or Reduced Fat baking mix

1 pound bulk pork sausage

4 cups shredded Cheddar cheese (16 ounces)

1/2 cup grated Parmesan cheese

1/2 teaspoon dried rosemary leaves

1/2 teaspoon parsley flakes

1. Heat oven to 350°. Lightly grease jelly roll pan, 15 1/2 x 10 1/2 x 1 inch.

2. Mix all ingredients thoroughly. Shape mixture into 1-inch balls. Place in pan.

3. Bake 20 to 25 minutes or until brown. Immediately remove from pan. Serve warm with store-bought sweet-and-sour sauce if desired.

1 APPETIZER: Calories 45 (Calories from Fat 25); Fat 3g (Saturated 2g); Cholesterol 5mg; Sodium 110mg; Carbohydrates 2g (Dietary Fiber 0g); Protein 2g.

Sausage-Cheese Balls

Waiyee Kennedy
Utica, New York

I am thirty-three years of age and of Chinese descent, having been born in Hong Kong. I have been in this country for twenty-five years and have learned many different cooking techniques from the different cultures I have encountered. My parents own a Chinese-Polynesian restaurant, and I have learned many wonderful lessons from them. I absolutely love to bake and cook; but baking is my specialty. I do not need a special reason or holiday to entice me to bake or cook, even though there is just my husband and I to cook for regularly.

My parish is always looking for donations of food to give to area refugees and the less fortunate. So on Wednesdays I make sandwiches and bake a variety of goodies to drop off at the church. I also volunteer as much of my time as I can to Hospice Care, Inc. I really enjoy doing this because it gives those terminally ill and unfortunate ones hope that there is a way to help them in their time of need. I work in a law office in Clinton, New York. After my day job, I go to my parents' restaurant to help them by waitressing. I often bake goodies for our customers, not to sell, but for them to try and also to show our appreciation for their patronage.

With my busy schedule, I often do not get to bake or cook until the late hours of the night. I usually start baking around 10:00 or 11:00 P.M. and don't finish until 1:00 A.M. I don't mind because it helps me unwind, and most of all, I enjoy it immensely! I cannot begin to tell you how much I have enjoyed all the Betty Crocker cookbooks I have. Every Betty Crocker recipe I tried has been my favorite. To choose one over the others would not be fair, because I have not found one I haven't enjoyed yet!

Chicken Pot Stickers

Legend has it that pot stickers, or pan-fried dumplings, were invented when a Chinese cook who was making boiled dumplings forgot to check them. The water in the dumpling pot had evaporated, leaving the dumpling bottoms fried to a crusty brown. The cook decided to serve them anyway, and they were a big success.

1 1/2 pounds ground chicken

1/2 cup shredded green cabbage

1/3 cup chopped green onions
(4 medium)

2 teaspoons chopped gingerroot

1 teaspoon sesame oil

1/4 teaspoon white pepper

1 small red bell pepper, finely
chopped (1/2 cup)

1 egg white

1 package (10 ounces) round
wonton skins

2 cups chicken broth

4 teaspoons soy sauce

1. Mix all ingredients except wonton skins, broth and soy sauce.

2. Brush each wonton skin with water. Place 1 scant tablespoon chicken mixture on center of wonton skin. Pinch 5 pleats on edge of one-half of circle. Fold circle in half over chicken mixture, pressing pleated edge of unpleated edge. Repeat with remaining skins and chicken mixture.

3. Spray 12-inch skillet with nonstick cooking spray; heat over medium heat. Cook 12 pot stickers at a time in skillet 3 minutes or until light brown; turn. Stir in 1/2 cup of the broth and 1 teaspoon of the soy sauce. Cover and cook 5 minutes. Uncover and cook 1 minute longer or until liquid has evaporated. Repeat with remaining pot stickers, broth and soy sauce.

3 POT STICKERS: Calories 110 (Calories from Fat 25); Fat 3g (Saturated 1g); Cholesterol 25mg; Sodium 350mg; Carbohydrates 11g (Dietary Fiber 1g); Protein 11g.

Stuffed Mushrooms

3 DOZEN MUSHROOMS

Make these tasty little tidbits ahead and store them in the refrigerator until you are ready to bake them. Or, rather than baking them, you can microwave them! Arrange the filled mushrooms, smallest mushrooms in the center, on a 10-inch microwavable plate. Microwave on high 3 to 4 minutes, rotating the plate 1/2 turn after 2 minutes, until the mushrooms are hot. Heat the mushrooms as you need them.

36 medium mushrooms (about 1 pound)

2 tablespoons margarine or butter

1 small onion, chopped (about 1/4 cup)

1/2 small green bell pepper, chopped (about 1/4 cup)

1 1/2 cups soft bread crumbs

2 teaspoons chopped fresh or 1/2 teaspoon dried thyme leaves

1/4 teaspoon salt

1/4 teaspoon ground turmeric

1/4 teaspoon pepper

1 tablespoon margarine or butter

1. Heat oven to 350°.

2. Remove stems from mushroom caps. Finely chop enough stems to measure 1/3 cup. Reserve mushroom caps.

3. Melt 2 tablespoons margarine in 10-inch skillet over medium-high heat. Cook chopped mushroom stems, onion and bell pepper in margarine about 3 minutes, stirring frequently, until onion is softened; remove from heat. Stir in bread crumbs, thyme, salt, turmeric and pepper. Fill mushroom caps with bread crumb mixture.

4. Melt 1 tablespoon margarine in shallow baking dish in oven. Place mushrooms, filled sides up, in dish.

5. Bake 15 minutes. Set oven control to broil. Broil with tops 3 to 4 inches from heat about 2 minutes or until tops are light brown. Serve hot.

1 MUSHROOM: Calories 30 (Calories from Fat 10); Fat 1g (Saturated 0g); Cholesterol 0mg; Sodium 65mg; Carbohydrates 4g (Dietary Fiber 0g); Protein 1g.

Deviled Eggs

This versatile dish is welcome as an appetizer, a snack, a main dish and even for breakfast. After cooking the eggs, be sure to run them under cold water to make peeling easier.

6 hard-cooked eggs, peeled

3 tablespoons mayonnaise, salad dressing or
   half-and-half

1/2 teaspoon ground mustard (dry)

1/8 teaspoon salt

1/4 teaspoon pepper

1. Cut eggs lengthwise in half. Slip out yolks and mash with fork.

2. Stir in mayonnaise, mustard, salt and pepper. Fill whites with egg yolk mixture, heaping it lightly. Cover and refrigerate up to 24 hours.

1 DEVILED EGG: Calories 55 (Calories from Fat 45); Fat 5g (Saturated 1g); Cholesterol 110mg; Sodium 75mg; Carbohydrates 0g (Dietary Fiber 0g); Protein 3g.

Betty Crocker Kitchen Tours? Follow the Red Spoons . . .

Are you one of the lucky ones who took a tour of the Betty Crocker Kitchens? Many people tell us they have fond memories of this little glimpse into the life of Betty Crocker. The tours were conducted from 1947 until 1985, and about 1.5 million visitors peeked into the famous kitchens during that time. The tours began with a multimedia presentation in the company auditorium, followed by a glimpse of Betty's official portraits, the cookbook library, and the formal Betty Crocker Dining Room. After viewing all of the seven kitchens, visitors received a "goody bag" of recipes, gadgets and products. They could then spend a few minutes shopping in the Betty Crocker Kitchens Boutique before ending the tour. The kitchen tours were very popular, and the company gets calls to this day wondering if they are still offered.

Favorite
Homemade Breads

Popovers
(page 303)

Herb Foccacia

6 FOCCACIA

The fresh herbs used in the glaze for this bread enlivens the wonderful, homey flavor of this bread. Make this traditional Italian bread the day before you plan on using it and warm before serving.

2 packages active dry yeast

1/4 teaspoon sugar

1 cup warm water

3 cups all-purpose flour

1/4 cup finely chopped onion

3 tablespoons vegetable oil

1 teaspoon salt

Herb Glaze (right)

1. Mix yeast, sugar and water in small bowl; let stand 5 minutes.

2. Blend remaining ingredients except Herb Glaze in large bowl; stir in yeast mixture to form a soft dough. Turn dough out onto floured surface. Knead dough 5 minutes until smooth and elastic. Place dough in greased bowl; cover and let rise in warm place 1 hour.

3. Grease baking sheet. Punch dough down; divide evenly into 6 pieces. Shape each piece into 5-inch circle; place on baking sheet. Cover; let rise 20 minutes.

4. Heat oven to 400°. Brush top of each bread with Herb Glaze. Bake 15 to 18 minutes until light golden brown.

HERB GLAZE

1 tablespoon chopped fresh or 1/2 teaspoon dried thyme leaves

1 tablespoon chopped fresh or 1/2 teaspoon dried basil leaves

1 egg, beaten

Mix all ingredients.

1 SERVING: Calories 300 (Calories from Fat 70); Fat 8g (Saturated 1g); Cholesterol 35mg; Sodium 410mg; Carbohydrates 50g (Dietary Fiber 2g); Protein 9g.

Bountiful Bread

Mmm, smell that? There's nothing like the fragrance of warm, homemade bread. Victorian cooks used 95 percent of the flour they bought for bread. Today, only 10 percent of flour is used to make bread, and many cooks say they cannot find the time to bake it. But the advent of automatic bread machines may change all that, because the appeal of that freshly baked, warm, aromatic bread, slathered in butter or honey, just can't be matched by anything else!

Carmelina Cockrell
Beaverton, Oregon

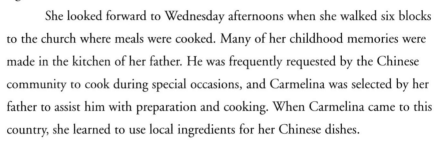

The seventeenth of May, 1984 was very cold when Carmelina Chan Cockrell arrived in this country from the steamy, bustling Philippine city of Cebu. As a newcomer, she experienced great difficulty in finding financial and banking work similar to her prior Philippine employment. Instead, she volunteered as a cook for the Catholic Church's community service program to assist the underprivileged.

She looked forward to Wednesday afternoons when she walked six blocks to the church where meals were cooked. Many of her childhood memories were made in the kitchen of her father. He was frequently requested by the Chinese community to cook during special occasions, and Carmelina was selected by her father to assist him with preparation and cooking. When Carmelina came to this country, she learned to use local ingredients for her Chinese dishes.

About seven years ago, Carmelina became a United States citizen and began working as a financial analyst in a government department. Each day she meets various challenges of budgets, paperwork, and politics in order to complete her projects. Also, she is a volunteer member of several committees dedicated to operating a local credit union more efficiently.

But not all of her time is spent on financial affairs. She still finds time to exercise her skills as a cook. Carmelina's favorite recipe is Honey-Wheat Bread featured in *Betty Crocker's Step-by-Step Cookbook*. She likes to treat her co-workers to Light Cornmeal Crescents (a Betty Crocker recipe) and her special Hum Bao (Dim Sum). Prior to my sister-in-law's death, her diet was highly restricted; nevertheless, she requested Carmelina's Hum Bao because they were her favorite treat.

Honey–Whole Wheat Bread

2 LOAVES, 6 SLICES EACH

Who can resist freshly baked bread, with the goodness of whole wheat, kissed with honey? Since this recipe makes two loaves, there is one to eat and one to freeze or give away!

3 cups stone-ground whole wheat or graham flour

1/3 cup honey

1/4 cup shortening

1 tablespoon salt

2 packages active dry yeast

2 1/4 cups very warm water (120° to 130°)

3 to 4 cups all-purpose or bread flour

Margarine or butter, melted, if desired

1. Mix whole wheat flour, honey, shortening, salt and yeast in large bowl. Add warm water. Beat with electric mixer on low speed 1 minute, scraping bowl frequently. Beat on medium speed 1 minute, scraping bowl frequently. Stir in enough all-purpose flour, 1 cup at a time, to make dough easy to handle.

2. Turn dough onto lightly floured surface. Knead about 10 minutes or until smooth and elastic. Place in greased bowl and turn greased side up. Cover and let rise in warm place 40 to 60 minutes or until double. Dough is ready if indentation remains when touched.

3. Grease bottoms and sides of 2 loaf pans, 8 1/2 x 4 1/2 x 2 1/2 or 9 x 5 x 3 inches, with shortening.

4. Punch down dough and divide in half. Flatten each half with hands or rolling pin into rectangle, 18 x 9 inches, on lightly floured surface. Roll dough up tightly, beginning at 9-inch side, to form a loaf. Press with thumbs to seal after each turn. Pinch edge of dough into roll to seal. Press each end with side of hand to seal. Fold ends under loaf. Place seam side down in pan. Brush loaves lightly with margarine. Cover and let rise in warm place 35 to 50 minutes or until double.

5. Move oven rack to low position so that tops of pans will be in center of oven. Heat oven to 375°.

6. Bake 40 to 45 minutes or until loaves are deep golden brown and sound hollow when tapped. Remove from pans to wire rack. Brush loaves with margarine, cool.

1 SLICE: Calories 105 (Calories from Fat 20); Fat 2g (Saturated 1g); Cholesterol 0mg; Sodium 210mg; Carbohydrates 21g (Dietary Fiber 2g); Protein 3g.

Traditional White Bread

2 LOAVES, 16 SLICES EACH

Do you have a need to use less salt in your diet? If so, decrease sugar to 2 tablespoons and salt to 4 teaspoons. Substitute vegetable oil for the shortening. Each rising time will be 10 to 15 minutes shorter.

6 to 7 cups all-purpose or bread flour

3 tablespoons sugar

1 tablespoon salt

2 tablespoons shortening

2 packages active dry yeast

2 1/4 cups very warm water (120° to 130°)

Margarine or butter, melted

1. Mix 3 1/2 cups of the flour, the sugar, salt, shortening and yeast in large bowl. Add warm water. Beat with electric mixer on low speed 1 minute, scraping bowl frequently. Beat on medium speed 1 minute, scraping bowl frequently. Stir in enough remaining flour, 1 cup at a time, to make dough easy to handle.

2. Turn dough onto lightly floured surface. Knead about 10 minutes or until smooth and elastic. Place in greased bowl and turn greased side up. Cover and let rise in warm place 40 to 60 minutes or until double. Dough is ready if indentation remains when touched.

3. Grease bottoms and sides of 2 loaf pans, 8 1/2 x 4 1/2 x 2 1/2 or 9 x 5 x 3 inches, with shortening.

4. Punch down dough and divide in half. Flatten each half with hands or rolling pin into rectangle, 18 x 9 inches, on lightly floured surface. Roll dough up tightly, beginning at 9-inch side, to form a loaf. Press with thumbs to seal after each turn. Pinch edge of dough into roll to seal. Press each end with side of hand to seal. Fold ends under loaf. Place seam side down in pan. Brush loaves lightly with margarine. Cover and let rise in warm place 25 to 50 minutes or until double.

5. Move oven rack to low position so that tops of pans will be in center of oven. Heat oven to 425°.

6. Bake 25 to 30 minutes or until loaves are deep golden brown and sound hollow when tapped. Remove from pans to wire rack. Brush loaves with margarine; cool.

1 SLICE: Calories 90 (Calories from Fat 10); Fat 1g (Saturated 0g); Cholesterol 0mg; Sodium 200mg; Carbohydrates 19g (Dietary Fiber 1g); Protein 2g.

Brown Bread

1 LOAF, 24 SLICES

Rye flour, which can be found in smaller bags where other flours are found, adds a hearty denseness to the bread. This is a great bread to serve with any soup or stew that has lots of broth to sop up.

1/2 cup all-purpose or rye flour

1/2 cup cornmeal

1/2 cup whole wheat flour

1/2 cup currants or chopped raisins

1 cup buttermilk

1/3 cup molasses

1 teaspoon baking soda

1 teaspoon grated orange peel

1/2 teaspoon salt

1. Grease loaf pan, 8 1/2 x 4 1/2 x 2 1/2 inches. Beat all ingredients in 3-quart bowl on low speed, scraping bowl constantly, 30 seconds. Beat on medium speed, scraping bowl constantly, 30 seconds longer. Pour into pan. Cover tightly with aluminum foil.

2. Place pan on rack in Dutch oven or steamer, pour boiling water into pan to level of rack. Cover Dutch oven. Keep water boiling over low heat until toothpick inserted in center of bread comes out clean, about 2 1/2 hours. (Add boiling water during steaming if necessary.) Remove pan from Dutch oven; immediately remove bread from pan. Serve warm.

1 SLICE: Calories 50 (Calories from Fat 0); Fat 0g (Saturated 0g); Cholesterol 0mg; Sodium 115mg; Carbohydrates 12g (Dietary Fiber 1g); Protein 1g.

Raisin-Oatmeal Bread

1 LOAF, 16 SLICES

Use this bread for unforgettable slices of warm, golden French toast, kissed with cinnamon and sweet, plump raisins.

1 1/2 cups water

1 1/2 teaspoons salt

1 1/2 cups quick-cooking oats

1/3 cup packed brown sugar

1 tablespoon shortening

1 package active dry yeast

1/4 cup warm water (105° to 115°)

1/2 cup raisins

3 to 3 1/4 cups all-purpose flour

1 egg white, slightly beaten

2 tablespoons quick-cooking oats

1. Heat water and salt to boiling in 3-quart saucepan. Stir in 1 1/2 cups oats, the brown sugar and shortening; cool to lukewarm. Dissolve yeast in 1/4 cup warm water. Stir into oat mixture. Stir in raisins. Mix in flour with spoon (dough will be sticky). Turn dough onto lightly floured surface; knead until smooth and elastic, about 10 minutes. Place in greased bowl; turn greased side up. Cover; let rise in warm place (85°) until double, about 1 1/2 hours. (If kitchen is cool, place dough on a rack over a bowl of hot water and cover completely with a towel.)

2. Grease loaf pan, 9 x 5 x 3 inches. Punch down dough; shape into rounded loaf. Place in pan. Brush top with egg white; sprinkle with 2 tablespoons oats. Cover; let rise in warm place until double, about 1 hour.

3. Heat oven to 375°. Bake until dark brown, 40 to 45 minutes. Remove from pan; cool on wire rack.

1 SLICE: Calories 155 (Calories from Fat 20); Fat 2g (Saturated 0g); Cholesterol 0mg; Sodium 230mg; Carbohydrates 32g (Dietary Fiber 2g); Protein 4g.

Evelyn Lawson
Victorville, California

Betty Crocker has been a cherished and important part of our household for over forty years. My mother almost single-handedly raised six of us on God, love, discipline, creativity, and Betty Crocker products. Her love for cooking and baking manifested itself into scrumptious feasts. When she could afford to do so, she

would always make "a little extra" to be donated to a neighboring soup kitchen. Even as children, we realized that financially our household income was quite limited, but Mom's imagination knew no bounds. Frequently, our house was filled with singing, laughter, and the incredible, tempting aroma of food that seemed to drift from every corner. Mom cooked up mouthwatering pies, cakes, breads, doughnuts, fudge, and casseroles that made us feel special even in hard times.

Down through the years mother always used Betty Crocker products. She would explain to us that quality made all the difference, and it never would be worth our time and money to skimp.

Today my mother is actively involved in feeding hungry families in our community. When she finds a family having trouble making ends meet, she tries to help them plan a sensible and feasible budget. She delivers loaves of bread, advice, and Betty Crocker recipes and products to make their lives easier.

I appreciate what my mother has taught me about Betty Crocker. She believes the Betty Crocker spirit is about people who have grown up with something tangible they can believe in and trust.

I believe this spirit definitely lives in my mother and has found a home there. I see it in the dishes of lovingly prepared food she shares with her loved ones. I see it in the quiet strength and character that flow from her at the end of each day.

We were saddened to hear of the passing of Evelyn Lawson and we offer our condolences to her family and friends.

Almond Honey–Whole Wheat Bread

Bread machines make it possible to have homemade bread with the press of a button! Savory almonds and honey combine to make this bread remarkable.

2/3 cup water

2 tablespoons honey

1 tablespoon margarine or
   butter, softened

1 cup bread flour

1 cup whole wheat flour

2 tablespoons toasted slivered
   almonds

3/4 teaspoon salt

1 teaspoon bread machine yeast

1 1/2-POUND RECIPE
(12 SLICES)

1 cup plus 2 tablespoons water

3 tablespoons honey

2 tablespoons margarine or
   butter, softened

1 1/2 cups bread flour

1 1/2 cups whole wheat flour

1/4 cup toasted slivered almonds

1 teaspoon salt

1 1/2 teaspoons bread machine
   yeast

1. Make 1 1/2-Pound Recipe with bread machines that use 3 cups flour, or make 1-Pound Recipe with bread machines that use 2 cups flour.

2. Measure carefully, placing all ingredients in bread machine pan in the order recommended by the manufacturer.

3. Select Whole Wheat or Basic/White cycle. Use Medium or Light crust color. Remove baked bread from pan and cool on wire rack.

1 SLICE: Calories 160 (Calories from Fat 35); Fat 4g (Saturated 1g); Cholesterol 0mg; Sodium 200mg; Carbohydrates 29g (Dietary Fiber 2g); Protein 4g.

The "Gold Medal" Flour

Many of Betty Crocker's recipes include flour, and she recommends Gold Medal, of course. "Gold Medal" was the name given to the flour that the Washburn Crosby Company entered into competition at the Millers' International Exhibition in Cincinnati, Ohio, in 1880. Cadwallader C. Washburn and his three grades of spring wheat swept the gold, silver and bronze medals, beating all other competitors at the exhibition. It seemed like a good idea to name the flour Gold Medal in celebration of the victory, and the first packages bearing that name were shipped in August 1880.

Pull-Apart Bread

1 LOAF, 12 SERVINGS

The delightful pull-apart loaf is also known as monkey bread or bubble loaf. For fun variations, after rolling the balls in butter, roll them in a cinnamon and sugar mixture or in a savory blend of fragrant herbs.

3 1/2 to 3 3/4 cups all-purpose flour

2 tablespoons sugar

1/2 teaspoon salt

1 package active dry yeast

1 cup milk

1/4 cup (1/2 stick) margarine or butter

1 egg

1/4 cup (1/2 stick) margarine or butter, melted

1. Grease 12-cup bundt cake pan or tube pan, 10 x 4 inches.

2. Mix 1 1/2 cups of the flour, the sugar, salt and yeast in 3-quart bowl. Heat milk and 1/4 cup margarine in 1-quart saucepan over medium-low heat, stirring frequently, until very warm (120° to 130°). Add milk mixture and egg to flour mixture. Beat on low speed until moistened; beat 3 minutes on medium speed. Stir in enough remaining flour to make dough easy to handle.

3. Turn dough onto lightly floured surface. Knead until smooth and elastic, about 5 minutes. Shape dough into 24 balls. Dip each ball of dough into the melted margarine. Layer evenly in pan. Cover and let rise in warm place until double, 20 to 30 minutes.

4. Heat oven to 350°. Bake until golden brown, 25 to 30 minutes. Cool 2 minutes; invert onto heatproof serving plate. Serve warm.

1 SERVING: Calories 220 (Calories from Fat 80); Fat 9g (Saturated 2g); Cholesterol 20mg; Sodium 220mg; Carbohydrates 31g (Dietary Fiber 1g); Protein 5g.

Pull-Apart Bread, Raisin-Oatmeal Bread (page 291)

Teri Hatch
Merrillville, Indiana

My wife, Teri, epitomizes America's woman of the 90s. She is active in the community, her church, her profession, and most of all, her family. The mother of three children, she is a little dark-haired dynamo.

Teri works in the dental profession as an oral surgery clinic supervisor of surgical assistants. One of the nicer touches she brings with her to the workplace is her practice of providing each co-worker a home-baked and decorated birthday cake on his or her birthday.

Teri has always been a believer in serving within her church. She has served in many capacities, including working in the children's ministry, hosting weekly Bible studies in our home, special activity nights, and food distribution to the poor. Her most touching experience was in El Paso, where she went out into the streets of the border ghetto areas to hand out groceries to the poor and homeless as part of the church food ministry.

Teri is firm about family tradition. She insists on family dinners, even now that the children are in high school, and routinely fixes big breakfasts on the weekends. Teri's schedule is quite full, yet she continues to prove more than capable of providing a nurturing atmosphere for a family on the go. This year, she was instrumental in applying for and acquiring permission to host a Russian foreign exchange student in our home. Due in large part to her own accomplishments and to the positive influence she had had on our children, our family was recognized as Family of the Year at Goodfellow Air Force Base and submitted as its nomination for the nation's Great American Familys competition. She is a professional woman on the go that still finds the time for the little things in life that make it all worth living!

Sunflower Seven-Grain Bread

1 LOAF, 6 SLICES

Using ready-to-eat-seven-grain cereal eliminates the need to buy seven different grains to make this wholesome bread.

1 1/2 cups all-purpose* or bread
   flour

3 tablespoons packed brown
   sugar

2 tablespoons vegetable oil

1 1/2 teaspoons salt

1 package regular or quick active
   dry yeast

1 cup very warm water (120° to
   130°)

1 1/2 cups 7-grain ready-to-eat
   cereal

1/2 cup raw sunflower nuts

1 to 1 1/2 cups whole wheat
   flour

Vegetable oil

1. Mix all-purpose flour, brown sugar, 2 tablespoons oil, the salt and yeast in large bowl. Add warm water. Beat with electric mixer on low speed 1 minute, scraping bowl frequently. Beat on medium speed 1 minute, scraping bowl frequently.

2. Stir in cereal and nuts. Stir in enough whole wheat flour, 1/2 cup at a time, to make dough easy to handle.

3. Turn dough onto lightly floured surface. Knead about 10 minutes or until smooth and elastic. Place in greased bowl and turn greased side up. Cover and let rise in warm place about 1 hour or until double. Dough is ready if indentation remains when touched.

4. Grease bottom and sides of loaf pan, 8 1/2 x 4 1/2 x 2 1/2 or 9 x 5 x 3 inches, with shortening.

5. Punch down dough. Flatten with hands or rolling pin into rectangle, 18 x 9 inches, on lightly floured surface. Roll dough up tightly, beginning at 9-inch side, to form a loaf. Press with thumbs to seal after each turn. Pinch edge of dough into roll to seal. Press each end with side of hand to seal. Fold ends under loaf. Place seam side down in pan. Brush loaves lightly with oil. Cover and let rise in warm place 45 minutes to 1 hour or until double.

6. Move oven rack to low position so that tops of pans will be in center of oven. Heat oven to 400°.

7. Bake 25 to 30 minutes or until loaf is deep golden brown and sounds hollow when tapped. Remove from pans to wire rack, cool.

1 SLICE: Calories 140 (Calories from Fat 35); Fat 4g (Saturated 1g); Cholesterol 0mg; Sodium 200mg; Carbohydrates 25g (Dietary Fiber 3g); Protein 4g.

*If using self-rising flour, omit salt.

Sally Chow
Clarksdale, Mississippi

Sally has been teaching home economics to seventh and eighth graders at Oakhurst Junior High School in Clarksdale, Mississippi, for the past six years. She teaches "life" skills to help those young people cope with today's problems and build their self-image and self-esteem.

Her interest in baking began early as she helped her mother at home. Her interest in food and cooking continued, and she began a part-time business producing original, distinctive cakes for special occasions. With her sister-in-law, they have earned a wonderful reputation throughout the Mississippi Delta region. Now, no Delta wedding would be complete without a "CHOW" cake.

Sally states that she has been a Betty Crocker fan for years. She is especially pleased with the frosting and the frosting mixes because of their smooth texture, excellent flavor, and ease of use. They work up the same each time, giving consistent results. This is so important for her students so that they can gain confidence in their work, even as neophyte bakers and cooks. The same could be said of many other Betty Crocker products.

When she isn't busy with her schoolwork, Sally can be heard playing the organ for her church's congregation. As an outstanding, active member of Oakhurst Baptist Church, she participated in a number of it's ministries, most recently as chairperson of the Scholarship Committee, and in other capacities as called on.

Sally and I just have celebrated our silver wedding anniversary this past August 30. We have two children, Lisa, twenty-two, and Bradley, twenty. She has been an ideal mother and wife for us, exhibiting great energy and resourcefulness to utilize her talents and skills to make and provide a wonderful, comfortable home.

Banana Bread

The next time you make this bread, save some for toasting. Spread it with cream cheese for something a little bit different. You might even enjoy a little smear of strawberry jam on top, too.

1 1/4 cups sugar

1/2 cup margarine or butter,
    softened

2 eggs

1 1/2 cups mashed ripe bananas
    (3 to 4 medium)

1/2 cup buttermilk

1 teaspoon vanilla

2 1/2 cups all-purpose flour

1 teaspoon baking soda

1 teaspoon salt

1 cup chopped nuts, if desired

1. Heat oven to 350°. Grease bottoms only of 2 loaf pans, 8 1/2 x 4 1/2 x 2 1/2 inches, or 1 loaf pan, 9 x 5 x 3 inches, with shortening.

2. Mix sugar and margarine in large bowl. Stir in eggs until well blended. Add bananas, buttermilk and vanilla. Beat until smooth. Stir in flour, baking soda and salt just until moistened. Stir in the nuts. Pour into pans.

3. Bake 8-inch loaves about 1 hour, 9-inch loaf about 1 1/4 hours, or until toothpick inserted in center comes out clean. Cool 5 minutes in pans on wire rack. Loosen sides of loaves from pans; remove from pans and place top side up on wire rack. Cool completely before slicing. Wrap tightly and store at room temperature up to 4 days, or refrigerate up to 10 days.

1 SLICE: Calories 70 (Calories from Fat 20); Fat 2g (Saturated 1g); Cholesterol 10mg; Sodium 100mg; Carbohydrates 12g (Dietary Fiber 0g); Protein 1g.

Traditional Corn Bread

12 SERVINGS

Corn bread is one of America's favorite quick breads. Easy and quick to make, it's a hearty way to satisfy a longing for warm-from-the-oven homemade bread. Delicious when hot, corn bread is also wonderful when cooled, sliced and thickly spread with butter or jam, or when toasted the next day.

1 1/2 cups yellow cornmeal

1/2 cup all-purpose flour

1/4 cup shortening

1 1/2 cups buttermilk

2 teaspoons baking powder

1 teaspoon sugar

1 teaspoon salt

1/2 teaspoon baking soda

2 eggs

1. Heat oven to 450°.

2. Grease round pan, 9 x 1 1/2 inches, or square pan, 8 x 8 x 2 inches. Mix all ingredients; beat vigorously 30 seconds.

3. Pour batter into pan. Bake until golden brown, 25 to 30 minutes. Serve warm.

1 SERVING: Calories 140 (Calories from Fat 55); Fat 6g (Saturated 2g); Cholesterol 38mg; Sodium 370mg; Carbohydrates 19g (Dietary Fiber 1g); Protein 4g.

Easy Garlic-Cheese Biscuits

10 TO 12 BISCUITS

These melt-in-your-mouth biscuits are especially good with any meal. The next time you make them, experiment with a different cheese, such as smoky Cheddar or pizza mozzarella.

2 cups Bisquick Original baking mix

2/3 cup milk

1/2 cup shredded Cheddar cheese (2 ounces)

1/4 cup margarine or butter, melted

1/4 teaspoon garlic powder

1. Heat oven to 450°.

2. Mix baking mix, milk and cheese to make a soft dough. Beat vigorously 30 seconds. Drop 10 to 12 spoonfuls dough onto ungreased cookie sheet.

3. Bake 8 to 10 minutes or until golden brown. Mix margarine and garlic powder; brush on warm biscuits before removing from cookie sheet. Serve warm.

1 BISCUIT: Calories 160 (Calories from Fat 90); Fat 10g (Saturated 3g); Cholesterol 10mg; Sodium 440mg; Carbohydrates 15g (Dietary Fiber 0g); Protein 3g.

Buttermilk Biscuits

ABOUT 10 BISCUITS

Buttermilk makes these biscuits tender and flavorful. The secret to fluffy biscuits is not overworking the dough. Once the shortening is cut into the flour, just a few quick stirs should make the dough form into a ball.

1/2 cup shortening

2 cups all-purpose flour

1 tablespoon sugar

2 teaspoons baking powder

1 teaspoon salt

1/4 teaspoon baking soda

About 3/4 cup buttermilk

1. Heat oven to 450°.

2. Cut shortening into remaining ingredients except buttermilk in large bowl, using pastry blender or crisscrossing 2 knives, until mixture resembles fine crumbs. Stir in just enough buttermilk so dough leaves side of bowl and forms a ball.

3. Turn dough onto lightly floured surface. Knead lightly 10 times. Roll or pat 1/2 inch thick. Cut with floured 2 1/2-inch biscuit cutter. Place about 1 inch apart on ungreased cookie sheet.

4. Bake 10 to 12 minutes or until golden brown. Immediately remove from cookie sheet. Serve hot.

1 BISCUIT: Calories 200 (Calories from Fat 100); Fat 11g (Saturated 3g); Cholesterol 2mg; Sodium 390mg; Carbohydrates 22g (Dietary Fiber 0g); Protein 3g.

Beaten Biscuits

24 BISCUITS

The beaten biscuit is a tradition down South that dates all the way back to the 1800s. Most biscuits are flaky and tender, but the beaten biscuit is hard and crisp. This texture is made when the dough is well-beaten until it is smooth and elastic. Our suggestion of a wooden spoon or mallet also works well for the beatings. If you put the baked ham in a biscuit, you'll recreate the ham-and-biscuit combination first found in the southern colonies.

1/4 cup shortening

2 cups all-purpose flour

2 teaspoons sugar

1/2 teaspoon salt

1/4 teaspoon baking powder

3/4 to 1 cup cold water

1. Heat oven to 400°.

2. Cut shortening into flour, sugar, salt and baking powder with pastry blender in large bowl until mixture resembles coarse crumbs. Stir in 3/4 cup water; stir in additional water to make a stiff dough.

3. Turn dough onto lightly floured board. Beat dough with wooden spoon or mallet 5 minutes, turning and folding dough constantly. Roll or pat dough to 1/4-inch thickness. Cut with 2-inch biscuit cutter.

4. Place biscuits on ungreased cookie sheet; prick tops with fork. Bake 18 to 20 minutes or until golden brown.

1 BISCUIT: Calories 55 (Calories from Fat 20); Fat 2g (Saturated 1g); Cholesterol 0mg; Sodium 55mg; Carbohydrates 8g (Dietary Fiber 0g); Protein 1g.

Mary Jane (Dottie) Brammer

Fairmont, Minnesota

As a bride in 1951, I received my first Betty Crocker cookbook. I still have it, and many other newer Betty Crocker cookbooks. My cooking improved (thanks Betty!) as we had five children and now six grandchildren. Everyone cooked in our family, and it is fun to visit our four married sons and find that they not only prepare meals, but have given me some great recipes.

Despite having multiple sclerosis (MS) since 1979, I can still cook anything. It has been necessary to change my kitchen so everything can be done from a sitting position; actually you get a closer look at what you're doing! In 1992 I moved to a one-bedroom condo but refused to get rid of any pots and pans. Since I love to cook and bake I needed them all. My neighbors are wonderful. They "gift" me with things like pecans so I'll make a pie. As a widow living alone, it's fun to share with my neighbors so there is no waste or stale cake or cookies. My favorite Betty Crocker recipe is for chocolate pie. Your new bar mixes are also delicious.

Betty Crocker taught me to cook and gave me confidence that if you can read; you can cook.

Popovers

Crusty on the outside and soft and moist on the inside, popovers are the perfect mate with roasts, beef stew or any meal where there's a little juice to sop.

1 cup all-purpose flour

1 cup milk

1/4 teaspoon salt

2 eggs

1. Heat oven to 450°. Generously grease six 6-ounce custard cups.

2. Mix all ingredients with hand beater just until smooth (do not overbeat). Fill cups about half full. Bake 20 minutes.

3. Reduce oven temperature to 350°. Bake 20 minutes longer. Immediately remove from cups. Serve hot.

1 POPOVER: Calories 120 (Calories from Fat 25); Fat 3g (Saturated 1g); Cholesterol 75mg; Sodium 140mg; Carbohydrates 18g (Dietary Fiber 0g); Protein 5g.

What Puts the *Pop* in Popovers?

One of your favorite special dinner breads may be popovers. Who can resist these puffy muffin-shaped breads served steaming and piping-hot from the oven? Do you know how they got their name? The batter, usually baked in muffin tins or special popover pans, rises and seems to *pop over* the sides of the pan during the baking process. These crusty breads have been around a long time; the first occurrence of the word in print was back in 1876. Early American bakers liked them because they were much quicker to make than yeast breads, which required long rising times. Popovers are very similar to the English Yorkshire pudding, and they're a close relative of the cream puff, as well.

Baking Powder Biscuits

12 BISCUITS

Add a bit of extra flavor to your biscuits by stirring in 2 teaspoons chopped fresh or 3/4 teaspoon dried dill weed or basil with the flour.

1/2 cup shortening

2 cups all-purpose flour

1 tablespoon sugar

3 teaspoons baking powder

1 teaspoon salt

3/4 cup milk

1. Heat oven to 450°.

2. Cut shortening into flour, sugar, baking powder and salt in medium bowl, using pastry blender or crisscrossing 2 knives, until mixture looks like fine crumbs. Stir in milk until dough leaves side of bowl (dough will be soft and sticky).

3. Turn dough onto lightly floured surface. Knead lightly 10 times. Roll or pat 1/2 inch thick. Cut with floured 2 1/2-inch round cutter. Place on ungreased cookie sheet about 1 inch apart for crusty sides, touching for soft sides.

4. Bake 10 to 12 minutes or until golden brown. Immediately remove from cookie sheet. Serve warm.

1 BISCUIT: Calories 160 (Calories from Fat 80); Fat 9g (Saturated 2g); Cholesterol 5mg; Sodium 310mg; Carbohydrates 18g (Dietary Fiber 0g); Protein 2g.

High-Rising Flour

Even as early as 1920, the folks at the Washburn Crosby Company (later General Mills) were interested in helping homemakers find easier ways to do things. In that year, they introduced self-rising flour, which had the correct proportions of salt and baking powder added to it, so that quick breads and biscuits could be mixed more conveniently. Special recipes for using this flour in other baked goods, such as cakes and cookies, were available, too.

Pepper-Cheese Twists

Freshly ground black pepper adds a nice spice kick to the twists. These are easy to make ahead; just cover them tightly with plastic wrap and refrigerate until ready to bake. They go great with clam chowder or tomato soup.

1/2 package (17 1/4 ounces) frozen puff pastry
   dough, thawed

1 egg, beaten

1 cup shredded Cheddar cheese

2 teaspoons black pepper

1. Heat oven to 425°.

2. Roll sheet of dough into 18 x 12-inch rectangle; brush with beaten egg. Sprinkle cheese over half of rectangle; fold remaining half over cheese and press edges to seal.

3. Brush dough with egg; sprinkle with pepper. Cut pastry lengthwise into 1/2-inch strips. Twist strips and place on cookie sheet. Bake 10 to 12 minutes or until light golden brown.

1 SERVING: Calories 110 (Calories from Fat 70); Fat 8g (Saturated 3g); Cholesterol 35mg; Sodium 75mg; Carbohydrates 6g (Dietary Fiber 0g); Protein 3g.

CHAPTER FIVE

Best-Loved Desserts

Perfect endings to perfect meals or an elegant finish to a lovely evening invites these memorable desserts to your table. You'll find a winning array of scrumptious treats for any grand finale. Moist cakes thick with creamy frosting, crispy cookies ready for a plunge in a glass of icy milk, fruit pies and desserts oozing with summer sweetness—it's all here, waiting to be served.

Chocolate Hazelnut Torte (page 338)

Cakes & Desserts

Best Chocolate Cake
with Fudge Frosting (page 317)

Applesauce Cake

The applesauce in this one-bowl cake makes for a moist and delicious cake. Want a really yummy idea? Serve this cake with warmed caramel topping drizzled over each slice. Pure heaven!

2 1/2 cups all-purpose flour

1 1/2 cups unsweetened applesauce

1 1/4 cups sugar

1/2 cup margarine or butter, softened

1/2 cup water

1 1/2 teaspoons baking soda

1 1/2 teaspoons pumpkin pie spice

1 teaspoon salt

3/4 teaspoon baking powder

2 eggs

1 cup raisins

2/3 cup chopped nuts

Maple-Nut Buttercream Frosting or Cream Cheese Frosting (right), if desired

1. Heat oven to 350°. Grease bottom and sides of rectangular pan, 13 x 9 x 2 inches, or 2 round pans, 8 x 1 1/2 or 9 x 1 1/2 inches, with shortening; lightly flour.

2. Beat all ingredients except raisins, nuts and Maple-Nut Frosting in large bowl with electric mixer on low speed 30 seconds, scraping bowl constantly. Beat on high speed 3 minutes, scraping bowl occasionally. Stir in raisins and nuts. Pour into pan(s).

3. Bake rectangle 45 to 50 minutes, rounds 40 to 45 minutes, or until toothpick inserted in center comes out clean. Cool rectangle in pan on wire rack. Cool rounds 10 minutes; remove from pans to wire rack. Cool completely.

4. Frost rectangle or fill and frost layers with Maple-Nut Buttercream Frosting.

MAPLE-NUT BUTTERCREAM FROSTING

3 cups powdered sugar

1/3 cup margarine or butter, softened

1/2 cup maple-flavored syrup

1 to 2 tablespoons milk

1/4 cup finely chopped nuts

1. Mix powdered sugar and margarine in medium bowl. Stir in syrup and milk.

2. Beat until smooth and spreadable. Stir in nuts.

CREAM CHEESE FROSTING

1 package (8 ounces) cream cheese, softened

1/4 cup margarine or butter, softened

2 teaspoons milk

1 teaspoon vanilla

4 cups powdered sugar

1. Beat cream cheese, margarine, milk and vanilla in medium bowl with electric mixer on low speed until smooth.

2. Gradually beat in powdered sugar on low speed, 1 cup at a time, until smooth and spreadable.

1 SERVING: Calories 265 (Calories from Fat 90); Fat 10g (Saturated 2g); Cholesterol 25mg; Sodium 350mg; Carbohydrates 42g (Dietary Fiber 1g); Protein 3g.

Becky Deutsch
Evansville, Indiana

Becky Deutsch is an all-around homemaker, housewife, mother, beautician, volunteer, and organizer. She is the mother of three sons, Michael, seventeen, Matthew, fourteen, and Nicholas, eight, all in Boy Scouts and 4-H. Becky is a full-time beautician yet still finds time to work for her church functions, baking hundreds of kuchens (coffee cakes), and making apple butter, burgoo (soup), and homemade ice cream for fund-raisers and fellowships.

Through her church, she and her husband were co-chairmen this past summer for the Habitat for Humanity housing project for the inner city. Becky and her family and church members built a house—one of twenty-six houses constructed in one week. She coordinated suppers, an auction, and an ice-cream social (to help in the cost of the home). This is the second Habitat for Humanity project she has been so heavily involved in, in four years' time.

Becky still finds time to belong to a Home Economics club, serve on the church board, can green beans and tomatoes, wash, iron, clean, wash cars, taxi, and help mow their five-acre lawn. She is a very loving, caring, respected, and delightful person.

Williamsburg Orange Cake

12 SERVINGS

It's not hard to make your own buttermilk. Try mixing 1 1/2 tablespoons of vinegar or lemon juice into regular milk and waiting a few minutes for it to thicken.

2 1/2 cups all-purpose flour or
    2 3/4 cups cake flour

1 1/2 cups sugar

1 1/2 teaspoons baking soda

3/4 teaspoon salt

1 1/2 cups buttermilk

1/2 cup margarine or butter,
    softened

1/4 cup shortening

3 eggs

1 1/2 teaspoons vanilla

1 cup golden raisins, cut up

1/2 cup finely chopped nuts

1 tablespoon grated orange peel

Williamsburg Butter Frosting
    (below)

1. Heat oven to 350°. Grease and flour oblong pan, 13 x 9 x 2 inches. Beat all ingredients except frosting in large mixer bowl on low speed, scraping bowl constantly, 30 seconds. Beat on high speed, scraping bowl occasionally, 3 minutes. Pour into pan(s).

2. Bake until toothpick inserted in center comes out clean, oblong 45 to 50 minutes; layers 30 to 35 minutes; cool. Frost with Williamsburg Butter Frosting.

WILLIAMSBURG BUTTER FROSTING

1/2 cup margarine or butter,
    softened

4 1/2 cups powdered sugar

4 to 5 tablespoons orange-
    flavored liqueur or orange
    juice

1 tablespoon grated orange peel

WILLIAMSBURG BUTTER FROSTING

Mix margarine and powdered sugar. Beat in liqueur and orange peel.

1 SERVING: Calories 500 (Calories from Fat 170); Fat 19g (Saturated 4g); Cholesterol 40mg; Sodium 420mg; Carbohydrates 78g (Dietary Fiber 1g); Protein 5g.

Sofia Schwarz
Seattle, Washington

Home, to me, was always a blend of deep Slavic tradition and new world culture, having been raised by a Croatian mother and Serbian father among nine siblings. My world, as a child of these early immigrants to America, was never easy, but my fondest memories always evoke the enjoyment of many old country recipes.

With this rich heritage of foods and customs, holidays and special occasions provided a strong identity for my three children. In addition to celebrating memorable get-togethers with extended family, they received the extra benefit of living and attending school in the former Yugoslavia for two years. This also became my long-awaited opportunity to reconnect with relatives from both Serbia and Croatia and to collect authentic recipes for my Slavic library.

Family interest in our ethnicity subsequently led to a long-term involvement by my children in a locally organized youth group where singing, dancing, and playing the original instruments of our homeland were taught. As their director, a highlight of their participation was a tour of the former Yugoslavia where the group performed in major cities and the significant villages of their ancestors.

Always providing sweet treats for my family was one expression of my passion for baking. For eighteen years my many co-workers have been supplied with "Monday morning blues" treats and, without exception, all of my real-estate open houses have included an array of freshly baked goodies from my kitchen!

Even though my greatest life energies have been expressed through my children and kitchen, I continue being of service at the annual city-wide Community Services Day to clean-up local playgrounds, paint schools, participate in heart walks, and maintain contact with elderly aunts, uncles, and friends in rest homes.

Countless families of East European immigrants currently celebrate their revered customs and traditions because of cherished family roots like mine. Collectively, their quiet commitment to preserve these values of hearth and home continues to contribute to the rich ethnic diversity enjoyed in America today!

Mahogany Chiffon Cake

This chiffon cake gets its mahogany color from the cocoa. Chocolate lovers can do double chocolate duty by using the chocolate glaze and topping the cake with big, luscious chocolate curls.

3/4 cup boiling water

1/2 cup baking cocoa

1 3/4 cups cake flour or

    1 1/2 cups all-purpose flour

1 3/4 cups sugar

1 1/2 teaspoons baking soda

1 teaspoon salt

1/2 cup vegetable oil

2 teaspoons vanilla

7 egg yolks

1 cup egg whites (7 or 8)

1/2 teaspoon cream of tartar

Chocolate Glaze (page 318)

1. Mix boiling water and cocoa; set aside to cool.

2. Move oven rack to lowest position. Heat oven to 325°.

3. Mix flour, sugar, baking soda and salt in large bowl. Beat in oil, vanilla, egg yolks and cooled cocoa mixture until smooth.

4. Beat egg whites and cream of tartar in large bowl with electric mixer on high speed until stiff peaks form. Do not underbeat. Gradually pour egg yolk mixture over beaten whites, gently folding just until blended. Pour into ungreased angel food cake pan (tube pan), 10 x 4 inches.

5. Bake 65 to 70 minutes or until top springs back when touched lightly. Immediately turn pan upside down onto heatproof funnel or bottle. Let hang about 2 hours or until cake is completely cool.

6. Spread or drizzle top of cake with Chocolate Glaze.

1 SERVING: Calories 320 (Calories from Fat 115); Fat 13g (Saturated 3g); Cholesterol 95mg; Sodium 330mg; Carbohydrates 48g (Dietary Fiber 1g); Protein 4g.

Cake Discovery of the Century

Many food authorities have declared that Chiffon Cake was the cake discovery of the century. This was an entirely new cake that combined the lightness of angel food cakes with the richness of butter cakes. The secret ingredient, discovered by an insurance salesman who enjoyed cooking, was cooking oil! Harry Baker made these cakes for special Hollywood occasions beginning in the late 1920s. He felt a special kinship with Betty Crocker, having listened to her radio program for a number of years, and decided that Betty should bring this new cake to the general public. He came to Minneapolis to offer the recipe to General Mills, and the deal was completed in 1947. After the home economists did some fine-tuning, the recipe and several variations were made public in a 1948 pamphlet. Betty had helped create the first really new cake in *100 years!*

Strawberry Shortcakes

Who can resist tender shortcakes covered in sweet strawberries and topped off with a bit of whipped cream! It's what summer days are made for. Blueberries, raspberries, fresh peaches, kiwi and cherries also make wonderful fruits for these shortcakes.

1 quart strawberries, sliced

1/2 cup sugar

1/3 cup shortening

2 cups all-purpose flour

2 tablespoons sugar

3 teaspoons baking powder

1 teaspoon salt

3/4 cup milk

Margarine or butter, softened

Sweetened whipped cream

1. Mix strawberries and 1/2 cup sugar. Let stand 1 hour.

2. Heat oven to 450°.

3. Cut shortening into flour, 2 tablespoons sugar, the baking powder and salt in medium bowl, using pastry blender or crisscrossing 2 knives, until mixture looks like fine crumbs. Stir in milk just until blended.

4. Turn dough onto lightly floured surface. Gently smooth into a ball. Knead 20 to 25 times. Roll 1/2 inch thick. Cut into 3-inch squares or use floured 3-inch cutter. Place about 1 inch apart on ungreased cookie sheet.

5. Bake 10 to 12 minutes or until golden brown.

6. Split shortcakes horizontally in half while hot. Spread margarine on split sides. Fill with strawberries; replace tops. Top with strawberries and sweetened whipped cream.

1 SERVING: Calories 400 (Calories from Fat 135); Fat 15g (Saturated 5g); Cholesterol 10mg; Sodium 630mg; Carbohydrates 63g (Dietary Fiber 8g); Protein 6g.

Strawberry Shortcakes

Heidi Devlin
Lebanon, Pennsylvania

I grew up in a large family, and my mother insisted that everyone (guys included) must learn to cook. One night a week each of us had to plan a well-balanced meal, cook, and then clean up afterward. Now, my sisters and I are excellent cooks, and my brothers tend to do most of the cooking in their homes, too. I am

well known among friends and family for my culinary skills, and baking is one of my favorite hobbies. I have always used and enjoyed Betty Crocker products. I especially enjoy the cake mixes both because of health consciousness and because of their versatility, particularly with my busy lifestyle.

My story is a bit different from most. Less than a dozen years ago, I was a single mother on welfare, and although I was at the bottom, I was not content to stay there. I started college in 1988 and received a BS in Biology (magna cum laude) in 1995. After graduation I was accepted as a doctoral candidate in the Cell and Molecular Biology graduate program at Penn State. I am currently doing cancer research for my doctoral thesis. I am recently married with a pre-teen son named Alex.

I have always had a strong sense of community involvement, and particularly due to my past dependence on the welfare system, I felt it was important to give back to the community. I've raised money for a senior citizen's center, registered people to vote, and participated in fund-raising for the American Lung Association and the American Cancer Association among others. But my two pet projects were the Berks County Commission for Women (BCCFW) and Berks AIDS Network (BAN). During the time in which I served, we accomplished a lot, including conducting and publishing a local mammography services survey, doing an intensive study of the problem of domestic abuse in Berks County, and working with the local Domestic Relations Office to help make their system more user-friendly. I've come a long way, and I owe a lot to those who believed in me and gave me the support I needed through the long and difficult years that it took for me to achieve my dream.

Best Chocolate Cake with Fudge Frosting

12 TO 16 SERVINGS

Looking for a great cake to make for someone's birthday? Here it is! For a special color and flavor treat, serve a few raspberries with each slice!

2 cups all-purpose flour

2 cups sugar

1/2 cup shortening

3/4 cup water

3/4 cup buttermilk

1 teaspoon baking soda

1 teaspoon salt

1 teaspoon vanilla

1/2 teaspoon baking powder

2 eggs

4 ounces unsweetened chocolate,
    melted and cooled

Fudge Frosting (below)

FUDGE FROSTING

2 cups sugar

1/2 cup shortening

3 ounces unsweetened chocolate

2/3 cup milk

1/2 teaspoon salt

2 teaspoons vanilla

1. Heat oven to 350°. Grease and flour rectangular pan, 13 x 9 x 2 inches, 3 round pans, 8 x 1 1/2 inches, or 2 round pans, 9 x 1 1/2 inches. Beat all ingredients except Fudge Frosting in large bowl on low speed 30 seconds, scraping bowl constantly. Beat on high speed 3 minutes, scraping bowl occasionally. Pour into pans.

2. Bake rectangular pan 40 to 45 minutes, round pans 30 to 35 minutes or until toothpick inserted in center comes out clean. Cool rounds 10 minutes; remove from pans. Cool completely. Prepare Fudge Frosting; frost cake. Fill layers with 1/3 cup frosting; frost side and top with remaining frosting.

FUDGE FROSTING

Mix all ingredients except vanilla in 2 1/2-quart saucepan. Heat to rolling boil, stirring occasionally. Boil 1 minute without stirring. Place saucepan in bowl of ice and water. Beat until frosting is smooth and of spreading consistency; stir in vanilla.

1 SERVING: Calories 620 (Calories from Fat 250); Fat 28g (Saturated 10g); Cholesterol 40mg; Sodium 450mg; Carbohydrates 89g (Dietary Fiber 3g); Protein 6g.

Angel Food Cake with Chocolate Glaze

16 SERVINGS

If you're looking for a delicious dessert that has done the skinny on fat and cholesterol, look no further. Angel food cake boasts zero to both! Serve it with cut-up fresh fruit or berries and a dollop of fluffy whipped topping and it will be a favorite with both young and old.

1 1/2 cups powdered sugar

1 cup cake flour

1 1/2 cups egg whites (about 12)

1 1/2 teaspoons cream of tartar

1 cup granulated sugar

1 1/2 teaspoons vanilla

1/2 teaspoon almond extract

1/4 teaspoon salt

Chocolate Glaze (right)

1. Move oven rack to lowest position. Heat oven to 375°.

2. Mix powdered sugar and flour; set aside. Beat egg whites and cream of tartar in large bowl with electric mixer on medium speed until foamy. Beat in granulated sugar, 2 tablespoons at a time, on high speed, adding vanilla, almond extract and salt with the last addition of sugar. Continue beating until stiff and glossy meringue forms. Do not underbeat.

3. Sprinkle sugar-flour mixture, 1/4 cup at a time, over meringue, folding in just until sugar-flour mixture disappears. Push batter into ungreased angel food cake pan (tube pan), 10 x 4 inches. Cut gently through batter with metal spatula.

4. Bake 30 to 35 minutes or until cracks feel dry and top springs back when touched lightly. Immediately turn pan upside down onto heat-proof funnel or bottle. Let stand about 2 hours or until cake is completely cool. Loosen side of cake with knife or long, metal spatula; remove from pan.

5. Spread or drizzle top of cake with Chocolate Glaze.

CHOCOLATE GLAZE

1/2 cup semisweet chocolate chips

2 tablespoons margarine or butter

2 tablespoons corn syrup

1 to 2 teaspoons hot water

Heat chocolate chips, margarine and corn syrup in 1-quart saucepan over low heat, stirring constantly, until chocolate chips are melted; cool slightly. Stir in hot water, 1 teaspoon at a time, until consistency of thick syrup.

1 SERVING: Calories 180 (Calories from Fat 25); Fat 3g (Saturated 1g); Cholesterol 0mg; Sodium 95mg; Carbohydrates 35g (Dietary Fiber 0g); Protein 3g.

Velvet Crumb Cake

8 SERVINGS

Enjoy the moment while it lasts! Nothing tastes better than the velvety sensation of this long-time favorite recipe melting on your taste-buds. Even better, you can make this cake in one pan. The broiled topping makes it a little crunchy, adding a pleasant texture to this tender cake.

1 1/2 cup Bisquick Original baking mix

1/2 cup sugar

1/2 cup milk or water

2 tablespoons shortening

1 teaspoon vanilla

1 egg

Broiled Topping (right)

1. Heat oven to 350°. Grease and flour square pan, 8 x 8 x 2 or 9 x 9 x 2 inches, or round pan, 9 x 1 1/2 inches.

2. Beat all ingredients except Broiled Topping in large bowl on low speed 30 seconds, scraping bowl constantly. Beat on medium speed 4 minutes, scraping bowl occasionally. Pour into pan.

3. Bake 9-inch square pan 25 to 30 minutes, 8-inch square or 9-inch round pan 30 to 35 minutes or until toothpick inserted in center comes out clean; cool slightly. Prepare Broiled Topping; spread over cake. Set oven control to broil. Broil cake about 3 inches from heat about 3 minutes or until topping is golden brown.

BROILED TOPPING

1/2 cup flaked coconut

1/3 cup packed brown sugar

1/4 cup chopped nuts

3 tablespoons margarine or butter, softened

2 tablespoons milk

Mix all ingredients.

1 SERVING: Calories 310 (Calories from Fat 145); Fat 16g (Saturated 5g); Cholesterol 30mg; Sodium 400mg; Carbohydrates 39g (Dietary Fiber 1g); Protein 3g.

Cake Mix

When research showed that Americans were baking nearly a billion cakes a year, Betty Crocker had to find a way to help make that job easier. Many years of research and testing were required to find the right recipe and to develop a mix that would retain its flavor and quality for many months. Also required was the development of new packages that could withstand the rigors of cross-country travel in railroad boxcars. After all that had been done, the mixes were tested in consumers' homes, and many voted Betty Crocker cake mixes better than scratch cakes made from treasured family recipes! Betty Crocker's devil's food and party layer cake mixes were introduced to the nation in 1949.

Peggy Rasmussen
Hamel, Minnesota

In the 1970s, Peggy Rasmussen would send home-baked cookies to her GI brother stationed overseas. "We shoot them out of the guns," he told her, "and they don't pulverize." Twenty years later, Peggy's recipes draw record response whenever she demonstrates her baking on a Minneapolis TV station.

When she bought a small cafe in Hamel, Minnesota, twenty years ago, Peggy thought she knew how to cook. But she quickly found out that she still had a lot to learn. She depended on her Betty Crocker cookbook for good basic instructions on how to prepare everything from meat loaf to apple pie. One of the secrets that a baker shared with her was that vintage Betty Crocker cookbooks had the best "from scratch" directions.

She always enjoyed cooking for the receptive customers in Hamel and still does. Baking was pretty tense during those learning years, but much to her surprise, she grew to love it. Her customers have become her friends, and she has had the privilege of sharing their joys and sorrow and laughs.

Peggy has had the opportunity to be involved with the local schools in a unique learning project that brings local sixth graders into the cafe to learn about small business and how to run a restaurant. They actually lease the Countryside Cafe for several nights each year and do all the jobs. The kids donate their profits to the local food shelves.

Her latest endeavor, a project called Kids Cafe, feeds 100 hungry kids a supper meal. She helped start the first "Cafe" in the Phillips neighborhood of Minneapolis and is now working with a group in St. Louis Park to start a site there.

She says you have to be resourceful if you want to be involved in the community and run a restaurant.

Bonnie Butter Cake

16 SERVINGS

Bonnie Butter Cake has been around for many years, a testament to the delicious flavor and delicate texture of this cake. Treat yourself and use real butter for a rich, old-fashioned taste!

1 3/4 cups sugar

2/3 cup margarine or butter, softened

1 1/2 teaspoons vanilla

2 eggs

3 cups cake flour or 2 3/4 cups all-purpose flour

2 1/2 teaspoons baking powder

1 teaspoon salt

1 1/4 cups milk

Fudge Frosting (page 317)

1. Heat oven to 350°. Grease bottom and sides of rectangular pan, 13 x 9 x 2 inches, or 2 round pans, 9 x 1 1/2 inches; lightly flour.

2. Beat sugar, margarine, vanilla and eggs in large bowl with electric mixer on low speed 30 seconds, scraping bowl constantly. Beat on high speed 5 minutes, scraping bowl occasionally. Beat in flour, baking powder and salt alternately with milk on low speed. Pour into pan(s).

3. Bake rectangle 45 to 50 minutes, layers 30 to 35 minutes or until toothpick inserted in center comes out clean. Cool rectangle in pan on wire rack. Cool rounds 10 minutes; remove from pans to wire rack. Cool completely.

4. Frost rectangle or fill and frost layers with Fudge Frosting.

1 SERVING: Calories 395 (Calories from Fat 135); Fat 15g (Saturated 8g); Cholesterol 50mg; Sodium 330mg; Carbohydrates 63g (Dietary Fiber 1g); Protein 4g.

Cake Making Made Easy

Always striving to help consumers save time, General Mills made cake-baking history in 1943 with its streamlined method for making cakes. It was called the one-bowl method, because the dry ingredients were sifted together, then shortening and liquid added, and it was all mixed in one bowl. There was no creaming or separate beating of eggs. The mixing time was cut in half!

Pumpkin Cheesecake

12 SERVINGS

Try this tempting alternative to the traditional Thanksgiving pumpkin pie. The gingersnap crust adds a nice spice to the moist, rich cheesecake. Dot whipped cream and garnish with pecan halves around the edges of the cake for a festive look.

1 1/4 cups gingersnap cookie crumbs (about twenty 2-inch cookies)

1/4 cup margarine or butter, melted

3 packages (8 ounces each) cream cheese, softened

1 cup sugar

1 teaspoon ground cinnamon

1 teaspoon ground ginger

1/2 teaspoon ground cloves

1 can (16 ounces) pumpkin

4 eggs

2 tablespoons sugar

12 walnut halves

3/4 cup chilled whipping cream

1. Heat oven to 350°.

2. Mix cookie crumbs and margarine. Press evenly on bottom of spring form pan, 9 x 3 inches. Bake 10 minutes; cool.

3. Reduce oven temperature to 300°.

4. Beat cream cheese, 1 cup sugar, the cinnamon, ginger and cloves in 4-quart bowl on medium speed until smooth and fluffy. Add pumpkin. Beat in eggs, one at a time on low speed. Pour over crumb mixture.

5. Bake until center is firm, about 1 1/4 hours. Cool to room temperature. Cover and refrigerate at least 3 hours but no longer than 48 hours.

6. Cook and stir 2 tablespoons sugar and the walnuts over medium heat until sugar is melted and nuts are coated. Immediately spread on a dinner plate or aluminum foil; cool. Carefully break nuts apart to separate if necessary. Cover tightly and store at room temperature up to 3 days.

7. Loosen cheesecake from side of pan; remove side of pan. Beat whipping cream in chilled 1 1/2-quart bowl until stiff. Pipe whipped cream around edge of cheesecake; arrange walnuts on top. Refrigerate any remaining cheesecake immediately.

1 PIECE: Calories 450 (Calories from Fat 290); Fat 32g (Saturated 17g); Cholesterol 150mg; Sodium 310mg; Carbohydrates 33g (Dietary Fiber 1g); Protein 8g.

Pumpkin Cheesecake

Eddie Murphy
Buena Park, California

Eddie Murphy, a single women in her mid-forties is the most sincere and kind human being I know. What she does to balance a busy life is remarkable, and no matter how busy she may be, her consideration to or remembrance of others is never secondary.

Having Eddie touch your life is a gift—and one of the gifts that she so often shares is her baking. As a young girl, she collected the Betty Crocker box tops for purchasing gifts. All this led to her interest in baking, which she has perfected over the years. As she often bakes from scratch, she prefers mixing with a wooden spoon. But of the Betty Crocker mixes, the brownie mix is her favorite.

Eddie's dedication to family and friends is noteworthy. In particular, she has a deep concern for the aged. Beginning with her hometown of Wellsville, Ohio, Eddie contributes a portion of her salary to assist some older people who are alone. In southern California where Eddie resides, she volunteers to a Second Careers Program, which assists retirees in gaining employment. She exhibits her consideration of others, old and young, by running in an annual 10 kilometer race to raise money for the Second Careers Program, coordinating an annual retiree picnic, and being a member of the International Society for Retirement Planning.

Two unselfish actions of note are her commitment to her paraplegic aunt and her volunteering to a "k-12" program that prompts education of students in the inner city.

She knows to allow for her favorite pastimes of baking, reading, and traveling, and she regularly attends church. When I asked Eddie why she enjoys baking, she said, "It is creating and I am concentrating on what I'm doing to make a product that will bring others pleasure."

Oatmeal Spice Cake with Browned Butter Frosting

16 SERVINGS

Sugar and spice and all things nice make this a cake to remember! Top with vanilla ice cream for a little a la mode. Keep an eye on the butter when you make the frosting. You'll have more control over the browning if you use a heavy skillet and just let the frosting get light golden brown to ensure it won't burn.

1 1/2 cups all-purpose flour

1 cup quick-cooking oats

1 cup packed brown sugar

1/2 cup granulated sugar

1 1/2 teaspoons baking soda

1 teaspoon ground cinnamon

1/2 teaspoon salt

1/2 teaspoon ground nutmeg, if desired

1/2 cup shortening

1 cup water

2 eggs

2 tablespoons molasses

Browned Butter Frosting (below)

1. Heat oven to 350°.

2. Grease rectangular pan, 13 x 9 x 2 inches with shortening; lightly flour.

3. Beat all ingredients except Browned Butter Frosting with electric mixer in large bowl 30 seconds on low speed, scraping bowl constantly. Beat on high speed 3 minutes, scraping bowl occasionally. Pour into pan.

4. Bake 35 to 40 minutes or until toothpick inserted in center comes out clean. Cool in pan on wire rack. Prepare Browned Butter Frosting; spread on cake.

BROWNED BUTTER FROSTING

1/3 cup butter

3 cups powdered sugar

1 1/2 teaspoons vanilla

About 2 tablespoons milk

BROWNED BUTTER FROSTING

Heat butter over medium heat until delicate brown. Mix in powdered sugar. Beat in vanilla and enough milk until smooth and spreadable.

1 SERVING: Calories 330 (Calories from Fat 100); Fat 11g (Saturated 4g); Cholesterol 35mg; Sodium 230mg; Carbohydrates 56g (Dietary Fiber 1g); Protein 3g.

Silver White Cake

16 SERVINGS

The silver white cake topped with a rich, chocolate frosting makes this a first-class cake. Why not polish up that silver platter that you've stored away and put it to good use!

2 1/4 cups all-purpose or 2 1/2 cups cake flour

1 2/3 cups sugar

2/3 cup shortening

1 1/4 cups milk

3 1/2 teaspoons baking powder

1 teaspoon salt

1 teaspoon vanilla or almond extract

5 egg whites

Mocha Frosting (right)

1. Heat oven to 350°. Grease bottom and sides of rectangular pan, 13 x 9 x 2 inches, 2 round pans, 9 x 1 1/2 inches, or 3 round pans, 8 x 1 1/2 inches, with shortening; lightly flour.

2. Beat all ingredients except egg whites and Mocha Frosting in large bowl with electric mixer on low speed 30 seconds, scraping bowl constantly. Beat on high speed 2 minutes, scraping bowl occasionally.

3. Beat in egg whites on high speed 2 minutes, scraping bowl occasionally. Pour into pan(s).

4. Bake rectangle 40 to 45 minutes, 9-inch rounds 30 to 35 minutes, 8-inch rounds 23 to 28 minutes, or until toothpick inserted in center comes out clean or until cake springs back when touched lightly in center. Cool rectangle in pan on wire rack. Cool rounds 10 minutes; remove from pans to wire rack. Cool completely.

5. Frost rectangle or fill and frost layers with Mocha Frosting.

MOCHA FROSTING

3 cups powdered sugar

2 1/2 teaspoons powdered instant coffee

1/3 cup stick margarine or butter, softened

2 teaspoons vanilla

3 ounces unsweetened baking chocolate, melted and cooled

2 to 3 tablespoons milk

1. Mix all ingredients except milk in medium bowl.

2. Stir in milk until smooth and spreadable.

1 SERVING: Calories 235 (Calories from Fat 80); Fat 9g (Saturated 3g); Cholesterol 2mg; Sodium 270mg; Carbohydrates 36g (Dietary Fiber 0g); Protein 3g.

Hot Fudge Sundae Cake

9 SERVINGS

Sound too good to be true? This moist, rich chocolate cake gets it name from the fact it makes it own sauce, which you can spoon over each warm, chocolatey piece. Wouldn't it be oh-so good topped with fresh strawberries or sweetened whipped cream?

1 cup all-purpose flour

3/4 cup granulated sugar

2 tablespoons baking cocoa

2 teaspoons baking powder

1/4 teaspoon salt

1/2 cup milk

2 tablespoons vegetable oil

1 teaspoon vanilla

1 cup chopped nuts, if desired

1 cup packed brown sugar

1/4 cup baking cocoa

1 3/4 cups very hot water

Ice cream, if desired

1. Heat oven to 350°.

2. Mix flour, granulated sugar, 2 tablespoons cocoa, the baking powder and salt in ungreased square pan, 9 x 9 x 2 inches. Mix in milk, oil and vanilla with fork until smooth. Stir in nuts. Spread in pan.

3. Sprinkle brown sugar and 1/4 cup cocoa over batter. Pour water over batter.

4. Bake 40 minutes or until top is dry.

5. Spoon warm cake into dessert dishes. Top with ice cream. Spoon sauce from pan onto each serving.

1 SERVING: Calories 400 (Calories from Fat 100); Fat 11g (Saturated 5g); Cholesterol 30mg; Sodium 240mg; Carbohydrates 71g (Dietary Fiber 1g); Protein 5g.

Hot Fudge Sundae Cake

A favorite Betty Crocker recipe has always been this hot, fudgy dessert. In fact, it has been in every basic Betty Crocker cookbook since the first one was published in 1950, although then it was called Hot Fudge Pudding. The current name better reflects the fact that two different layers form during the baking process. Even before it was published in the cookbooks, the recipe was recommended to homemakers who were concerned about food rationing and shortages during World War II. This cake requires no eggs or butter—two items that were in short supply during the war. Even today, those who are watching their cholesterol intake will find this dessert appealing. It is also one of the few recipes that lends itself very well to cooking in the microwave. What an all-purpose recipe!

Marcille (Marci) Faye Zietlow

Oshkosh, Wisconsin

Marci is a young career women of the nineties, excelling in all facets of life. Marci, twenty-four, is a chemical engineering honors graduate and is employed as a research scientist. Besides her job, she always manages to find time for cooking/baking, family/friends, and community service.

Food has always been of interest to Marci. From the time she was in preschool, she was rolling out cookie dough and cutting out cookies. Later, at the age of nine, she became involved in the 4-H food nutrition project. The Betty Crocker cookbook became her textbook with all the helpful hints and easy-to-follow recipes. Some of her favorites included coffee cake, strawberry shortcake, standard pastry, apple pie, pumpkin pie, cream puffs, and meat loaf. During the nine years that she exhibited at the county fair, she received numerous blue ribbons and received top exhibit awards for pastry, apple pie, and yeast rolls (recipes from the Betty Crocker cookbook).

Because of her love of cooking, she became a 4-H foods leader for three years, was a five county 4-H camp counselor outdoor cooking demonstrator. Upon her graduation from 4-H, at the age of seventeen, Marci received the highest, most prestigious 4-H award, the National 4-H Congress award for the Food Nutrition Project.

Community service has always been a part of Marci's life. After four months on the job, she began serving as a volunteer primary Drug/Alcohol and Wellness representative for the Absorbent Technology Department. In addition, she is also a Junior Achievement consultant. Last spring, she taught a six week program focused on business basics.

Marci's family appreciates all the special foods she has made in the past. And she continues to help making foods for special holidays. She never misses a special occasions and now lives within easy driving distance to her family's home farm. Before her grandfather's death in 1986, she visited her grandfather in the nursing home almost everyday. Later, she became a nursing home volunteer. Also, Marci's friends are important to her. She has always been there for them should they have a personal problem to discuss or just to help them with school work.

Cranberry-Orange Pound Cake

16 SERVINGS

Enjoy this moist, tender cake all year by purchasing bags of fresh cranberries in season and putting them in the freezer for later use. Quickly chop fresh or frozen cranberries, using a food processor with a metal blade.

1 (18.25 ounce) package golden vanilla or yellow cake mix with pudding

1 package (4-serving size) vanilla instant pudding and pie filling mix

1 cup water

1/2 cup margarine or butter, melted

1 teaspoon grated orange peel

4 eggs

1 1/2 cups fresh or frozen cranberries, chopped (do not thaw)

Orange Butter Sauce (below)

1. Heat oven to 350°. Grease bottom and side of 12-cup bundt cake pan; lightly flour.

2. Beat cake mix (dry), pudding mix (dry), water, margarine, orange peel and eggs in large bowl with electric mixer on low speed 30 seconds, scraping bowl constantly. Beat on medium speed 2 minutes. Fold in cranberries. Spread in pan.

3. Bake 1 hour 5 minutes to 1 hour 10 minutes or until cake springs back when touched lightly in center. Cool 10 minutes; remove from pan. Cool completely. Serve with warm Orange Butter Sauce.

ORANGE BUTTER SAUCE

1 cup sugar

1 tablespoon all-purpose flour

1/2 cup orange juice

1/2 cup butter (do not use margarine)

ORANGE BUTTER SAUCE

Mix sugar and flour in 1-quart saucepan. Stir in orange juice. Add butter. Cook over medium heat, stirring constantly, until thickened and bubbly.

1 SERVING: Calories 340 (Calories from Fat 145); Fat 16g (Saturated 6g); Cholesterol 70mg; Sodium 400mg; Carbohydrates 47g (Dietary Fiber 0g); Protein 2g.

Bread Pudding with Whiskey Sauce

8 SERVINGS

Don't let day old bread go to waste. In addition to white bread, try whole wheat, cinnamon-raisin, egg bread or other flavors of bread that appeal to you. For a family dessert, instead of the whiskey sauce, serve warm caramel sauce to drizzle over each warm, gooey serving.

2 cups milk

1/4 cup margarine or butter

1/2 cup sugar

1 teaspoon ground cinnamon or nutmeg

1/4 teaspoon salt

2 eggs, slightly beaten

6 cups dry bread cubes (8 slices bread)

1/2 cup raisins, if desired

Whiskey Sauce (right)

1. Heat oven to 350°.

2. Heat milk and margarine in 2-quart saucepan over medium heat until margarine is melted and milk is hot.

3. Mix sugar, cinnamon, salt and eggs in large bowl with wire whisk until well blended. Stir in bread cubes and raisins. Stir in milk mixture. Pour into ungreased 1 1/2-quart casserole or square baking dish, 8 x 8 x 2 inches. Place casserole in rectangular pan, 13 x 9 x 2 inches; pour boiling water into rectangular pan until 1 inch deep.

4. Bake uncovered 40 to 45 minutes or until knife inserted 1 inch from edge of casserole comes out clean.

5. Prepare Whiskey Sauce. Serve sauce over warm bread pudding. Refrigerate any remaining dessert.

WHISKEY SAUCE

1 cup packed brown sugar

1/2 cup stick margarine or butter

3 to 4 tablespoons bourbon or 2 teaspoons brandy extract

Heat all ingredients to boiling in heavy 1-quart saucepan over medium heat, stirring constantly, until sugar is dissolved. Serve warm or cool.

1 SERVING: Calories 665 (Calories from Fat 215); Fat 24g (Saturated 6g); Cholesterol 60mg; Sodium 1020mg; Carbohydrates 101g (Dietary Fiber 3g); Protein 14g.

Bread Pudding with Whiskey Sauce

Sue Stauffer

Rockford, Illinois

It seems as if I have always been interested in food preparation. As a result, I chose to major in foods and nutrition. Healthful eating has always been important to me even before it became "fashionable," therefore, I have enjoyed teaching cooking classes and working in consumer service, as well as cooking and baking for my family and friends. Many of my friends call me their "answer lady" on any question relating to food or nutrition, and it has been my pleasure many times to help them.

I became involved with one of our local community soup kitchens thirteen years ago. We now serve two hundred meals four times a week. Everyone involved is a volunteer. It has been a very humbling experience to serve the hungry in our city and also very gratifying.

Five years ago I was asked by a local not-for-profit to consider working for them. Their clients are pregnant and parenting adolescents. One of their programs is an emergency homeless shelter, and I began my work there as nutritionist. I planned menus and taught cooking and nutrition to the residents. Healthful foods for mom and baby are just about the last thing they want to hear about. I feel, however, that when information is presented in an interesting and casual way, they can and will learn and will have a good time. I visit the moms in their homes to teach independent living skills, too. My favorite part of the job is helping a young mom bake something or prepare a meal for the first time. What a feeling of accomplishment she has!

My favorite Betty Crocker product is Hamburger Helper®. As a working mom, it was a great time saver for me and a meal that my family loved. It was also a product that I could adapt to our own tastes. It also helped us out because, at the time, we were on a tight budget and it was an inexpensive dinner for us. I suggest this product to the young moms I work with for the very same reasons. It is a great way to get their feet wet in the kitchen and a good base for planning a dinner menu. It is a product you can count on to be successful time after time.

Cheesecake with Cherry Glaze

Sue testifies this is a "never fail" cheesecake and always a real crowd-pleaser. We're sure you'll receive rave reviews as well! You might want to use a 15 ounce can of cherry, or blueberry, pie filling instead of making the cherry glaze.

1/2 cup fine zwieback or graham cracker crumbs

1 tablespoon sugar

1/4 teaspoon ground cinnamon

1/4 teaspoon ground nutmeg

5 eggs, separated

1 cup sugar

2 packages (8 ounces each) cream cheese, softened

1 cup sour cream

2 tablespoons all-purpose flour

1 teaspoon vanilla

Cherry Glaze (below)

1. Heat oven to 275°. Butter springform pan, 9 x 3 inches.

2. Mix cracker crumbs, 1 tablespoon sugar, the cinnamon and nutmeg. Dust bottom and side of springform pan with crumb mixture.

3. Beat egg yolks in large bowl with electric mixer on high speed or until thick and lemon-colored. Gradually beat in 1 cup sugar. Beat in cream cheese until smooth. Beat in sour cream, flour and vanilla until smooth.

4. Beat egg whites in large bowl with electric mixer on high speed until stiff but not dry. Gently fold into cream cheese mixture. Pour into pan.

5. Bake 1 hour 10 minutes. Turn off oven and leave cheesecake in oven 1 hour. Cool in pan on wire rack 15 minutes. Refrigerate about 3 hours or until chilled.

6. Spread top of cheesecake with Cherry Glaze. Refrigerate until glaze is set. Remove cheesecake from pan just before serving.

CHERRY GLAZE

1 can (16 ounces) pitted red tart cherries, drained and liquid reserved

1/2 cup sugar

2 tablespoons cornstarch

Few drops red food color, if desired

CHERRY GLAZE

Add enough water to cherry liquid to measure 1 cup. Mix sugar and cornstarch in 1 1/2-quart saucepan. Gradually stir in cherry liquid. Cook over medium heat, stirring constantly, until mixture thickens and boils. Boil and stir 1 minute; remove from heat. Stir in cherries and food color; cool.

1 SERVING: Calories 275 (Calories from Fat 135); Fat 15g (Saturated 9g); Cholesterol 105mg; Sodium 115mg; Carbohydrates 30g (Dietary Fiber 0g); Protein 5g.

Connie Licón
Kankakee, Illinois

Superwoman describes my wife, Connie Licón, both in our home, with her family, or at work. She still has time to bake and save the Betty Crocker coupons off all of the box tops for her mother.

She loves to bake strawberry-rhubarb pies (my favorite) with Betty Crocker pie crusts, and there is always a supply of Betty Crocker cakes and brownies going to events. My mother remarks daily that Connie is the only mom she knows that can make a complete meal in a three-piece suit, high heels, grab an apron if one is handy, and never gets a thing on her clothes. Often a gift from her to a new bride will be a Betty Crocker cookbook. I have called her Betty Crocker so many times that it is a passing joke between us.

She is the mother of one son who is an honor student at Kankakee High School. She was the T-Ball coach when the fathers could not get off work early enough for practice; she missed one basketball game in four years as a basketball mom and is a mentor for area students looking at a future in business. She is a public speaker on behalf of meeting planning and tourism, is active in many women in business groups, and writes state grants.

How she has so much energy no one knows, but she always makes sure everyone has a good breakfast before going to school, lunches are packed, and dinner is ready even if she has a meeting in the evening. She is truly amazing and a model for us all.

Fresh Peach Cobbler

Cobblers are a homey way to use fruit in season. Short on time? Try using blueberries instead—
there's no peeling or pitting!

1/2 cup sugar

1 tablespoon cornstarch

1/4 teaspoon ground cinnamon

4 cups sliced peaches
  (6 medium)

1 teaspoon lemon juice

3 tablespoons shortening

1 cup all-purpose flour

1 tablespoon sugar

1 1/2 teaspoons baking powder

1/2 teaspoon salt

1/2 cup milk

1. Heat oven to 400°.

2. Mix 1/2 cup sugar, the cornstarch and cinnamon in 2-quart saucepan. Stir in peaches and lemon juice. Cook, stirring constantly, until mixture thickens and boils. Boil and stir 1 minute. Pour into ungreased 2-quart casserole; keep peach mixture hot in oven.

3. Cut shortening into flour, 1 tablespoon sugar, the baking powder and salt in medium bowl, using pastry blender or crisscrossing 2 knives, until mixture looks like fine crumbs. Stir in milk. Drop dough by 6 spoonfuls onto hot peach mixture.

4. Bake 25 to 30 minutes or until topping is golden brown. Serve warm and, if desired, with sweetened whipped cream.

1 SERVING: Calories 260 (Calories from Fat 65); Fat 7g (Saturated 2g); Cholesterol 5mg; Sodium 310mg; Carbohydrates 48g (Dietary Fiber 2g); Protein 3g.

Carrie Moses
Portland, Oregon

Carrie has been my wife and loving companion for forty-four years. Together we have happily raised six wonderful children (three boys and three girls) and have also welcomed several of our teenagers' friends who needed a home.

Carrie's favorite recipes include Peach Kuchen made with Betty Crocker cake mix, and Springerle Cookies from *Betty Crocker's Cookie Book*. She uses an old wooden springerle rolling pin that belonged to my German grandmother. Carrie and I both love to have dinner parties. The Peach Kuchen is often served for dessert at these parties. (People clamor for it!)

Since our four-year-old grandson Rudy was diagnosed with juvenile diabetes I, Carrie has ridden each year in the American Diabetes Association's twenty-mile bike ride, Tour de Cure. She tells everyone, "I'm going to ride each year until they either find a cure or I turn 103"—and I believe she will.

Carrie organizes fun-filled get-togethers for her five sisters and F.B.I.'s. (fine brothers-in-law). The sisters often dress alike and are apt to break out in a song or routine at any moment. (Beware!) Carrie lost one sister to breast cancer, and the other sisters now walk in the Susan G. Komen 5 K "Race for the Cure" in her memory.

Carrie is now serving as secretary for the Women's Club at Ascension Church. Her first project was assisting the new president in revising the outdated by-laws, to better serve today's women.

That's how Carrie is. She revels in the sheer joy of living. Her motto has always been her Four H's: Heart, Humor, Hope, and Health.

Peach-Custard Kuchen

9 SERVINGS

This sweet peaches-and-cream dessert starts as an easy-to-mix-up base. Sprinkled with cinnamon-sugar, the peaches partially bake to release some of their juices before the creamy custard is poured over them to finish baking. Mmmmm.

1 cup all-purpose flour

2 tablespoons sugar

1/4 teaspoon salt

1/8 teaspoon baking powder

1/4 cup margarine or butter, softened

1 1/2 cups sliced fresh peaches (about 3 medium)*

1/3 cup sugar

1 teaspoon ground cinnamon

2 egg yolks

1 cup whipping cream

1. Heat oven to 400°.

2. Stir together flour, 2 tablespoons sugar, the salt and baking powder. Work in margarine until mixture is crumbly.

3. Pat mixture firmly and evenly in bottom and halfway up sides of ungreased square pan, 8 x 8 x 2 inches. Arrange peaches in pan. Mix 1/3 cup sugar and the cinnamon; sprinkle over peaches. Bake 15 minutes.

4. Blend egg yolks and whipping cream; pour over peaches. Bake 25 to 30 minutes or until custard is set and edges are light brown. Serve warm. Refrigerate any remaining dessert.

1 SERVING: Calories 245 (Calories from Fat 135); Fat 15g (Saturated 9g); Cholesterol 90mg; Sodium 115mg; Carbohydrates 25g (Dietary Fiber 1g); Protein 3g.

*1 package (8 ounces frozen sliced peaches, thawed and drained, or 1 can (16 ounces) sliced peaches drained, can be substituted for the fresh peaches.

Rice Pudding

Why not enjoy rice pudding for breakfast as well as dessert? This is comfort food for any time of day.

1/2 cup uncooked regular long grain rice

1 cup water

2 eggs or 4 egg yolks

1/2 cup sugar

1/2 cup raisins or chopped dried apricots

2 1/2 cups milk

1 teaspoon vanilla

1/4 teaspoon salt

Ground cinnamon or nutmeg

Whipped cream, if desired

1. Heat rice and water to boiling in 1 1/2-quart saucepan, stirring once or twice; reduce heat to low. Cover and simmer 14 minutes (do not lift cover or stir). All water should be absorbed.

2. Heat oven to 325°.

3. Beat eggs in ungreased 1 1/2-quart casserole. Stir in sugar, raisins, milk, vanilla, salt and hot rice. Sprinkle with cinnamon.

4. Bake uncovered 45 minutes, stirring every 15 minutes. (Overbaking may cause pudding to curdle.) Top of pudding will be very wet and not set.

5. Stir well; let stand 15 minutes. Enough liquid will be absorbed while standing to make pudding creamy. Serve warm, or cover and refrigerate about 3 hours or until chilled. Serve with whipped cream. Refrigerate remaining dessert.

1 SERVING: Calories 195 (Calories from Fat 25); Fat 3g (Saturated 1g); Cholesterol 60mg; Sodium 115mg; Carbohydrates 37g (Dietary Fiber 0g); Protein 5g.

Chocolate Hazelnut Torte

Save some time by preparing this stunning, rich torte a day ahead; it keeps well covered in the refrigerator. Try grinding the nuts 1/4 cup at a time—it will keep them from getting too oily!

6 ounces sweet cooking chocolate

3/4 cup margarine or butter

4 eggs, separated

1/8 teaspoon salt

3/4 cup sugar

3/4 cup ground hazelnuts

2 tablespoons hazelnut liqueur or coffee

Whole hazelnuts

1. Heat oven to 375°. Grease and flour springform pan, 8 x 2 1/2 inches.

2. Heat chocolate and margarine in medium saucepan over low heat until melted; cool 5 minutes.

3. Beat egg whites and salt in medium bowl on high speed until stiff. Beat egg yolks and sugar on medium speed until lemon colored; stir into chocolate mixture. Stir in ground hazelnuts and liqueur. Gently fold chocolate mixture into egg whites; pour into pan.

4. Bake 40 to 45 minutes until top is dry and knife inserted in center comes out slightly wet. Cool completely; remove from pan. Garnish with whole hazelnuts.

1 SERVING: Calories 340 (Calories from Fat 215); Fat 24g (Saturated 6g); Cholesterol 85mg; Sodium 240mg; Carbohydrates 28g (Dietary Fiber 1g); Protein 4g.

Pies, Cookies & Treats

Strawberry Ice Cream
(page 368)

Sour Cream–Raisin Pie

8 SERVINGS

Using brown sugar instead of granulated sugar gives this meringue a light satiny beige color. Be decorative—use a spoon to spread and swoop the meringue up over the filling, forming soft points and swirls.

Baked Pie Crust (page 349)

1 cup plus 2 tablespoons sugar

1 1/2 tablespoons cornstarch

1/4 teaspoon salt

3/4 teaspoon ground nutmeg

1 1/2 cups sour cream

3 egg yolks

1 1/2 cups raisins

1 tablespoon lemon juice

Brown Sugar Meringue (right)

1. Prepare Baked Pie Crust.

2. Heat oven to 400°. Mix sugar, cornstarch, salt and nutmeg in 2-quart saucepan. Stir in sour cream. Stir in egg yolks, raisins and lemon juice.

3. Cook over medium heat, stirring constantly, until mixture thickens and boils. Boil and stir 1 minute. Pour into pie crust.

4. Prepare Brown Sugar Meringue. Spoon onto hot pie filling. Spread over filling, carefully sealing meringue to edge of crust to prevent shrinking or weeping.

5. Bake 8 to 10 minutes or until meringue is light brown. Cool away from draft. Cover and refrigerate cooled pie until serving time. Refrigerate any remaining pie after serving.

BROWN SUGAR MERINGUE

3 egg whites

1/4 teaspoon cream of tartar

6 tablespoons packed brown sugar

1/2 teaspoon vanilla

Beat egg whites and cream of tartar in medium bowl with electric mixer on high speed until foamy. Beat in brown sugar, 1 tablespoon at a time; continue beating until stiff and glossy. Do not underbeat. Beat in vanilla.

1 SERVING: Calories 515 (Calories from Fat 190); Fat 21g (Saturated 10g); Cholesterol 115mg; Sodium 270mg; Carbohydrates 77g (Dietary Fiber 1g); Protein 6g.

Lemon Meringue Pie

Carefully measure the water and lemon juice in the filling. That way you'll get the right consistency to hold a cut.

Baked Pie Crust (page 349)

3 egg yolks

1 1/2 cups sugar

1/3 cup plus 1 tablespoon cornstarch

1 1/2 cups water

3 tablespoon margarine or butter

2 teaspoons grated lemon peel

1/2 cup lemon juice

2 drops yellow food color, if desired

Meringue (right)

1. Prepare Baked Pie Crust.

2. Heat oven to 400°.

3. Beat egg yolks with fork in small bowl. Mix sugar and cornstarch in 2-quart saucepan. Gradually stir in water. Cook over medium heat, stirring constantly, until mixture thickens and boils. Boil and stir 1 minute.

4. Immediately stir at least half of the hot mixture into egg yolks; stir back into hot mixture in saucepan. Boil and stir 1 minute; remove from heat. Stir in margarine, lemon peel, lemon juice and food color. Pour into pie crust.

5. Prepare Meringue. Spoon onto hot pie filling. Spread over filling, carefully sealing meringue to edge of crust to prevent shrinking or weeping.

6. Bake 8 to 12 minutes or until meringue is light brown. Cool away from draft. Cover and refrigerate cooled pie until serving. Immediately refrigerate any remaining pie.

MERINGUE

3 egg whites

1/4 teaspoon cream of tartar

6 tablespoons sugar

1/2 teaspoon vanilla

1. Beat egg whites and cream of tartar in medium bowl with electric mixer on high speed until foamy.

2. Beat in sugar, 1 tablespoon at a time; continue beating until stiff and glossy. Do not underbeat. Beat in vanilla.

1 SERVING: Calories 425 (Calories from Fat 145); Fat 16g (Saturated 4g); Cholesterol 80mg; Sodium 210mg; Carbohydrates 66g (Dietary Fiber 0g); Protein 4g.

Tiffany Haugen
Walterville, Oregon

Two weeks after Tiffany and Scott were married, they moved to a small village, Point Lay, Alaska, where they began teaching. In six years of teaching, Tiffany has taught over twenty different subjects ranging from beginning reading with first graders to geometry and advanced sociology to high school seniors.

Tiffany's favorite classes to teach are home economics (she designs her own curriculum) and health. Tiffany uses her Betty Crocker cookbook as well as the one I received as a wedding present thirty-three years ago. She has introduced recipes to the community elders, utilizing their traditional subsistence foods. This effort has changed the style in which many traditional foods were previously prepared.

Tiffany also tutors first through twelfth graders on computer skills every day after school for three hours. She also supervises recreational swimming three nights a week and is one of two people certified to do so in the village. Tiffany organizes many other events for the school/community, which includes carnivals, dinners at the school for the village elders, rummage sales, movie nights, and she also volunteers at Sunday school in the village church.

She is one of the most positive people I have ever met. She always looks at a challenge as an opportunity. She has been able to open so many minds, young and old, showing them new ways in which to expand upon their daily lives. All of the villagers love her for her positive helpful ways. She indeed brings such joy to all those around her. She is the best wife, teacher, daughter, homemaker, cook, modern/pioneer woman I know.

Strawberry-Rhubarb Pie

8 SERVINGS

Heralded as the pie plant by early pioneers, this tart fruit was used in countless pies, sauces, jams and desserts. Early pink rhubarb provides a more mild flavor than more mature red rhubarb. If fresh is out of season, you can use 4 cups unsweetened frozen rhubarb, thawed and drained.

Pastry for Two-Crust Pie
(below)

2 cups sugar

2/3 cup all-purpose flour

1 teaspoon grated orange peel, if desired

3 cups sliced strawberries

3 cups cut-up rhubarb (1/2-inch pieces)

1 tablespoon margarine or butter

PASTRY FOR
TWO-CRUST PIE

2/3 cup plus 2 tablespoons shortening

2 cups all-purpose flour

1 teaspoon salt

4 to 5 tablespoons cold water

1. Heat oven to 425°. Prepare pastry.

2. Mix sugar, flour and orange peel in large bowl. Stir in strawberries and rhubarb. Turn pastry-lined pie plate. Dot with margarine. Cover with top pastry that has slits cut in it; seal and flute. Sprinkle with sugar if desired. Cover edge with 2- to 3-inch strip of aluminum foil to prevent excessive browning. Remove foil during last 15 minutes of baking.

3. Bake about 55 minutes or until crust is brown and juice begins to bubble through slits in crust. Cool in pie plate on wire rack.

PASTRY FOR TWO-CRUST PIE

1. Cut shortening into flour and salt, using pastry blender or crisscrossing 2 knives, until particles are size of coarse crumbs. Sprinkle with cold water, 1 tablespoon at a time, tossing with fork until all flour is moistened and pastry almost cleans side of bowl (1 to 2 teaspoons water can be added if necessary).

2. Gather pastry into a ball. Shape into flattened round on lightly floured cloth-covered board. Divide pastry in half and shape into 2 rounds. Roll one round into circle 2 inches larger than upside-down pie plate, 9 x 1 1/4 inches, with floured cloth-covered rolling pin. Fold pastry into fourths; place in pie plate. Unfold and ease into plate, pressing firmly against bottom and side. Place filling in pastry. Trim overhanging edge of pastry 1/2 inch from rim of plate. Roll other round of pastry. Fold into fourths and cut slits so steam can escape.

1 SERVING: Calories 560 (Calories from Fat 200); Fat 22g (Saturated 5g); Cholesterol 0mg; Sodium 310mg; Carbohydrates 88g (Dietary Fiber 3g); Protein 5g.

Cherry-Berries on a Cloud

Lots of requests come in for this recipe and we know why! You, too, will be on cloud nine after one bite of this sweet very-berry pie. The juicy cherries and fresh fruit sit on a cloud of marshmallow and whipped cream, making this dessert irresistibly good.

Pastry Crust (right)

1 package (8 ounces) cream cheese, softened

3/4 cup sugar

1 teaspoon vanilla

2 cups whipping (heavy) cream

2 1/2 cups miniature marshmallows

1 can (21 ounces) cherry pie filling

1 teaspoon lemon juice

2 cups sliced strawberries (1 pint) or 1 package (16 ounces) frozen strawberries, thawed

1 cup fresh or frozen (thawed) sliced peaches

1. Prepare and bake Pastry Crust.

2. Beat cream cheese, sugar and vanilla in large bowl with electric mixer on medium speed until smooth. Beat whipping cream in chilled medium bowl with electric mixer on high speed until stiff. Fold whipped cream and marshmallows into cream cheese mixture; spread over crust.

3. Cover and refrigerate at least 8 hours but no longer than 48 hours.

4. Mix pie filling, lemon juice, strawberries and peaches. Cut dessert into serving pieces; serve with fruit mixture. Cover and refrigerate any remaining dessert.

PASTRY CRUST

1 1/2 cups all-purpose flour

1 cup margarine or butter, softened

1/2 cup powdered sugar

1. Heat oven to 400°.

2. Beat all ingredients with electric mixer on low speed 1 minute, scraping bowl constantly. Beat on medium speed about 2 minutes or until creamy.

3. Spread in ungreased rectangular pan, 13 x 9 x 2 inches. Bake 12 to 15 minutes or until edges are golden brown. Cool completely. (For quick cooling, place in freezer 10 to 15 minutes.)

1 SERVING: Calories 650 (Calories from Fat 370); Fat 41g (Saturated 19g); Cholesterol 80mg; Sodium 310mg; Carbohydrates 67g (Dietary Fiber 2g); Protein 5g.

Cherry-Berries on a Cloud

Susan Senes
Trumbull, Connecticut

We have been calling my sister, Susan Senes, Betty Crocker for many years. Our father died when she was eleven years old, and our mother when she was twelve, and she has been cooking ever since. She not only did put loving tender care into her cooking, but became one of the best cooks I know. Whenever we get

together, her assignment is desserts, and they look better than their picture. We also look forward to the Salmon Loaf, her favorite recipe from the Betty Crocker cookbook (held together with pieces of cellophane tape).

Susan is a mother of four children and grandmother of Emily. All her children are college graduates, and Susan's husband of thirty-two years is a financial director. Susan is a nursery school teacher at St. Paul's Child Development Center. It is an inner-city day care center in Bridgeport, Connecticut. She is also a eucharist minister at St. Stephen's Roman Catholic Church and helps out at the nursery during masses. Susan could easily teach school anywhere she chooses, since she is a credited teacher and college graduate, but she chose to go into Bridgeport and help the children of all socioeconomic backgrounds. The school is part of the church, and it stays open due to the hard work of Susan and other like her.

So often you hear excuses from people, how sad their childhood was and therefore why bother? Well our family and my sister are proof that it doesn't have to be that way. She has always been a most unselfish person with never an unkind word for anyone.

Apple Pie

For a creamy Dutch Apple Pie, make extra-large slits in the top crust. Five minutes before the end of baking, pour 1/2 cup whipping (heavy) cream through the slits in the crust.

Pastry for Two-Crust Pie

(page 343)

1/3 to 2/3 cup sugar

1/4 cup all-purpose flour

1/2 teaspoon ground cinnamon

1/2 teaspoon ground nutmeg

Dash of salt

8 cups thinly sliced peeled tart apples (8 medium)

2 tablespoons margarine or butter

1. Heat oven to 425°. Prepare pastry.

2. Mix sugar, flour, cinnamon, nutmeg and salt in large bowl. Stir in apples. Turn into pastry-lined pie plate. Dot with margarine. Cover with top pastry that has slits cut in it; seal and flute. Cover edge with 3-inch strip of aluminum foil to prevent excessive browning. Remove foil during last 15 minutes of baking.

3. Bake 40 to 50 minutes or until crust is brown and juice begins to bubble through slits in crust. Cool in pie plate on wire rack. Serve warm if desired.

1 SERVING: Calories 430 (Calories from Fat 215); Fat 24g (Saturated 6g); Cholesterol 0mg; Sodium 370mg; Carbohydrates 54g (Dietary Fiber 4g); Protein 4g.

Gold Medal Flour Cookbooks

Washburn Crosby Company, Betty Crocker's original parent company, realized early on that it needed to provide homemakers with recipes for using its flour. So in 1894, it published *Washburn, Crosby Co.'s New Cook Book*, followed by the *Gold Medal Flour Cook Book* in 1903. The 1917 version of that book announced, "This Book has been Carefully Revised, Rearranged and Amplified by the Best Talent Obtainable. . . . Over a million American housewives and bakers can testify to perfect satisfaction in using Washburn-Crosby's GOLD MEDAL FLOUR. Therefore, do not be troubled about your bread, rolls or pastry but buy GOLD MEDAL FLOUR and find that with it there are no baking troubles." Who could ask for more?

Impossible Coconut Pie

6 TO 8 SERVINGS

To make this creamy coconut pie even more delicious, try pouring a little melted chocolate over each slice before serving.

2 cups milk

1/4 cup margarine or butter, softened

4 eggs

3/4 cup sugar

1/2 cup Bisquick Original baking mix

1 1/2 teaspoons vanilla

1 cup flaked or shredded coconut

1. Heat oven to 350°. Grease glass pie plate, 9 x 1 1/4 or 10 x 1 1/2 inches.

2. Stir all ingredients with fork until blended. Pour into pie plate.

3. Bake 50 to 55 minutes or until golden brown and knife inserted in center comes out clean. Refrigerate any remaining pie.

1 SERVING: Calories 360 (Calories from Fat 160); Fat 18g (Saturated 8g); Cholesterol 150mg; Sodium 350mg; Carbohydrates 41g (Dietary Fiber 0g); Protein 8g.

Other Betty Crocker Cookbooks

Perhaps the best-known Betty Crocker cookbooks are the big, red, basic cookbooks, of which eight editions have been published since 1950. But Betty has written many more than that! In fact more than 200 cookbooks bearing her name have been published. Many are specialty books devoted to one topic, such as cookies, Christmas, or cooking with children. Some are designed to help the change to a new lifestyle or a more healthful diet. She has even published large-print and Braille cookbooks. As your best friend in the kitchen, Betty tries to provide you with the most up-to-date recipes.

Strawberry Glacé Pie

When backyard gardens and farmer's markets flourish with summer fruits, use other seasonal fruits in this pie.
Try 6 cups of raspberries or 5 cups of sliced fresh peaches for the strawberries.

Baked Pie Crust (right)

1 1/2 quarts strawberries

1 cup sugar

3 tablespoons cornstarch

1/2 cup water

1 package (3 ounces) cream cheese, softened

1. Prepare Baked Pie Crust.

2. Mash enough strawberries to measure 1 cup. Mix sugar and cornstarch in 2-quart saucepan. Gradually stir in water and mashed strawberries. Cook over medium heat, stirring constantly, until mixture thickens and boils. Boil and stir 1 minute; cool.

3. Beat cream cheese until smooth. Spread in pie shell. Fill shell with whole strawberries. Pour cooked strawberry mixture over top. Refrigerate about 3 hours or until set. Refrigerate any remaining pie after serving.

BAKED PIE CRUST

1/3 cup plus 1 tablespoon shortening or 1/3 cup lard

1 cup all-purpose flour

1/4 teaspoon salt

2 to 3 tablespoons cold water

1. Heat oven to 475°.

2. Cut shortening into flour and salt, using pastry blender or crisscrossing 2 knives, until particles are size of coarse crumbs. Sprinkle with cold water, 1 tablespoon at a time, tossing with fork until all flour is moistened and pastry almost cleans side of bowl (1 to 2 teaspoons water can be added if necessary). Gather pastry into a ball.

3. Shape into flattened round on lightly floured cloth-covered board. Roll pastry into circle 2 inches larger than upside-down pie plate, 9 x 1 1/4 inches, with floured cloth-covered rolling pin. Fold pastry into fourths; place in pie plate.

4. Unfold and ease into plate, pressing firmly against bottom and side. Trim overhanging edge of pastry 1 inch from rim of plate. Fold and roll pastry under, even with plate; flute.

5. Prick bottom and side thoroughly with fork. Bake 8 to 10 minutes or until light brown; cool on wire rack.

1 SERVING: Calories 315 (Calories from Fat 125); Fat 14g (Saturated 5g); Cholesterol 10mg; Sodium 180mg; Carbohydrates 47g (Dietary Fiber 3g); Protein 3g.

Correna Wilson
Wilson, Oklahoma

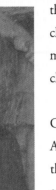

I am a white-haired, fifty-eight-year-old grandmother of fifteen, who whips up no-fail Betty Crocker angel food cakes every chance I get!

I've used Betty Crocker mixes for delicious desserts to serve to the local Rotarians when I served as the first woman president of the sixty-five-year-old former all-male local civic club. The members of my church have enjoyed some of Betty Crocker's best mixes turned quickly into mouth-watering, fast disappearing desserts for special church socials and bake sales.

In past years, my Betty Crocker desserts have shown up at Eastern Star Chapter meetings, political meetings, holidays, family reunions, and family meals! As far as I'm concerned, Betty Crocker can't be beat! In my busy, hectic schedule, they fit right in with time to spare! Even karate champ, film actor Chuck Norris asked for the last piece of my angel food cake, after already eating a large slice, while I was staying with his mother.

I am one of the largest segments of today's society in America, who still prepares meals at home, striving to provide good-quality family-time memories, and wholesome food, with Betty Crocker as my helper! These good family-time memories are so very special to me, with each added year, especially due to my husband's illness and my survival of breast cancer seventeen years ago.

Grandparents are an important factor in the lives of today's children! Grandmothers have learned the meaning of true family values and memories of coming home to a warm kitchen smelling of freshly baked desserts, to which nothing can compare! A smile always beams across my face because, "This is the day the Lord hath made, rejoice and be glad in it," and have some of my Betty Crocker foods!

Chocolate Brownies

16 BROWNIES

You can make colorful Thanksgiving turkeys, festive holiday wreaths or delicate Valentine hearts, but any day you bake up these tender cookies becomes a holiday.

2/3 cup margarine or butter

5 ounces unsweetened baking chocolate, cut into pieces

1 3/4 cups sugar

2 teaspoons vanilla

3 eggs

1 cup all-purpose flour

1 cup chopped walnuts

Fudge Frosting (page 317), if desired

1. Heat oven to 350°. Grease bottom and sides of square pan, 9 x 9 x 2 inches, with shortening.

2. Melt margarine and chocolate in 1-quart saucepan over low heat, stirring constantly. Cool slightly.

3. Beat sugar, vanilla and eggs in medium bowl with electric mixer on high speed 5 minutes. Beat in chocolate mixture on low speed. Beat in flour just until blended. Stir in walnuts. Spread in pan.

4. Bake 40 to 45 minutes or just until brownies begin to pull away from sides of pan. Cool completely in pan on wire rack. Spread with Fudge Frosting. Cut into about 2-inch squares.

1 BROWNIE: Calories 300 (Calories from Fat 160); Fat 18g (Saturated 5g); Cholesterol 40mg; Sodium 100mg; Carbohydrates 32g (Dietary Fiber 2g); Protein 4g.

Expanding Betty's *Sphere* of Influence

Did you know Betty had her own magazine in 1972? Dedicated to "the young-minded homemaker of today, whose interest and influence, while centered in the home, go far beyond its boundaries," it was *Sphere, The Betty Crocker Magazine.* In addition to providing food articles and recipes, *Sphere* also had information on crafts, decorating, fashion, beauty, and more. The Betty Crocker Kitchens still gets requests for recipes and articles from this popular magazine, especially for the 1972 article on the "heritage wedding," including the recipe for a wedding cake decorated with meringue mushrooms. Today, thousands of consumers enjoy Betty Crocker recipe magazines, which are available at their favorite supermarket.

Mary Baer
Hallandale, Florida

The four qualities that Betty Crocker possesses are all wrapped up in my wonderful grandmother, Mrs. Mary Baer. She is an eighty-year-old dynamo who enjoys cooking and baking, is completely devoted to her family and friends, expertly handles everyday tasks in a resourceful and creative manner, and is extremely involved in her community.

She bakes in the middle of the night, in the morning, and invariably—all the hours in between. She bakes as a form of relaxation and to feed the unexpected visitors who are constantly filling her sweet-smelling kitchen. More important, she bakes as an expression of her love.

My grandmother is much more than a wonderful cook. She has been a long-time president of her condominium association in Florida and even now, answers calls twenty-four hours a day from her fellow senior citizens to console bereaved families, analyze problems, soothe heartaches, or assist sickly residents. To ensure their well-being, she is in daily contact with a lengthy list of ill residents.

My grandmother volunteers her time and sits with the "elderly" and infirm. She plays cards with and reads to those people who are in need of the most precious gifts of companionship and kindness. I will always know that she encompasses the true definition of love.

Cashew Brownie Bars

36 BARS

Everyone will be impressed and delighted when you present them with these yummy sweet treats. Using a brownie mix to start with not only makes it a snap to make these rich, nutty bars but also allows you to whip them up at a moments notice.

1 package (15.5 ounces) Betty Crocker fudge brownie mix

Brown Butter Frosting (below)

1 square (1 ounce) unsweetened chocolate

1 tablespoon butter

1/2 cup chopped cashews

BROWN BUTTER FROSTING

1/4 cup butter

2 cups confectioners' sugar

2 tablespoons light cream

1 teaspoon vanilla

1. Bake Fudgy or Cake-like Brownies as directed on package. Cool.

2. Frost with Brown Butter Frosting. Melt chocolate and butter over low heat. When cool, spread over frosting; sprinkle with nuts. When topping is set, cut into bars, 2 1/4 x 1 inch.

BROWN BUTTER FROSTING

In 1-quart saucepan, heat butter over medium heat until delicate brown. Blend in sugar. Beat in light cream and vanilla until smooth and of spreading consistency.

1 BAR: Calories 120 (Calories from Fat 45); Fat 5g (Saturated 2g); Cholesterol 5mg; Sodium 65mg; Carbohydrates 17g (Dietary Fiber 0g); Protein 2g.

Pumpkin Pie

Be sure to use canned pumpkin and not pumpkin pie mix for this pie. The canned pumpkin is just puree, while the pie mix has spices already added to the puree. For a special garnish, cut leftover pastry into special shapes and bake separately on a cookie sheet until light golden brown. Arrange cut outs over baked filling.

Pastry for Baked Pie Crust (page 349)

2 eggs

1/2 cup sugar

1 teaspoon ground cinnamon

1/2 teaspoon salt

1/2 teaspoon ground ginger

1/8 teaspoon ground cloves

1 can (16 ounces) pumpkin

1 can (12 ounces) evaporated milk

Sweetened whipped cream

1. Heat oven to 425°. Prepare Pastry for Baked Pie Crust through step 4.

2. Beat eggs slightly in medium bowl with wire whisk or hand beater. Beat in remaining ingredients except sweetened whipped cream.

3. To prevent spilling, place pastry-lined pie plate on oven rack. Pour filling into pie plate. Bake 15 minutes.

4. Reduce oven temperature to 350°. Bake about 45 minutes longer or until knife inserted in center comes out clean. Refrigerate about 4 hours or until chilled. Serve with sweetened whipped cream. Immediately refrigerate any remaining pie after serving.

1 SERVING: Calories 295 (Calories from Fat 135); Fat 15g (Saturated 5g); Cholesterol 65mg; Sodium 330mg; Carbohydrates 34g (Dietary Fiber 1g); Protein 7g.

Power Grocery Shopping

One of the more unusual jobs in the Betty Crocker Kitchens is that of professional grocery shopper. The shopper is responsible for purchasing all the groceries needed each day in the busy kitchens. She makes several trips, filling her minivan with many, many bags of food selected from her multipage shopping list. She keeps Betty's pantry full of the same staples and products that you might buy for your kitchen. She must also purchase foods for the photography kitchens. This part of the shopper's job requires her to find the most beautiful and photogenic produce available, no matter where it is. This can be a tough job, but she does it—and does it well! (She lets her husband do the family shopping, however!)

Pumpkin Pie

Sandra A. Collins-Burnham

Eagle River, Alaska

Ever since she received her first "easy bake" oven for her fifth birthday, Sandy has been leafing through the batter-speckled pages of her mother's 1950 edition of *Betty Crocker's Cook Book*. It is nestled safely between the Betty Crocker cookbook her mother gave her for Christmas when she was twelve and the more modern, loose-leaf copy that I gave her a few years ago. Sandy cooks every chance that she gets, frequently creating her own recipes. The fact that she is a career women and the primary provider for our family doesn't deter her from cooking dinner every night.

Sandy's interest in food and nutrition led her into a career as a registered dietitian, but another influence drove her to want to get her master's degree in public health. Since Sandy was old enough to walk, she has been taking care of her younger brother, Jeff, who has Down's syndrome. Sandy worked with the developmentally disabled, supervising Jeff and his schoolmates at summer programs and camps, and as a volunteer for the special Olympics.

Sandy is also a loving wife and mother. We have been married for ten wonderful years, and in October 1994, Sandy gave birth to our first child, Maggie. We live in Alaska. Virtually everyone is separated from family by several thousand miles. As a result, surrogate families develop fostered by this shared isolation. Sandy has done a great deal to forge these bonds of friendship and support.

Sandy was three months pregnant when we started building a cabin on a lake and well into her last trimester when we finished, but she was actively involved with the whole project. But Sandy has a myriad of her own hobbies as well as being a heck of a carpenter. She does beadwork, which she learned from Native Alaskan Indians, she paints, does cross-stitch, and most recently has taken up spinning wool to make yarn for her knitting.

Sandy is a wonderful person, terrific wife, adoring mother, excellent bread winner, and faithful friend. Through her work and with her free time, she serves her community. An avid and superb cook she epitomizes the qualities of Betty Crocker.

Chocolate Chip Cookies

Make someone's day a little bit brighter when you share these all-American cookies with them. Don't forget it's best to wash them down with a nice glass of cold milk!

1 1/2 cups margarine or butter, softened

1 1/4 cups granulated sugar

1 1/4 cups packed brown sugar

1 tablespoon vanilla

2 eggs

4 cups all-purpose flour

2 teaspoons baking soda

1/2 teaspoon salt

2 cups coarsely chopped nuts, if desired

1 package (24 ounces) semisweet chocolate chips (4 cups)

1. Heat oven to 375°.

2. Beat margarine, sugars, vanilla and eggs in large bowl with electric mixer on medium speed, or mix with spoon. Stir in flour, baking soda and salt (dough will be stiff). Stir in nuts and chocolate chips.

3. Drop dough by level 1/4 cupfuls or #16 cookie/ice-cream scoop about 2 inches apart onto ungreased cookie sheet. Flatten slightly with fork.

4. Bake 13 to 15 minutes or until light brown (centers will be soft). Cool 1 to 2 minutes; remove from cookie sheet to wire rack.

1 COOKIE: Calories 240 (Calories from Fat 110); Fat 12g (Saturated 4g); Cholesterol 15mg; Sodium 170mg; Carbohydrate 32g (Dietary Fiber 1g); Protein 2g.

The Cookie Jar

The popularity of cookies is worldwide: In Italy, they're *biscotti;* in England, *biscuits.* Germans call them *keks* and Spaniards munch on *galletas.* The Dutch call them *koekje* (pronounced *cookie*). American colonists kept that name, and all the immigrants who came later brought their own beloved versions with them. With this melting pot of people came the melding of different cookie recipes, making up today's favorites. Whether your preference is for drop, shaped, molded, refrigerator, or bar cookies, Betty's got a recipe that is sure to please.

Nancy Busch
Pittsburgh, Pennsylvania

Writing and cooking are among my favorite pastimes. I am certainly not a professional at either of these but truly enjoy both. I have scoliosis (spine curvature) and have had four major back surgeries, but I am still able to do many things. Actually, it is because of my scoliosis that I do a lot of writing. I have three

pen pals (even one in England) who also have this ailment, and we compare our progress and treatment.

I am fifty-three years old, very happily married for almost thirty-four years, have two grown children (a son and daughter), am a grandmother to two little boys, and have been a homemaker all of our married life. My husband and I both grew up in small towns, and family life and quality time are very important to us. We never had a lot of extras, but we had everything that we consider important—lots of love and time spent with our children. We always had meals together, vacationed together, and enjoyed being a family. Our children mention these good times often, even to this day. To us, this is true wealth!

Over the years, I have come to truly love all aspects of cooking. My husband still chuckles about when we first got married, my main accomplishment was gelatin. My very favorite cookbook is *Betty Crocker's New Good and Easy,* 1962 (a great year—the year of our marriage).

I volunteer in the Physical Therapy Department of our local nursing home and am active in our neighborhood civic association. The bulk of my time is now spent with the "Shepherds," a caring ministry of laity at our church. I have been chairperson for almost nine years now since it was organized. We are very active in many other ways in our church, and cooking is a big part of many gatherings. Just this past week, the ladies made apple pies and dumplings as a fund-raiser for our women's group. I am one of the "resident crust makers."

Brown Sugar Drops

ABOUT 6 DOZEN COOKIES

An old-fashioned favorite, we think this drop cookie shouts versatility! Stir in 1 cup of your favorite chopped nuts or shredded coconut or 3 cups of cut-up gumdrops for a fun twist.

2 cups packed brown sugar

1 cup shortening

2 eggs

1/2 cup buttermilk or water

3 1/2 cups all-purpose flour

1 teaspoon baking soda

1/2 teaspoon salt

1. Mix brown sugar, shortening, eggs and buttermilk. Stir in remaining ingredients. Cover and refrigerate at least 1 hour.

2. Heat oven to 400°. Grease cookie sheet.

3. Drop dough by rounded teaspoonfuls about 2 inches apart onto cookie sheet.

4. Bake 8 to 10 minutes or until almost no indentation remains when touched. Immediately remove from cookie sheet. Cool on wire rack.

1 COOKIE: **Calories 75** (Calories from Fat 25); **Fat 3g** (Saturated 1g); **Cholesterol 5mg; Sodium 40mg; Carbohydrates 11g** (Dietary Fiber 0g); **Protein 1g.**

Remodeling the Kitchens

Does your kitchen need a face lift? Would you like to make room for some newer, more efficient appliances? That same problem has faced the Betty Crocker Kitchens, and many changes have occurred over time. In the 1950s, there was the Terrace Kitchen, the Polka Dot Kitchen, the Kitchen of Tomorrow, and the Kamera Kitchen, where food photography was done. Over the years, there have also been a Japanese Kitchen, a New Orleans Kitchen, a New England Kitchen, a Latin American Kitchen, a Scandinavian Kitchen, and a Mediterranean Kitchen. Today's Betty Crocker Kitchens number seven: the Arizona Desert Kitchen, the California Kitchen, the Cape Cod Kitchen, the Chinatown Kitchen, the Hawaiian Kitchen, the Pennsylvania Dutch Kitchen, and the Williamsburg Kitchen, plus three camera kitchens. Each is decorated to represent the region of the United States for which it is named.

BEST-LOVED DESSERTS   359

Betty Crocker

Salt Lake City, Utah

Betty Crocker is alive and well! My Aunt Betty Specht married David Crocker fifty-three years ago. Aunt Betty fits her namesake perfectly! She loves to cook and bake anything. She shares the products of her enjoyment with family, friends, neighbors, church, and basically everyone. In elementary school, one of her sons was even found out to be selling his mom's cookies at lunch for fifteen cents a piece. After all, they *were* Betty Crocker originals!

She uses many of the recipes from her favorite gift: a Betty Crocker cookbook. Aunt Betty has won many awards and recognitions for her cooking and baking, including the Sweepstakes at the Utah State Fair with her breads. Aunt Betty has taken each of her grandchildren and one-on-one taught them to bake. Cookies are always overflowing in Grandma Crocker's kitchen.

This Betty Crocker is not only a wonderful cook and baker, but also an accomplished seamstress and knitter. She has always knitted hats, mittens, afghans, etc., for those less fortunate than we are, and she has taught many people to knit, men as well as women.

Betty Crocker is known as the Best Neighbor in Salt Lake. However, she would be the first one to tell you that she and Uncle Dave are a team. Together they visit neighbors, the sick, the lonely, and the needy. They are volunteer drivers for people needing rides and have been long-time deliverers of Meals on Wheels. She has given many demonstrations for making candy and breads. They have had their own personal trials and tragedies, but with their faith in God, their commitment to each other, and their love for life, they have risen above them. My Aunt Betty Crocker, with her heart of gold, generosity, and contagious energy definitely fits the qualities of the image of Betty Crocker.

Snickerdoodles

They are as fun to say as they are to eat. This can be a great way to get the kids involved in helping to roll the dough in the cinnamon-sugar mixture. Or, for a colorful twist, roll the dough in colored sugar instead of white granulated sugar.

1 1/2 cups sugar

1/2 cup margarine or butter,
   softened

1/2 cup shortening

2 eggs

2 3/4 cups all-purpose flour

2 teaspoons cream of tartar

1 teaspoon baking soda

1/4 teaspoon salt

2 tablespoons sugar

2 teaspoons ground cinnamon

1. Heat oven to 400°.

2. Mix 1 1/2 cups sugar, the margarine, shortening and eggs thoroughly in 3-quart bowl. Stir in flour, cream of tartar, baking soda and salt until blended. Shape dough by rounded teaspoonfuls into balls.

3. Mix 2 tablespoons sugar and the cinnamon; roll balls in sugar mixture. Place about 2 inches apart on ungreased cookie sheet. Bake until set, 8 to 10 minutes. Immediately remove from cookie sheet.

1 COOKIE: Calories 65 (Calories from Fat 25); Fat 3g (Saturated 1g); Cholesterol 5mg; Sodium 45mg; Carbohydrates 8g (Dietary Fiber 0g); Protein 1g.

Russian Tea Cakes

The powdered sugar gives these cookies a wonderful melt-in-your-mouth texture. Walnuts or almonds are often used when making these cookies, which are also known as Mexican Wedding Cakes. Try toasting the nuts very lightly for a more pronounced flavor.

1 cup margarine or butter, softened

1/2 cup powdered sugar

1 teaspoon vanilla

2 1/4 cups all-purpose flour

3/4 cup finely chopped nuts

1/4 teaspoon salt

Powdered sugar

1. Heat oven to 400°.

2. Mix margarine, 1/2 cup powdered sugar and the vanilla in large bowl. Stir in flour, nuts and salt until dough holds together.

3. Shape dough into 1-inch balls. Place about 1 inch apart on ungreased cookie sheet.

4. Bake 10 to 12 minutes or until set but not brown. Remove from cookie sheet. Cool slightly on wire rack.

5. Roll warm cookies in powdered sugar; cool on wire rack. Roll in powdered sugar again.

1 COOKIE: Calories 75 (Calories from Fat 45); Fat 5g (Saturated 1g); Cholesterol 0mg; Sodium 55mg; Carbohydrates 7g (Dietary Fiber 0g); Protein 1g.

Raisin Crisscross Cookies

A potato masher dipped into flour is also a quick way to flatten these cookies. Chocolate lovers can use 1/2 cup semisweet chocolate chips or chocolate-covered raisins for the plain raisins.

3/4 cup sugar

1/4 cup shortening

1/4 cup margarine or butter, softened

1 egg

1/2 teaspoon lemon extract or vanilla

1 3/4 cups all-purpose flour

3/4 teaspoon cream of tartar

3/4 teaspoon baking soda

1/4 teaspoon salt

1 cup raisins

1. Heat oven to 400°.

2. Mix sugar, shortening, margarine, egg and lemon extract in large bowl. Stir in remaining ingredients.

3. Shape dough by rounded teaspoonfuls into balls. Place 3 inches apart on ungreased cookie sheet. Flatten in crisscross pattern with fork dipped in flour.

4. Bake 8 to 10 minutes or until light brown. Remove from cookie sheet. Cool on wire rack.

1 COOKIE: Calories 75 (Calories from Fat 25); Fat 3g (Saturated 1g); Cholesterol 10mg; Sodium 55mg; Carbohydrates 12g (Dietary Fiber 0g); Protein 0g.

Lemon Squares

25 SQUARES

You'll love these tart and creamy lemon bars. Be sure to grate the lemon peel first. Then firmly roll the lemon on your countertop before squeezing to get the most juice you can from the lemon.

1 cup all-purpose flour

1/2 cup margarine or butter, softened

1/4 cup powdered sugar

1 cup granulated sugar

2 teaspoons grated lemon peel, if desired

2 tablespoons lemon juice

1/2 teaspoon baking powder

1/4 teaspoon salt

2 eggs

1. Heat oven to 350°.

2. Mix flour, margarine and powdered sugar. Press in ungreased square pan, 8 x 8 x 2 or 9 x 9 x 2 inches, building up 1/2-inch edges.

3. Bake crust 20 minutes.

4. Beat remaining ingredients with electric mixer on high speed about 3 minutes or until light and fluffy. Pour over hot crust.

5. Bake 25 to 30 minutes or until no indentation remains when touched lightly in center. Cool in pan on wire rack. Cut into about 1 1/2-inch squares

1 SERVING: Calories 90 (Calories from Fat 35); Fat 4g (Saturated 1g); Cholesterol 15mg; Sodium 80mg; Carbohydrates 13g (Dietary Fiber 0g); Protein 1g.

Delores Vacarro

Pueblo, Colorado

Dolores Vaccaro has been a loyal 4-H foods leader for eighteen years and has provided leadership and support to hundreds of youth. Dolores is loved and respected by all. She has been the main cook at 4-H camp for many years, and through donations from the community, she has saved enough to send many other 4-H leaders to various activities and trips.

While her children attended a Catholic school, Dolores raised enough money to add on an additional classroom. Dolores also organized a very large project at our local nature center to build a trail for handicapped access to the river.

Her home is full of homemade crafts. She formed a club to help some of her friends, who have been widowed, earn extra money. Dolores sponsors a craft show once a year to sell all the craft items they have made.

Dolores is also very dedicated to her family. Dolores was raised by a single mom, after the death of her father. Dolores is the mother of three successful, grown children and is the grandmother of two. Dolores believes in strong family ties and cooks a family meal every Sunday that all of her family attends. You are never a stranger in her home, and she and her husband of forty-nine years always have their home open to all!

Dolores has been winning at state and county fairs since 1951 and has over three hundred ribbons as proof. Dolores literally tests hundreds of recipes a year in her kitchen. She is up every morning by 5:00 A.M., making fresh bread and other baked items.

When our city was on the verge of loosing the Colorado State Fair, Dolores went into action. She organized a "Save the Fair" campaign that reached many people; among them, Willie Nelson who did a benefit to help save the fair; Dolores presented Mr. Nelson with a large thank-you card signed by thousands. All work and materials were donated, and Dolores cooked for approximately fifteen hundred that weekend. The community all pulled together, and with people like Dolores, Pueblo is still proud to be the home of the Colorado State Fair.

She exemplifies the traditional homemaker and, at the same time, is in tune with the present-day working woman. She is truly remarkable.

Oatmeal-Raisin Cookies

ABOUT 3 DOZEN COOKIES

Looking for something to replace the raisins? Try dried cherries or dried cranberries for a refreshing change of flavor and color.

2/3 cup granulated sugar

2/3 cup packed brown sugar

1/2 cup margarine or butter, softened

1/2 cup shortening

1 teaspoon baking soda

1 teaspoon ground cinnamon

1 teaspoon vanilla

1/2 teaspoon baking powder

1/2 teaspoon salt

2 eggs

3 cups quick-cooking or old-fashioned oats

1 cup all-purpose flour

1 cup raisins, chopped nuts or semisweet chocolate chips, if desired

1. Heat oven to 375°.

2. Mix all ingredients except oats, flour and raisins in large bowl. Stir in oats, flour and raisins.

3. Drop dough by rounded tablespoonfuls about 2 inches apart onto ungreased cookie sheet.

4. Bake 9 to 11 minutes or until light brown. Immediately remove from cookie sheet. Cool on wire rack.

1 COOKIE: Calories 120 (Calories from Fat 55); Fat 6g (Saturated 1g); Cholesterol 10mg; Sodium 110mg; Carbohydrates 15g (Dietary Fiber 1g); Protein 2g.

Barbara (B.J.) Jones

Albuquerque, New Mexico

SPIRIT OF BETTY CROCKER CONTEST
Winner

My wife embodies very successfully the modern working woman. She is a hardworking human resources manager at a large defense contractor in Albuquerque and, at the same time, is a wonderful wife, mother, and community volunteer.

My wife has always enjoyed cooking and was busy in the kitchen helping her family since she was in her early teens. She is an avid collector of cookbooks and subscribes to five cooking magazines. In fact, my wife is such a good cook that we don't eat out very much any more, because we can always have a better meal at home.

Our three-and-half-year-old daughter has inherited her mother's love of the kitchen, and together they laugh and cook and make messes in the kitchen. Our daughter's name means "star" in Spanish. One of their favorite activities is to bake a star-shaped cake, using Betty Crocker cake mix, of course, and then frost it and decorate it. My wife's favorite Betty Crocker products are the cake mixes and frostings, and one of our family's real favorites is Au Gratin Potatoes.

My wife has developed a special Christmas tradition. Throughout the year, she collects our favorite new recipes, including those that she creates herself, and makes an annual cookbook that we share with our most special friends.

My wife makes time for a variety of community activities. She has served on the boards of the local children's museum, the Stanford Alumni Club, and Leadership Albuquerque (a local leadership development program). We have also been involved with a variety of ministries in our church parish. She has worked as a mentor to high school students as well as to black student interns.

In this day and age a woman has to fulfill many different roles, and it is difficult to juggle all of them successfully. My wife is one of those rare individuals who I believe does successfully manage and excel at all her roles.

Deluxe Sugar Cookies

You can make colorful Thanksgiving turkeys, festive holiday wreaths or delicate Valentine hearts, but any day you bake up these tender cookies becomes a holiday.

1 1/2 cups powdered sugar

1 cup margarine or butter, softened

1 teaspoon vanilla

1/2 teaspoon almond extract

1 egg

2 1/2 cups all-purpose flour

1 teaspoon baking soda

1 teaspoon cream of tartar

Granulated sugar

1. Mix powdered sugar, margarine, vanilla, almond extract and egg in large bowl. Stir in flour, baking soda and cream of tartar. Cover and refrigerate at least 2 hours.

2. Heat oven to 375°. Lightly grease cookie sheet.

3. Divide dough in half. Roll each half 1/4-inch thick on lightly floured surface. Cut into desired shapes with 2- to 2 1/2-inch cookie cutters. Sprinkle with granulated sugar. Place on cookie sheet.

4. Bake 7 to 8 minutes or until edges are light brown. Remove from cookie sheet. Cool on wire rack.

1 COOKIE: Calories 65 (Calories from Fat 25); Fat 3g (Saturated 1g); Cholesterol 5mg; Sodium 60mg; Carbohydrates 8g (Dietary Fiber 0g); Protein 1g.

Caramel Corn

This confection was hardly an overnight success. Known as "popcorn candy," it was sold from an outdoor popcorn stand for twenty years before it took off at the 1893 World's Fair in Chicago. Early recipes used that staple from colonial days, molasses, but the irresistible combination of butter and sugar made the caramel the more popular formula.

3 3/4 quarts (15 cups) popped corn

1 cup packed brown sugar

1/2 cup margarine or butter

1/4 cup light corn syrup

1/2 teaspoon salt

1/2 teaspoon baking soda

1. Heat oven to 200°. Divide popped corn between 2 ungreased rectangular pans, 13 x 9 x 2 inches.

2. Heat brown sugar, margarine, corn syrup and salt, stirring occasionally, in saucepan until bubbly around edge. Cook over medium heat 5 minutes; remove from heat.

3. Stir in baking soda until foamy. Pour over popped corn, stirring until corn is well coated. Bake 1 hour, stirring every 15 minutes.

1 CUP SERVING: Calories 155 (Calories from Fat 55); Fat 6g (Saturated 4g); Cholesterol 15mg; Sodium 170mg; Carbohydrates 25g (Dietary Fiber 1g); Protein 1g.

Strawberry Ice Cream

Great summertime memories are made when you bring out the homemade ice cream maker. Look for berries with a deep red color and no white. The riper the strawberry, the more flavorful this ice cream will be!

1 quart fresh strawberries, washed and hulled

1/2 cup sugar

2 cups whipping (heavy) cream

1 cup milk

1/4 cup sugar

1/2 teaspoon vanilla

2 eggs

1. Mix strawberries and 1/2 cup sugar in bowl; let stand about 1 hour, stirring occasionally. Mash strawberries.

2. Whisk together remaining ingredients. Cook in medium saucepan over low heat, stirring constantly, about 8 minutes until mixture thickens. Stir in strawberry mixture.

3. Chill mixture about 2 hours. Pour into ice-cream freezer; freeze according to manufacturer's directions.

1/2 CUP SERVING: Calories 330 (Calories from Fat 215); Fat 24g (Saturated 15g); Cholesterol 135mg; Sodium 55mg; Carbohydrates 27g (Dietary Fiber 2g); Protein 4g.

NUTRITION GUIDELINES:

We provide nutrition information for each recipe that includes calories, fat, cholesterol, sodium, carbohydrate, fiber and protein. Individual food choices can be based on this information

Recommended intake for a daily diet of 2,000 calories as set by the Food and Drug Organization

Total Fat	Less than 65g
Saturated Fat	Less than 20g
Cholesterol	Less than 300mg
Sodium	Less than 2,400mg
Total Carbohydrate	300g
Dietary Fiber	25g

CRITERIA USED FOR CALCULATING NUTRITION INFORMATION:

- The first ingredient was used wherever a choice is given (such as ⅓ cup sour cream or plain yogurt).

- The first ingredient amount was used wherever a range is given (such as 3 to 3½ pound cut-up broiler-fryer chicken).

- The first serving number was used wherever a range is given (such as 4 to 6 servings).

- "If desired" ingredients (such as sprinkle with brown sugar if desired) and recipe variations were not inclued .

- Only the amount of a marinade or frying oil that is estimated to be absorbed by the food during preparation or cooking was calculated.

Cooking Terms Glossary:

Beat: Mix ingredients vigorously with spoon, fork, wire whisk, hand beater or electric mixer until smooth and uniform.

Boil: Heat liquid until bubbles rise continuously and break on the surface and steam is given off. For rolling boil, the bubbles form rapidly.

Chop: Cut into coarse or fine irregular pieces with a knife, food chopper, blender or food processor.

Cube: Cut into squares 1/2 inch or larger.

Dice: Cut into squares smaller than 1/2 inch.

Grate: Cut into tiny particles using small rough holes of grater (citrus peel or chocolate).

Grease: Rub the inside surface of a pan with shortening, using pastry brush, piece of waxed paper or paper towel, to prevent food from sticking during baking (as for some casseroles).

Julienne: Cut into thin, matchlike strips, using knife or food processor (vegetables, fruits, meats).

Mix: Combine ingredients in any way that distributes them evenly.

Sauté: Cook foods in hot oil or margarine over medium-high heat with frequent tossing and turning motion.

Shred: Cut into long thin pieces by rubbing food across the holes of a shredder, as for cheese, or by using a knife to slice very thinly, as for cabbage.

Simmer: Cook in liquid just below the boiling point on top of the stove; usually after reducing heat from a boil. Bubbles will rise slowly and break just below the surface.

Stir: Mix ingredients until uniform consistency. Stir once in a while for stirring occasionally, often for stirring frequently and continuously for stirring constantly.

Toss: Tumble ingredients lightly with a lifting motion (such as green salad), usually to coat evenly or mix with another food.

Ingredients Used in Recipe Testing and Nutrition Calculations:

- Ingredients used for testing represent those that the majority of consumers use in their homes: large eggs, 2% milk, 80% lean ground beef, canned ready-to-use chicken broth, and vegetable oil spread containing *not less than 65% fat.*

- Fat-free, low-fat or low-sodium products are not used, unless otherwise indicated.

- Solid vegetable shortening (not butter, margarine, nonstick cooking sprays or vegetable oil spread as they can cause sticking problems) is used to grease pans, unless otherwise indicated.

Equipment Used in Recipe Testing:

We use equipment for testing that the majority of consumers use in their homes. If a specific piece of equipment (such as a wire whisk) is necessary for recipe success, it will be listed in the recipe.

- Cookware and bakeware **without** nonstick coatings were used, unless otherwise indicated.

- No dark colored, black or insulated bakeware was used.

- When a baking *pan* is specified in a recipe, a *metal* pan was used; a baking *dish* or pie *plate* means oven-proof glass was used.

- An electric hand mixer was used for mixing *only when mixer speeds are specified* in the recipe directions. When a mixer speed is not given, a spoon or fork was used.

Metric Conversion Guide

VOLUME

U.S. Units	Canadian Metric	Australian Metric
¼ teaspoon	1 mL	1 ml
½ teaspoon	2 mL	2 ml
1 teaspoon	5 mL	5 ml
1 tablespoon	15 mL	20 ml
¼ cup	50 mL	60 ml
⅓ cup	75 mL	80 ml
½ cup	125 mL	125 ml
⅔ cup	150 mL	170 ml
¾ cup	175 mL	190 ml
1 cup	250 mL	250 ml
1 quart	1 liter	1 liter
1½ quarts	1.5 liters	1.5 liters
2 quarts	2 liters	2 liters
2½ quarts	2.5 liters	2.5 liters
3 quarts	3 liters	3 liters
4 quarts	4 liters	4 liters

WEIGHT

U.S. Units	Canadian Metric	Australian Metric
1 ounce	30 grams	30 grams
2 ounces	55 grams	60 grams
3 ounces	85 grams	90 grams
4 ounces (¼ pound)	115 grams	125 grams
8 ounces (½ pound)	225 grams	225 grams
16 ounces (1 pound)	455 grams	500 grams
1 pound	455 grams	½ kilogram

MEASUREMENTS

Inches	Centimeters
1	2.5
2	5.0
3	7.5
4	10.0
5	12.5
6	15.0
7	17.5
8	20.5
9	23.0
10	25.5
11	28.0
12	30.5
13	33.0

TEMPERATURES

Fahrenheit	Celsius
32°	0°
212°	100°
250°	120°
275°	140°
300°	150°
325°	160°
350°	180°
375°	190°
400°	200°
425°	220°
450°	230°
475°	240°
500°	260°

Note: The recipes in this cookbook have not been developed or tested using metric measures. When converting recipes to metric, some variations in quality may be noted.

Index